19.95

A Field Guide to

GOLD, GEMSTONE
& MINERAL SITES
of British Columbia

A Field Guide to

GOLD, GEMSTONE & MINERAL SITES
of British Columbia

Volume 2

Sites Within A Day's Drive of Vancouver

RICK HUDSON

ORCA BOOK PUBLISHERS

Canadian Cataloguing in Publication Data
Hudson, Richard (Richard Dennis), 1947–
Gold, gemstone and mineral sites of British Columbia

Includes bibliographical references and index.
Contents: Vol. I, Vancouver Island – v. 2, Sites within a day's drive of Vancouver.

ISBN 1-55143-057-6 (v. 1) – ISBN 1-55143-150-5 (v. 2)
1. Mines and mineral resources – British Columbia – Handbooks, manuals, etc.
2. Prospecting – British Columbia. I. Title. II. Title, Gold, gemstone & mineral sites of British Columbia.
TN27B9H82 1997 553.4'09711   C96-910287-9

Orca Book Publishers gratefully acknowledges the support of our publishing programs provided by the following agencies: The Government of Canada through the Book Publishing Industry Development Program (BPIDP).
Canadä

Cover design by Jim Brennan
All photographs and maps by the author
Printed and bound in Canada

Orca Book Publishers   **Orca Book Publishers**
PO Box 5626, Station B   PO Box 468
Victoria, BC Canada   Custer, WA USA
V8R 6S4   98240-0468

01 00 99   5 4 3 2 1

Dedicated to
Simon Deane
1951 – 1997
who was my rockhounding buddy for much
of *Volume I* (Vancouver Island),
appearing on both the front and back
covers of the first edition.

ACKNOWLEDGMENTS

This book draws from the work of many people. In the 1970s, Ann Sabina, Howard Pearsons, Stan and Chris Leaming and Ron Purvis published books about rocks and minerals in BC. They made my task much easier.

Regarding field trips: my thanks to Peter Thorne of Vancouver for his knowledge of fossil sites; and to Alice and Elmer Clark, Cliff and Dorothy Smith, David Singleton, Yvonne Evans, Harley and Livia Waterson, Don Stebbing, Adam Villazambo and Frank Tierney in the lower Mainland. A special thanks to Win Robertson, who digitized numerous reports from old *Rockhound* magazines, and suggested other sites based on her extensive experience rockhounding around the province. Karen Vanderwolf and Ailsa Lamont of Lillooet helped with site localities. And thanks to John Garrett of Bralorne for a fine afternoon of prospecting reminiscences. In Princeton, my thanks to the Willis family who have ranched for three generations under the slide on Agate Mountain; to Bob Bouvette, retired Lillooet prospector now settled near Hedley, who produced a wonderful Bralorne gold specimen; and to Edith and Doug Currie for being charming hosts, with a view from their house second to none.

On Texada Island, my particular thanks to old-time prospectors Ed Johanson and Bob Duker for advice and samples. Thanks also to John McDonald, Ann Wild and the staff at AXYS Corporation of Sidney, BC, whose excellent QUIKMAP program allowed me to draw some of the maps, and to Terry Ridings at Applied Microsystems Ltd., and Mike Rebitt at Terra Surveys Ltd. for advice with AutoDesk's AutoCAD.

Thanks to many of the staff at BC's Geological Survey Branch offices in Victoria; in particular, Larry Jones and the MINFILE group, without whom this project would have been impossible. Thanks to Dr. George Simandl for advice and ideas; and particular thanks to Dr. Nick Massey for long discussions. Thanks also to Sharon Ferris, Head Librarian at the Jack Davis Geological Library. At the Pacific Geoscience Centre, my thanks to Roy Hyndman, Earl Davis and Jane Wynne for help on matters geophysical. I am particularly indebted to Gilles Lebrun of the Victoria Lapidary and Mineral Society for his willingness to identify the unidentifiable, and for his continual enthusiasm in matters geological.

Finally, my thanks to my editor Andrew Wooldridge, Christine Toller, Susan Adamson, and editor-in-chief Bob Tyrrell for their help, support, suggestions and improvements on turning this manuscript into what you see today.

FOREWORD

One and a half million years ago, our ancestors worked the first simple carvings in stone, to make images of gods and to record events in their lives. They learned that some varieties of stone could be fashioned into tools for food gathering, making clothing, lighting fires and otherwise improving living conditions. As life became easier for these ancient people, they began to notice that some stones were colourful or contained interesting patterns and could be fashioned for personal adornment. Crudely fashioned beads and amulets made from bone, ivory, shell and stone have been dated back to 38,000 BC. By 6,000 BC, semi-precious and precious gems were being shaped into polished beads and art objects. As these early techniques evolved they became known as the lapidary arts.

Until the Industrial Revolution released workers from endless drudgery, and workers found themselves with more leisure time, collecting semi-precious stones was only undertaken by those making a living from the practice. But spare time allowed people to develop hobbies, and soon ordinary people were becoming interested in finding gemstones, fossils and minerals. They were the first rockhounds.

During the 1950s, with the abundance and variety of available material in British Columbia, rockhounding became one of our foremost hobbies. Clubs were formed throughout the province by people interested in collecting rocks and learning the lapidary arts. A number of how-to books were written on cutting and polishing stones, cleaning crystals, faceting and other area of interest but there were very few on field collecting. As rockhounds made discoveries, rough maps of the locations were drawn and made available through club newsletters, but their circulation was obviously limited. Since 1972, there has been no comprehensive publication on the province's Interior gem sites at all. Yet much has changed or been discovered since then. This book fills an important void in the knowledge base of our hobby, covering the area around the Lower Mainland.

Remember that rockhounding requires no expensive equipment: A rock hammer, a pair of good hiking boots, and most importantly, a good field guide are all you need. And rockhounding is a hobby for all seasons. In good weather there is the pleasure of roaming the hills, enjoying the scenery and collecting. Long winter days are brightened by sorting the summer finds, discovering the rainbows of colour and patterns within the rocks and gems, and working them in the lapidary arts.

Welcome to a wonderful hobby.

Win Robertson
Vice President
Lapidary Rock & Mineral Society of British Columbia

TABLE OF CONTENTS

Introduction   1

1. Geology   3
   1.1 All about rocks and minerals   3
   1.2 The shape of BC (geomorphology)   4
   1.3 The rocks of BC (petrology)   6
      1.3.1 Igneous rocks   6
      1.3.2 Sedimentary rocks   7
      1.3.3 Metamorphic rocks   7
   1.4 A brief geological history of SW British Columbia   8
   1.5 Where to look when rockhounding   9
   1.6 Ethics   10

2. A short history of BC prospecting   12
   2.1 The gold rush started everything   12
   2.2 Defining a province   12
   2.3 A network of civilization developed   13
   2.4 Mining built the province   13
   2.5 The little guy is still a key player   13

3. Prospecting techniques   14
   3.1 What to wear   15
   3.2 What tools to carry   15
   3.3 Caring for your specimens   16
   3.4 Safety tips   17

4. Access Rights   18
   4.1 Access rights   18

5. Rock & mineral identification   20
   5.1 Hardness   22
   5.2 Colour   22
   5.3 Lustre   23
   5.4 Specific gravity, or density   24
   5.5 Cleavage   24
   5.6 Fracture   24
   5.7 Streak   25
   5.8 Magnetism   25
   5.9 Electrical properties   25
   5.10 Radioactivity   25

6. Gemstones & minerals of BC   26

7. Gold!   52
    7.1 Recognizing gold   53
    7.2 Panning for gold   53
    7.3 Where to look   54
    7.4 Equipment   55
    7.5 Weights and measures   56

8. Other treasures   57
    8.1 Fossils   57
        8.1.1 Collecting fossils   57
    8.2 Meteorites   58
    8.3 Jade   59
        8.3.1 What is jade?   60
        8.3.2 The history of jade in BC 60
        8.3.3 Jade prospecting methods 62
    8.4 Agate   63
        8.4.1 What is agate?   63
        8.4.2 Hunting for agate   64
        8.4.3 Thundereggs   65
    8.5 Other material   65

9. Prospecting sites   67
    9.1 Greater Vancouver area   71
    9.2 Georgia Strait   74
    9.3 Howe Sound – Whistler Valley   88
    9.4 Fraser Valley   103
    9.5 Fraser River   116
    9.6 Thompson River   130
    9.7 Cariboo Country   145
    9.8 Lillooet area   150
    9.9 Upper Bridge River   169
    9.10 Hope – Merritt   192
    9.11 East of Merritt   206
    9.12 North of Merritt   215
    9.13 Hope – Princeton   226
    9.14 Princeton   238
    9.15 Coalmont – Tulameen   253

10. Addresses   268

11. Glossary of terms   276

12. Bibliography   282

13. Index   285

INTRODUCTION

*The countries of North America have busied themselves for so many
years with digging vast quantities of coal, leveling mountains of iron
ore, and tapping subterranean lakes of oil, that their considerable
gemstone resources have often been ignored.*

John Sinkankas, *Gemstones of North America*, 1959

The centre of Canada is made up of rocks of the Canadian Shield. On the
east and west it is flanked by mountain belts. The province of British Columbia is within the Cordilleran Belt, which makes up the western margin of
the continent, from Mexico to Alaska.

The eastern side of the Cordillera (close to the Alberta border) is a fold
and thrust belt, deformed and broken, that is comprised mostly of sedimentary rocks eroded from North America. The western part (the Coastal
Belt) consists of a series of volcanic segments (or *terranes*) that evolved as
a result of interactions between the Pacific and North America tectonic
plates. The buildup of each new terrane has extended the edge of the continent westward.

The complex processes that formed the Cordillera are reflected in the
distribution of its minerals and other resources. Belts of distinct rocks, each
with their own deposits, run NW-SE through the province, parallel to the
present coastline and the Continental Divide. As a result, the province's
geology varies considerably when you travel W-E. The mainly volcanic
terranes of the west contain gold, silver, iron, copper and molybdenum,
while the generally sedimentary rocks of the eastern terranes are rich in
lead, zinc, silver and, beyond the eastern margin, oil and gas.

This book looks at the area within a day's drive of Vancouver and,
traffic jams in the Fraser Valley notwithstanding, covers a region that is
almost exclusively within the Coastal Belt. It extends as far northwest as
Powell River on the Sunshine Coast, as far north as Gold Bridge and Clinton,

and takes in Cache Creek, Ashcroft, Merritt and Princeton. Within this area lie some fascinating mineral deposits, old mines, placer beaches, cliffs, outcroppings, deep gorges and exposed bedrock. In short, the perfect places for a rockhound to spend an enjoyable (and hopefully rewarding) weekend, or, better still, summer week away from it all.

Happy prospecting!

CHAPTER 1: GEOLOGY

1.1 ALL ABOUT ROCKS AND MINERALS

Everything around us, and of us, is made up of just 106 elements (sulfur, gold and iron are typical elements). Together, these elements form a bewildering number of compounds. And the compounds can form minerals. Fortunately, in the field of mineralogy, there are only about 3,600 different minerals, and we need to know only about 50–100 to sound like an expert!

These minerals are found on that thin layer of the earth's outer hard surface known as the crust. The continents are islands, composed of lighter rocks, floating on an inner mass of heavier ones, far below the surface and still at very high temperatures.

The most common elements by weight of the earth's crust are believed to be oxygen at 53%, silicon at 26%, then aluminum 7.5%, iron 4.2%, calcium 3.3%, potassium 3%, hydrogen 1%, carbon 0.4% and so on down the list. It's hardly surprising, then, that *silica* (silicon dioxide or SiO_2, which is what glass, sand and quartz are all made from) is one of the most common compounds in the crust.

A given rock may be formed from one or several minerals, and its properties will depend on its components. It may be plastic like clay, malleable like gold, powdery like sand or liquid like mercury.

The study of rocks includes many different fields. The *geologist* identifies the rock formations and determines how and when they were formed. *Petrologists* identify the structure and history of the rocks themselves; the *mineralogist* identifies and studies the minerals that make up the rocks. There are lots of other *-ologists* dealing in other aspects of geology, but we are most interested in these three subjects.

It is well worth learning as much as you can about the science of rocks, even if you believe you will never go beyond identifying the occasional rock found in a river bed. The fact is, you don't need to understand how an engine works to drive a car, but, if you do, it will make you a better driver. So too with rockhounding: A basic understanding of the processes and minerals makes you more likely to find "the big one" that we all know is out there, with our name written all over it! And remember, only a century ago when the first prospectors were looking for oil in the United States, they used to throw a hat in the air, and drill where it landed! We've come quite a way in a hundred years!

Learning about rocks can take place at many levels. There's a lot to be said for joining a local lapidary or rockhounding club (see Chapter 10: Addresses). They organize field trips and offer lots of hands-on learning opportunities. For those wanting something a bit more thorough, colleges, institutes and universities offer night classes.

1.2 THE SHAPE OF BC (GEOMORPHOLOGY)

The earth's surface is constantly being changed, either catastrophically (like the eruption of Mount St. Helens), or gradually, in the form of upthrusting or erosion. The main agents in erosion are water, ice, wind and chemical breakdown. In the recent past, within the province of BC, glacial ice has played a major role in shaping the land and depositing sediments. Today, rivers are the major erosion force.

Bedrock also affects the shape of the land. Whether it's hard or soft, cracked or massive, makes a big difference. Climate has an effect too—in a desert area, limestone will last much longer than in a high rainfall zone, where it slowly dissolves.

There are four major physiographic divisions in the province. Reading from left to right on the map, they are the Western, Central, Eastern and Alberta Plains divisions. See **Figure 1.1** for details.

The *Western System* is made up of two ranges: the outer mountains of the Queen Charlotte Islands and Vancouver Island, and the inner Coastal Ranges that back onto the city of Vancouver, and run up the coast to the Alaskan Panhandle. The two ranges are separated by the Coastal Trough (Georgia Strait up to Hecate Strait). This is an active area; in the past 10 million years volcanoes have been formed along the margin (Mt. Garibaldi, Black Tusk Peak).

The *Interior System* is a blend of plateaux and mountain areas that formed from about 200 million years ago onwards, and is the result of recurring glacial ice, as well as volcanic activity. For example, the basalts south of Ashcroft are 200 million years old, while those at Spences Bridge not far away are only 100 million years old. By and large, the mountainous areas of the Interior System are underlain with old rocks, including igneous, metamorphic and Pre-Cambrian sedimentary. The plateaux, on the other hand, are generally younger. This is a great mineral hunting area.

The *Eastern System* is quite different; it is made up of the Rocky and Mackenzie mountains, and is bounded on the western side by the Rocky Mountain Trench, which has the towns of Kimberley and Golden in it.

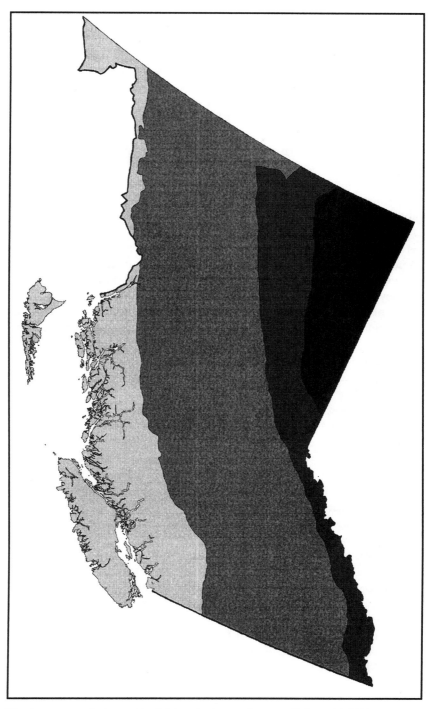

The four major physiographic divisions in the province are: (left to right) Western, Central, Eastern and Alberta Plains.

Granites are uncommon; instead, the records show massive piling up of slabs of rock that were pushed and slid from the west, mostly during a time of between 100 million and 40 million years ago. This created thick strata of sedimentary rocks, such as Mount Robson near Jasper, and Mount Rundle near Banff. In some places, old rocks have been pushed up over younger ones. In most, there is a tendency for the southwest slopes to be gentle, the northeast to be steep or even cliff-like, resulting in grand scenery. This is world-class fossil country.

The *Alberta Plain* is a sedimentary basin that intrudes into the northeastern corner of the province, on the east side of the Rocky Mountain ranges. Drained by the Peace River, sediments here are thousands of metres thick, and are known best for their oil and gas production. Fossils abound.

1.3   THE ROCKS OF BC (PETROLOGY)

A noted university professor of geology used to begin his introductory lecture with the words, "There are only two kinds of rocks—those you make money out of, and those you don't."

This is rather an over-simplification! Instead, you could say there are three kinds of rocks: *igneous, sedimentary* and *metamorphic*. Let's explain:

1.3.1   Igneous rocks

Igneous rocks are those that have come from molten matter deep inside the earth. They may be *intrusive*, which means they never reached the surface, but squeeze into cracks on the way up (as *dykes* or *sills*), and are later exposed due to weathering or uplifting. Granite is a typical intrusive rock, being coarse-grained. It cooled slowly deep down, allowing feldspar, quartz and usually mica and hornblende to crystallize in the rock matrix. The mountains in the Bugaboo Range (to the west of Windermere) are granites, as is the Stawamus Chief, that huge cliff that overhangs the highway as you reach Squamish at the top of Howe Sound. Other important intrusives are *pegmatites*, which frequently house the best gemstones, *syenite*, which is a granite without quartz, *diorite*, *gabbro* and *peridotite*, the latter often containing important commercial minerals. Mountaineers often prefer intrusives because they offer hard, well-cracked rock faces to climb.

Igneous rocks can be *extrusive* too, which means they reached the surface as lava or magma flows and cooled quickly to form fine-grained material. Hawaii and Iceland are ongoing examples of this process. The lava flows below Black Tusk and Garibaldi Park, above Highway #99, are this type, where you would expect to find *obsidian*, *basalt* and *rhyolite*. Basalt and rhyolite have much the same chemistry as granite but, by cooling more quickly, do not allow crystals to form and grow. When rhyolite is blown by hot gases into a sponge texture, it is called *pumice*, which is a volcanic froth. There are deposits northwest of Pemberton. Pumice has so many air pockets, it floats on water!

There are a wide variety of extrusive rocks in British Columbia. The most important, from a mineral collecting point of view, are the basalts, which are commonly *vesicular* (full of voids). These gaps may later be filled with agate, calcite or zeolite minerals, to become *amygdaloidal* lavas. The most prolific flows are those that formed during the Tertiary Age from about 20 million to 65 million years ago. Most rockhounds have heard of the prolific agate beds within the area of Kamloops-Vernon-Princeton, but other areas to the north have similar geology, but have not been explored to any extent. Large areas are unfortunately covered by overburden (often glacial till). New localities may be found by prospecting creeks, talus slopes and outcrops.

1.3.2   Sedimentary rocks

Sedimentary rocks are surprisingly varied, and are produced by fluid (usually water, but sometimes wind) depositing them in layers. Sedimentary rocks are therefore formed in *strata* or beds, and are initially flat. Some are formed from pre-existing rocks by erosion, and can be fine-grained like the sandstone beaches found along the shores of the Gulf and Georgia Strait islands, or coarse-grained conglomerates, which look like piles of river pebbles glued together with concrete. The Rocky Mountains along the BC-Alberta border are fine examples of sedimentary processes, with their obvious "layer cake" look, often tilted due to recent thrusting.

Some sedimentary rocks are formed by chemical precipitation (e.g. gypsum) while others are formed by compacting the shells of marine animals to form limestone. A lot of chalk and limestone cliffs (including the famous White Cliffs of Dover in England) are actually countless marine organisms piled into layers hundreds of metres thick.

1.3.3   Metamorphic rocks

The third type is *metamorphic rock*, and basically refers to any rock that has been changed after being formed. Thus, both igneous and sedimentary rocks can be *metamorphosed* into something new. The change can be small (slate is simply shale that has been cooked for a few millennia), or it can be so dramatic you can't tell what the original material was (sometimes known as *fubar*ite = "fudged up beyond all recognition")! Pressure, chemical penetration and heat are the great metamorphic forces. Marble is metamorphosed limestone, and quartzites were usually sandstones once. *Schists* and *gneisses* (pronounced "shists" and "nices") are often heavily changed shales and granites, after other material has invaded or permeated them. Geologists spend years arguing about what happened, when and to whom.

1.4 A BRIEF GEOLOGICAL HISTORY OF SW BRITISH COLUMBIA

The mountains of the Canadian Cordillera formed as a result of *plate tectonics*. The outer skin of the Earth, to a depth of about 150 km, consists of seven major and some minor *plates*. These plates move in response to great currents far down inside the planet. Major surface formations, such as mountains, form at or near plate boundaries.

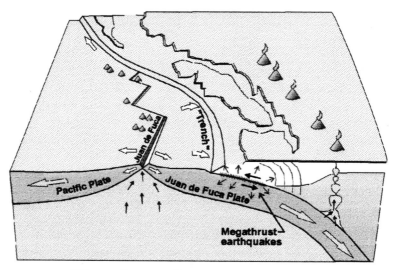

West Coast Great Earthquakes

In **Figure 1.2**, the three kinds of plate boundaries are shown. The diagram shows the relationships at the surface and at depth of the continental North America Plate and the oceanic Juan de Fuca and Pacific plates.

On the left, an *ocean ridge* is formed by magma rising to the surface, where the plates spread apart.

Along the "Trench" there is a *subduction zone* where the Juan de Fuca Plate converges with the North America Plate and dives beneath it. A chain of volcanoes forms on the overriding plate on the right of the figure. These can be seen at Black Tusk, Mount Garibaldi, Mount Baker, Mount Rainier aand Mount St. Helens.

Further north, a *transform plate* occurs, where two plates (the Juan de Fuca and the North America) slide past each other. These *shear faults*, often located close to a country's shoreline, have the potential to do considerable damage through massive earthquakes. On the other hand, there's nothing like a good subduction-induced earthquake to set the teeth rattling, as has been the case many times in Chile, Alaska and Japan.

The Canadian Cordillera is the product of natural processes that have been operating for millions of years, and are still happening. Mountain uplift is primarily the result of the plates converging, which thickens the Earth's crust. In addition, volcanic eruptions add large amounts of rock, spreading out from local hot spots.

Countering these uplift processes are the forces of erosion. Rain, snow, wind, ice and chemical attack all wear down the land. Enormous amounts of sand, gravel and boulders move down BC's rivers every day. During spring runoff, you can often hear the din of rocks rolling down creek beds. In BC, ice ages (of which there have been many in the past two million years) have further scoured the landscape in a way that no precipitation can do. Cirques, hanging valleys, U-shaped valleys and fiords are all the result, from Juan de Fuca Strait in the south to the Alaskan Panhandle and beyond. As recently as 15,000 years ago, most of the Canadian Cordillera was buried under 2 km of ice from the last great continental ice sheet. You wouldn't have recognized Stanley Park.

1.5 WHERE TO LOOK WHEN ROCKHOUNDING

There are abandoned mines and prospects all over the province. Why are they abandoned? Because the required concentration of ore was missing. For every hundred prospects, only one will become a mine. Where does this leave the rockhound? While the prospect might be unsatisfactory for the miner, there may be tonnes of good material for the collector, recovered from trenches, shallow adits (tunnels) or even just from exposed bedrock.

I wonder how many times I've heard someone say, "Oh, that place! It's been picked over for years. There's nothing left there." In fact, that's very rarely the case. Even small dumps contain huge amounts of great "stuff". All it takes is a little effort to recover it. And don't forget that mine roads are often made from surplus "stuff" too.

Remember that even when this guidebook lists a particular site at "Point X", it may only be the centre of the mineralized area. Spurs and extensions may extend in several different directions, something that others often choose to ignore, because the "official" site is at Point X. Perhaps Point X is on the bank of a river. In which case, what about checking the other bank? You may be surprised to find all sorts of comparable material that hasn't been picked over. If it's difficult to get to the other bank, so much the better: not many others will have made the effort.

What if the site is at the foot of a hill? The strata may reappear on the other side of the same hill, at a comparable level. Except no one has bothered to check yet. You'd be surprised how often idleness sets in when the sun is hot, or the bugs are bad, or ... you get the picture. Often, nobody has bothered to check it out.

Knowing a bit about basic geology helps too. Contact zones, where one formation meets another (say a granite plug touches a limestone deposit) are of great interest, because where strata meet is where minerals concentrate, and crystals can form.

Gravity is another great help to the prospector. Material weathering out of a cliff will fall and stop, or fall and roll great distances. Talus slopes become sorting grounds for interesting material. Rivers do the same thing, settling dense metals (gold, barite, magnetite) deep into bedrock cracks, and moving the light materials on over the top.

Road and railway cuttings are easily accessible sources of material. They are often active (mini-slides), revealing fresh faces to examine. And, of course, they are frequently rearranged by road maintenance, so that major new surfaces are exposed, all without you lifting a shovel! Actually, some of the very best sites have been found by forestry or highway crews while building new roads or upgrading old ones. So, cultivate your local road engineers—they can be invaluable.

Cliffs are good sites, as are the shores of the sea, lakes and river beds. Quarries, mine workings and mine dumps are usually productive places to search for minerals, but be careful! **Shafts and tunnels in old mines are frequently unsafe, and should be avoided.** It's usually safe to work the old parts of a mine dump; dig in from the side, if you can, to avoid having to remove the newer, overburden. Examine boulders—there may be stuff in them that was missed. When you find something, note the circumstances, and try finding similar conditions elsewhere.

In the field, know what host rocks are associated with what you're trying to find. For example, jade is associated with serpentine, although not all serpentine will contain jade. But it's a lot easier to look for large serpentine deposits than individual jade boulders. Beryl is found in pegmatite, but not every pegmatite has beryl … and so on.

1.6 ETHICS

Common courtesy dictates that you ask permission before entering a mine site, quarry or other private property. There may be old adits or drifts that are hidden, but poorly protected. Falling down a mine shaft could ruin your whole day. Access rights are discussed in Chapter 4. For more detailed information, talk to a Gold Commissioner.

★ If the property is privately owned, it is common to pay some daily fee, or percentage of the take.

★ Be cautious about bringing along a dog. Bears, porcupines and ranchers may not share your admiration for the family pet.

★ Respect all wildlife. Before you go into an area, try to figure out what you're likely to meet, and what the best way to react would be if you do. A few moments' forethought can avoid a lot of discomfort later.

★ Be extra careful with fire.

★ Close gates.

★ Take out your garbage.

★ Don't contaminate the creeks.

★ Fill in your holes. Animals, including valuable stock, could fall into them. And besides, you don't want to show everyone where you've been working.

★ Stay off crop and grass land.

★ No firearms or blasting unless the owner agrees.

★ If the owner allows you to prospect for free (many do), then a gift made from something taken off the property (some tumbled stones, or a pretty agate slice) makes a valued "thank you" the next time you visit.

★ Tell someone where you're going and when you're coming home. If you change your mind before leaving the vehicle, leave a note on the dashboard, so potential rescue parties have a clue which way you went.

★ Be honest. Without honesty, the whole access question gets bogged down, and wonderful collecting sites can be put off limits, sometimes for decades.

CHAPTER 2: A SHORT HISTORY OF BC PROSPECTING

2.1 THE GOLD RUSH STARTED EVERYTHING

The 1858 gold rush in BC followed on the heels of the 1849 rush in California. It's true that the Haida had discovered gold in the Queen Charlotte Islands as early as 1850, but the production was low and the locals hostile, so little activity followed. In 1852 native Indians found gold on the Thompson River, but for five years little happened. Then, in 1858, some 75 American miners arrived and set up operations at Hills Bar, below what we know today as Yale, in the Fraser Canyon.

Within a year, the gold rush had swelled from a trickle to a flood. In Victoria, the capital city of Vancouver Island (but not the Mainland), the population jumped from 225 to 450 in a single day, and swelled to 5,000 within a month. Any vessel capable of being patched and rendered semi-seaworthy, set sail from California, crammed to the railings with men dreaming of riches in the gold fields of British Columbia.

2.2 DEFINING A PROVINCE

The Governor, Sir James Douglas, quickly realized that if he did not establish a system to control this influx of southerners, both the gold and the interior of the province would default to the United States, since the border at that time was still undefined. As a result, he claimed ownership of the gold fields in the name of the Crown, established a system of miner's licenses, and enforced the law. Anyone venturing into the interior to prospect had to buy a license in Victoria (at a cost of ten shillings per month). Under the terms of this license, a man could stake a claim 12 feet by 12 feet.

By 1860, prospectors had discovered the Cariboo fields, and word quickly spread of incredible finds. At the same time, the placer deposits along the Fraser and Thompson rivers were being worked out as men moved huge volumes of gravel and sand with little more than hand tools.

Further gold discoveries followed: in 1862 the Stikine; the Kootenays and Leech River (near Victoria) in 1864; Big Bend in 1866; the Peace-Omineca in 1869; and finally the Cassiar district in 1872.

2.3 A NETWORK OF CIVILIZATION DEVELOPED

As the gold rush progressed, the law, in the form of the North West Mounted Police, locally appointed magistrates, Victoria appointed judges, and Gold Commissioners established a system of records and government that was quite unlike the cheerful lawlessness of the California and Nome gold rushes. Behind them, the Royal Engineers followed, establishing roads, bridges, ferries and infrastructure.

Once the surface placers began to peter out, most of the miners left for other pastures, leaving behind them a string of new towns and networks which were quickly expanded by ranchers, businessmen and fisheries. Saw-mills and logging started, followed by housing, hotels, entertainment and more. In short, in just two decades the non-existent province of British Columbia came into existence, was included into the new federation of Canada, gained a network of roads and railway lines, a dynamic population, and a booming economy.

There had been early coal discoveries at Nanaimo on Vancouver Island in the 1850s, but with the gold decline in the 1880s, its importance in the interior grew. Lead and silver, often found in association with gold, were also developed, and copper was discovered in large quantities in the early 1900s.

2.4 MINING BUILT THE PROVINCE

Many towns were founded on mining. For example, Yale, Barkerville and Atlin were the result of gold placer mining; Nelson was silver mining; Rossland on copper-gold; Kimberley on the Sullivan lead-zinc mine; Kaslo on lead-silver; Greenwood and Britannia on copper; Endako on molybdenum; Nanaimo, Comox, Fort St. John and Cumberland on coal mining.

Times have changed a great deal in just one short century. Where the old sourdoughs struggled into the interior of the province over terrible trails, enduring scorching summer heat and flies, and arctic winters that killed them in droves, today mining is the forte of large corporations who can raise the huge sums of money needed to move 100,000 t of rock a day to get at the minerals.

2.5 THE LITTLE GUY IS STILL A KEY PLAYER

Yet the prospector still has an important role to play. Despite all the sophisticated technology used in modern exploration, new mineral showings are still being turned up by prospectors; just ordinary people with determination, an independent streak and a dream. The province is vast; its potential barely tapped. It could happen to you, just as easily as it happened to Billy Barker at Barkerville.

CHAPTER 3:
PROSPECTING TECHNIQUES

Go, my sons, buy stout shoes, climb the mountains, search the valleys, the deserts, the sea shores, and the deep recesses of the earth. Mark well the various kinds of minerals, note their properties and their mode of origin.

– Petrus Severinus (1571)

Rockhounding takes you into the boonies, so here are some tips to make things more comfortable when you're out there.

★ Don't prospect alone. Three is the best number—in the event of an accident, one can stay with the patient while the other goes for help.

★ Make sure your vehicle is in good shape; there might not be anyone along for a while to find you if you break down. Four wheel drive is a lot better than two. And have enough gas!

★ Bring food and water; you may want to stay longer than planned. And bring candles for light and warmth.

★ Carry decent maps—the 1:250,000 and the 1:50,000 series are useful, and give plenty of detail.

★ Get local information from the Gold Commissioner's Offices, local rock shops and rockhounding clubs.

★ Don't be too ambitious—hounding takes time, and the more time spent driving between sites, the less time there is to enjoy what you really want to do: hunt for that prize specimen.

★ Don't ignore the seasons. Winter in the Interior is serious. Even summer in the high country can be bitterly cold. Digging hot gravels in mid-summer should be done in the cool of the morning and evening.

3.1 WHAT TO WEAR

Wear the same sort of clothes as you would to hunt or hike. Tough, comfortable shoes or boots are a must. When working near water, take along a pair of gumboots. If you don't have to worry about getting your feet wet, you'll often go into places that others may have overlooked. Spare socks are appreciated by everyone when you get back to the vehicle.

A canvas or nylon vest full of pockets is handy. They can be bought at most outfitting stores (for hunters or fishermen), or ordered from a mining supplier, where they are called geologist's vests.

A lot of prospecting involves bending over. Knee pads are sometimes handy (the skateboard type are great), and a waterproof jacket to protect your horizontal back is a must if you plan to have some comfort. A spare sweater is also handy—gullies, cracks and mine shafts can be cool to downright freezing, even in mid-summer.

3.2 WHAT TOOLS TO CARRY

Take a pair of safety goggles; you can buy them at hardware stores, or a pair of old ski goggles work well. Wear them whenever you're chipping rock. Work gloves are necessary. Insect repellent is also handy. Some people prefer bug-hats with a wide brim and mesh. Let's face it, when things are bad, nothing seems to work. It makes you wonder how the sourdoughs managed a hundred years ago.

Brawn Tools: A hammer is essential. One with a chisel-shaped back is handy for trimming specimens. A carpenter's hammer is no good—it will chip. A prybar, a shovel, a set of hardened chisels, a smaller trenching tool, a pointed pick and a spoon are all useful for different jobs. A heavy hammer (8 lb is about best) can convince hard samples to relax a bit. A small plastic gold pan weighs nothing yet can provide hours of fun. But remember, the more you have to carry, the less distance you'll be prepared to hike from the road.

Brain Tools: A tough bag with a shoulder strap is indispensable, together with a pocket knife. A leather carpenter's apron is preferred by some. A hardness testing kit (see Chapter 5.1 for materials to use) is handy for identifying specimens by hardness. A magnifying glass (*loupe*) in the X10 to X16 range is useful for checking inclusions and crystallography.

Bring a flashlight, and make sure it can't switch on by accident (put a disk of cardboard between the spring and back battery). A compass and map(s) are vital. I find I use an altimeter a lot, not only to figure out how far up-slope I am, but as a barometer. Overnight, it is a much more reliable gauge of the weather than the radio (if the altitude apparently drops, the weather is improving). Bring newspaper to wrap your specimens (and to read, when your partner is still way up the hill). A magnet and a streak plate (unglazed side of a bathroom tile) are also helpful in identifying an unknown sample.

If you're into chemistry, a dropper bottle containing one part concentrated hydrochloric acid to 19 parts water (a 5% solution) is handy for testing reactivity. Just make sure that the cap doesn't leak, or you'll be looking for new pockets.

A notebook and pencil (you can buy "Write in the Rain" paper from some stationers), camera and labels are a good idea to keep accurate records. You might also like to know that the average person's index finger measures approximately 2.5 cm (1 in) between knuckle joints, which means that you can measure the width of a mineral vein, or the length of a chrysotile fibre with considerable accuracy, simply by bringing a hand along on field trips.

A recent arrival on the scene is the Global Positional System (GPS) receiver. About the size of a calculator, it receives radio signals from up to 12 orbiting satellites, and calculates its position in latitude, longitude and altitude with an accuracy of between 30 m to 300 m. While this may seem an unnecessary refinement when you are working in open country (like Alberta), in the thick forests and box canyons of BC you can walk within 50 m of a site and never even see it. GPS receivers (now under $300 and the prices are still dropping), when used with common sense, can save you a lot of wasted time.

And, of course, bring this book!

3.3 CARING FOR YOUR SPECIMENS

There's always a temptation to take too much, with the result you end up with a basement full of stuff you'll never really use. That's not fair on the next guy to try his luck, and it often irritates the landowner when he sees huge chunks of his property disappearing into the back of a pickup—sort of makes him wonder what he's missing. Trim your specimens to a practical size. Wrap them individually in newspaper, and label them with place, time, and other relevant information. If you don't, it's funny how often they all look the same when you get back to the road and start gloating! Pack them very carefully to avoid later disappointments, especially if the hike out is rough.

Once home, wash the specimens in water. Don't use stiff brushes on soft materials. Label each clearly. You can paint a small white patch on an inconspicuous surface, using typist's white-out liquid, and then number with an indelible felt-tip pen. Note all the details in your field book.

As your collection grows, you may want to arrange it in some sort of system (by area, or date, or colour or material), so loose labels may get misplaced, and numbering sequences interrupted. Many serious collectors use Dana's system of mineralogy, a system of mineral classification based on chemical properties. Developed by James Dwight Dana, a Yale professor, it was first published in 1837 and significantly revised in 1854.

3.4 SAFETY TIPS

Old mines sites are hazardous places; hidden shafts and unstable walls lurk in vegetation and underfoot. In coal areas, shafts fill with methane gas that is odourless and deadly.

★   Avoid entering old workings, but if you do, LOOK UP! Always have a buddy within earshot. Don't hammer or walk up-slope of your friend. Well, not if you want him to stay a friend.

★   Wear safety glasses, and check that your hammer's head is secure.

★   Before visiting an area for the first time, talk with someone who knows the area. Features change and new roads make easier access (I once climbed 3,000 m in 13 hours to find a new jeep track that could have been driven in an hour!)

★   Carry a first aid kit. And check it's complete BEFORE you start.

★   Respect the weather. It's bigger than you.

CHAPTER 4. ACCESS RIGHTS

4.1 ACCESS RIGHTS

First, a bit of legalese to explain what rights exist for property owner and prospector:

Most land owners in BC hold clear title to their property, but their Certificate of Title seldom includes what lies beneath the surface. Surface and subsurface rights are separate and distinct. Unless otherwise excluded by the property title, the land owner's rights usually only extend to soil, sand and gravel. Under normal circumstances, the Crown reserves the rights to the subsurface, which may include coal, petroleum, natural gas and minerals (both base and precious). The rights to these substances may be granted by the Crown separately under different legislation. The land owner's rights are defined in the **Land Act**. Any person disregarding those rights is subject to the **Trespass Act**. A person may be entitled to enter private lands, however, in order to acquire subsurface rights, under the **Mineral Tenure Act**.

Many of the sites listed in this guidebook are on unoccupied Crown Land, so you don't need any paperwork just to have a look around. Anyone can hand pan or prospect on most Crown Lands, with the following exceptions:

★   in parks, except as permitted by the Mineral Tenure Act
★   on a valid Placer Claim or Placer
★   on an Indian Reserve
★   on land occupied by a building
★   up to 75 m around a dwelling house
★   orchards and cultivated lands.

Recreational hand panning and prospecting are allowed without holding a Free Miner's Certificate (obtainable from your local Gold Commissioner's Office). Hand panning equipment is restricted to a hand shovel and a hand pan. The key word here is *hand*. You can't use mechanical equipment for recreational purposes. In particular, portable suction dredges are strictly regulated in BC; you should check with your nearest Gold Commissioner before taking one into the field.

If you think this is limiting, pity the poor Albertans. According to their laws, rockhounds may only pick up what is on the surface! If you need to dig ("excavate" is what the lawyers call it) you need an excavation permit.

Beware of disturbing archaeological sites or artifacts. These are protected under the **Heritage Conservation Act**. And going even further back in time, palaeontological artifacts and fossils are additionally covered under the **Cultural Properties Import & Export Act** which, among a lot of other details, advises you that you cannot export Canadian fossils valued at more than $200 without a permit.

Another reason for leaving archaeological sites alone is the matter of completeness. If you found a jade axe, for example, you'd be delighted. For a while, it would sit on your mantleshelf in a place of honour. It would be shown to friends, and the story of its discovery told repeatedly. Maybe too repeatedly. But after a while, it will get dusty. The grandchildren will be found using it to crack nuts on the back porch ... You get the idea. OK, so instead, you take it to a museum for evaluation. Museums are underfunded these days. They don't have the manpower to check out the site. But, without a detailed, professional assessment of the site, one artifact (however spectacular) is just one artifact. And archaeological artifacts can't stand on their own—they must be part of a carefully researched, painstakingly detailed study of a complete site. Unless you're prepared to do that, leave the sites to those who are.

Then, of course, there is the **Trespass Act**, which everyone thinks they know, but probably don't really. Here are the two key sections:

Section 4.1: A person found inside enclosed land without the consent of its owner, lessee or occupier shall be deemed a trespasser.

Section 6: A person who is, within the meaning of this act, a trespasser or who continues or who enters again an enclosed land after having been notified, or required by or on behalf of its owner, lessee or occupier to quit the land commits an offence.

Think that through for a minute. What the act is saying is (a) the property must be **enclosed** (usually fenced or walled), **and** (b) you are only trespassing if you (i) refuse to leave when told to, or (ii) return after being told to leave.

Finally (if you are still capable of reading), there are laws preventing the collection of minerals in federal and provincial parks, and ecological reserves. These restrictions apply whether the goodies are in, on or growing out of, the ground, and may be covered under the **Ecological Reserve Act**. Tread softly.

CHAPTER 5: ROCK & MINERAL IDENTIFICATION

Most gemstones are minerals, made up of elements or compounds, occurring naturally. This means they are not man-made or otherwise manufactured; they have a definite chemical composition; often, they have a distinct crystal form. They differ from rocks, in that rocks are made up of minerals in various mixtures. When I explain that concept to kids, I use the analogy of pizza—olives, ham and cheese are the "minerals" and always look the same; the final mixture or "rock" is the pizza itself, and can vary quite considerably while still having the same ingredients.

There are exceptions to the rule above, of course. Amber is plant-made, pearl is animal-made, and they're both gems. Granite and unakite are rocks without crystal form (or *habit*), but are often used in jewelry.

In case you've ever wondered why minerals and rocks sometimes have such wacky names, you should know that since 1959 the International Mineralogical Association Commission on New Minerals and New Names calls the shots. If someone wants to have a name recognized internationally, he or she must submit a full description of the new species, complete with chemical composition, properties and a lot more. At the same time, he or she can propose a name of their choice. Then, after suitable mumbling, the name and species are adopted, or not.

There are two schools of thought when it comes to naming a new mineral: *rational* and *irrational*. *Rational* names are based on some property of the new species; for instance, "fluorite" fluoresces, and "naphoite" is made of sodium (chemical symbol *Na*) and phosphate (*PhO*). Incidentally, the "*ite*" on the end of so many minerals and rocks comes from the Greek word *lithos*, meaning rock or stone.

Irrational names don't tell you anything about the material itself, but usually honour some person or thing who may have contributed to its identification, or was the finder of the first sample. Examples are *bauxite*, named after the region near Baux in France where it was first identified, and *wicksite*, named after Dr F.J. Wicks, curator of the Royal Ontario Museum.

To date, about 3,600 minerals have been identified. Of these, fewer than a hundred are gemstone material, and you'll be lucky to see more than 30 in a jewelry store. So, don't despair, it's not as complex as you might first think!

GEMSTONES — A SPECIAL CASE

Gem material must be rare, beautiful and wear-resistant. Fashion also plays an important part in the demand for gemstones. In ancient Greece, yellow stones were much in demand, but in Roman times green was considered the epitome of fashion. Today, clear brilliance is highly prized: "A diamond is forever." Rarity makes a stone precious, but if it is too rare, not enough people know about it, and there's little demand.

The trouble with most gems and minerals is that in the rough they don't look anything like they do when you see them in a jewelry store. Ah, the prizes we've walked over in big boots, and never even suspected, eh? To solve that problem, rockhounds have developed a number of field tests. Some gems can be identified by their colours, but many have weathered or oxidized outer shells and so have no colour at all. Others have lots of colours, which is just as confusing. So we try to identify the gem through elimination.

Many gemstones are crystals, and so show a distinct arrangement of smooth faces and angles formed by those faces. These are the result of the atoms aligning themselves in repetitive patterns. Crystallography is a huge field, and not something that can be covered in a guide like this. Let's just say that, in theory, crystals grow perfectly, usually over prolonged periods of time. To give you some idea of the rate of crystal growth, consider a surface that grows by one millimeter per day. (That's about the thickness of your fingernail.) To maintain this incredibly rapid rate, over 100 atomic layers have to align themselves (perfectly) *per second*! It's hardly surprising that crystals are (a) rare, (b) small, and (c) take a long time to form.

In the real world, of course, there are impurities and other factors that result in crystals growing in all sorts of variations. Suffice it to say, mineralogists have reduced all crystal shapes to just six systems:

isometric – fluorite, octahedral diamond, trisoctahedral garnet, halite, galena

tetragonal – zircon, rutile, cassiterite

hexagonal – quartz, apatite, calcite, tourmaline, beryl

orthorhombic – barite, topaz, sulfur, staurolite, olivine

monoclinic – orthoclase feldspar, gypsum, epidote, mica

triclinic – rhodonite, plagioclase feldspar

There are exceptions to every rule, of course. Opal and obsidian, for example, don't have a crystal structure at all, and are just gemmological Jell-O.

5.1 HARDNESS

Mohs' scale of hardness is named after the German mineralogist Friederich Mohs (1773-1839) who devised a simple standard of comparison, ranging from 1 (soft) to 10 (hard) that determines relative "scratchability". Anything having, for example, a hardness of 6, will scratch anything having a lower number of 1 through 5. Minerals having typical hardnesses are:

1 talc
2 gypsum
3 calcite
4 fluorite
5 apatite
6 orthoclase
7 quartz
8 topaz
9 corundum (ruby, sapphire)
10 diamond

The easiest way to remember the sequence is "*The girls can flirt and other queer things can do*." Gypsum is harder than talc, but not twice as hard. Fluorite is harder than calcite, but is less hard than apatite. If a material scratches everything up to fluorite, but not apatite, then it has a hardness between 4 and 5. For field work, you can buy hardness pencils that come equipped with known stones, or you can make your own. Other useful hardness tools are:

2.5 fingernail
4 penny, common nail
5.5 window glass, penknife blade
6.5 metal file
7 quartz crystal

Remember not to scratch a prize specimen in a visible place! When examining a scratch, make sure you are looking at the scratch, and not some loose powder that has been scraped off. Wash the specimen and see that the scratch scores the real rock.

5.2 COLOUR

Recognizing a rock by its outer colour can be pretty deceiving, as surfaces oxidize and tarnish, fooling the most experienced prospector. You have to look at a clean break to get an honest sample, and even then, there are plenty of variations on the colour theme:

Asterism is the result of an alignment of atoms in the stone so that the reflected light is in the form of a star (four or six points are common). Star ruby and quartz are well known.

Chatoyant is a form of asterism where a single line of light is reflected, forming a cat's eye effect. A much admired gem is chrysoberyl, while tiger eye is more common.

Colour change is how a material changes colour as the light falls on it from different angles. Labradorite and tiger eye are typical examples.

Colour play is how an opal's fire changes as the stone is turned; the stone's prismatic lenses catch the light and refract it in various hues.

Fluorescence is the ability of a mineral to glow in the dark when exposed to invisible light, such as an ultraviolet lamp. An obvious stone is fluorite, named for that very reason.

Iridescence is the play of light produced by tiny cracks and fractures in an otherwise transparent crystal. It's not uncommon to see rainbows in quartz, for example, caused this way.

Opalescence is a milky or mother-of-pearl appearance that seems to glow from the inside. Australian fire opal, for example, often looks like it's being lit from within by a hot coal.

Phosphorescence is a property that allows a stone to radiate light even after the light source (a bright lamp, for example) has been removed.

5.3 LUSTRE

Lustre depends on the absorption, reflection or refraction of the light by the mineral's surface. Common terms are:

adamantine – brilliant, glittering, like a diamond

greasy – appears oil smeared

metallic – smooth and gleaming like a typical metal. Hematite and galena are typical

resinous – looks a bit like egg-shell porcelain

silky – looks fibrous, like asbestos

vitreous – smooth and glossy like glass

5.4 SPECIFIC GRAVITY, OR DENSITY

Specific gravity (or SG, also called density) is the ratio of the weight of a known volume of mineral, compared to an equal volume of pure water. Water has a density of 1. Most rocks have an SG between 2 and 5, but some minerals are a dead give-away when you pick them up. There's no substitute for a gold nugget—even a pebble pup can recognize it because its SG is 19.3! That's heavy! Other dense minerals are cinnabar (8) and uraninite (9.5). At the other end of the scale, pumice is a volcanic rock containing gas bubbles, and has an SG of 0.9, so it's one of the few rocks that floats!

SG is best done in a lab, although you can rig up a density scale quite easily if you have a triple beam balance at home. It's usually used as a "clincher" to identify a mineral when all other tests have already been done to reduce the options. Weigh the sample in air (*air weight*). Let's suppose it weighs 327 gm. Now tie a thin thread around it and lower it into a bowl of water so it is completely submerged. Tie the top end of the thread (somehow) to the scale's weigh pan. Suppose the scale now reads 206 gm (*water weight*). Then the SG = the air weight divided by the difference between the air and water weights = $327 / (327 - 206) = 327 / 121 = 2.7$

Another way to measure SG is to make up liquids of different densities. Since most rocks of interest are in the range 2 to 5, that does not make it too difficult. Archimedes years ago realized that an object that floated in a liquid, had the same density as that liquid. That's why we just float in sea water—we're about the same SG of 1.024. In fresh water (SG = 1.00) we frequently sink. So, by dropping your unknown specimen into different SG mixes, you can determine fairly accurately what the density is.

5.5 CLEAVAGE

Cleavage has nothing to do with ladies in cocktail dresses. It's the way some minerals split along planes related to the molecular structure of the mineral, and parallel to possible crystal faces. Cleavage perfection is described in five steps from *poor* (such as bornite), *fair, good, perfect* and *eminent*, such as in mica, which will flake and flake into thinner and thinner slices. Materials like galena cleave into beautiful cubes, while calcite cleaves into rhombohedrals. Diamond have perfect cleavage, meaning a diamond can be split along planes to form a classic octahedral.

5.6 FRACTURE

Any break along non-cleavage planes is called a fracture. There are several characteristic fractures. A *conchoidal break* leaves a clam shell shape of arcs. Obsidian or flint (often used by early peoples worldwide for arrow and spear heads) is typical. An *earthy break* looks ragged, like a broken brick.

5.7 STREAK

Streak generally refers to the colour left when a material is rubbed across a piece of unglazed tile or porcelain. In metals especially, the streak may be a clue to the mineral. For example, hematite (a ferric oxide mineral with as much as 70% iron in it) streaks red, not metal/silver, as you'd expect. As a result, the Greeks called it "bloodstone"; hence the name *haema*(blood)*tite*. Streaking only works, obviously, on minerals softer than an unglazed tile (about 4.5). For harder materials, you will need to get a powder sample (crush), and view against a white background.

5.8 MAGNETISM

Only a few minerals are magnetic, but since magnetism is easy to test for, and the results can be both fun to watch and exciting to find, it's mentioned here. Don't, whatever you do, shove a magnet into the material. If you do, you could be picking chips off that magnet for hours! Instead, place your sample on a piece of paper, and slide the magnet underneath. It'll be obvious if any part of the mineral is magnetic—it'll slide after the magnet but, thanks to the paper, won't stick to it. An alternate method is to bring a compass close to the specimen. Does the needle swing erratically? If so the material is magnetic.

Why is it exciting to find magnetic material? Well, the gold rush sourdoughs knew that placer gold was often found in association with black sand, which is powdered magnetite. So, if the black sand you pan is magnetic, you may be getting close to a motherlode.

5.9 ELECTRICAL PROPERTIES

Some minerals, such as amber, sulfur and topaz, develop a static charge when rubbed (they make your hair stand on end, if held close to your arm). Other minerals, such as quartz, are *piezoelectric*, meaning if you apply mechanical pressure, they produce a tiny electric charge. Vice versa, if given an electrical charge, they produce a mechanical push. This property is exploited in radio crystals and digital (quartz) watches, but requires special equipment to detect.

5.10 RADIOACTIVITY

Measuring radioactivity is not something the average rockhound is likely to get into. Suffice to say, certain "heavy" elements break down over a period of time (seconds to centuries), giving off energy particles that can be detected using a Geiger counter. Uranium and thorium are probably the best known elements.

Actually, lots of minerals are slightly radioactive. The granite slabs facing city buildings, for example, push out low levels (that are within human tolerance). Radioactive sands are quite common in the Lytton area of the Fraser Canyon.

CHAPTER 6: GEMSTONES
& MINERALS OF BC

I wouldn't want to be a rock.
I wouldn't, no, not me.
Some rockhound just might pick me up
And then look where I'd be!

Anon., *Rock Rustler's News*

There are a bewildering number of names for a bewildering number of minerals. When you start, it all seems a bit overwhelming. Don't worry about it. It's a bit like your first day in grade school—you'll get through it, and before the end of the first week you'll have figured out most of the major players. The others? You can learn them slowly, when and if needed.

Whenever possible, only the simple or generic name is used here. There are a multitude of specialty names and even local names that you will come across. Some will be synonyms. For example, "mutton fat" jade in one area may be referred to as "spit" jade elsewhere (I'm not making this up!), and exotic names such as "chicken guts" jade and "parrot wing" jasper just cry out for you to discover them in the rough. Well, perhaps not.

For a fairly complete alphabetical list of mineral names identified in the province, see Chapter 11.

AGATE
Agate is one of the most popular BC gemstones, and is found throughout the province. It is a quartz with microscopic crystals (*cryptocrystalline quartz*) which give each piece its unique colouring. It belongs to the *chalcedony* group, a waxy, smooth form of quartz, often found lining cavities, filling cracks or forming crusts. Agate can be *banded*, usually in concentric circles with the bands wavy or smooth, depending on how it formed; or it can be

brecciated, where it has other crystals or material included in the matrix. Petrified wood is often an agatized wood.

Agate has a hardness of 6.5–7.5 (harder than a steel file), so you can't scratch it with a knife. In the rough, it is deposited in veins and seams, or may form egg-shaped nodules. When found in place (in the hills), it usually has a hard, nondescript "rind" on its outside that can disguise it well; when found in river beds and along beaches, the outer shell is often stripped off, and some of the colour may show through.

Agate is extremely varied, with names to describe its forms: *lace, fortification, plume, polka dot, dendritic, moss* and more. In all, the dots, layers or patterns are inclusions. The plume (French for "feather") and moss agates are the result of hot liquids being squeezed into cracks, leaving fernlike shapes as they cool. To be worth collecting, agate must be free of cracks, so no wild hammering on a nodule! Since it's quite a common material, the quality of the individual piece depends largely on the colour, any interesting patterns, and how it was cut and mounted. Agate can be sliced into thin, translucent slabs, or matched as bookends. In jewelry, agate looks great in cabochons or pendants. Because every piece is unique, many collectors treasure good agates as much as gems like diamonds and sapphires.

Some of the better known agate areas are around Monte and Douglas lakes southeast of Kamloops; Agate Creek south of Shaw Springs; near Indian Garden Ranch south of Savona; near the Barnhartvale Road and Buse Lake southeast of Kamloops; in Charcoal Creek near Pillar Lake; on south side of Squilax Mountain; on the Perry Ranch east of Cache Creek; on the Green Mountain Road west of Penticton; on Agate Mountain near Princeton; on the banks of the Tranquille and Chris creeks; on the Nicoamen Plateau near Shaw Springs; and elsewhere.

ALABASTER

Alabaster is a massive, fine-grained gypsum, easily worked, having a hardness of 2. Throughout history, it has been shaped into vases and other decorative forms. Workshop tools are all you need to work with it, and the material's brilliant white, gray or pink makes it an attractive addition to any collector's cabinet. Found at Falkland near Kamloops.

AMBER

Yellow amber up to 2.5 cm in size has been found, sometimes with a greenish tinge and occasional plant inclusions along the Quesnel River near Quesnel. Nodules are found in shaly sandstone along the Peace River Canyon, and sizable nodules off the Pacific Coast on Graham Island of the Queen Charlottes.

In BC, amber is often associated with coal deposits. It is generally believed that amber is a fossil resin, of vegetable origin, that was buried and metamorphosed under special conditions of heat and pressure. Amber often contains inclusions of sticks or insects, which make it all the more interesting. The colour varies from milk to gold to brown. It's pretty soft, at 2.5 on the Mohs scale, so can be worked with ordinary tools.

Amber is enjoying a lot of renewed interest recently, and amber necklaces and other beadwork are popular. The problem is, there are lots of plastics that look like amber, and it's not always easy to recognize the real thing. Three quick tests are (1) rub the sample on a woolen sleeve and see if it becomes electrically charged enough to attract tiny pieces of styrofoam (amber is electrostatic); (2) place the sample in very salty water — with a density of only 1.1, amber will float, while most plastics will sink; (3) heat a pin to red hot, then push it into a non-obvious spot (such as the inside of the hole in a bead) and sniff the smoke ... amber smells resinous, while plastic smells like—well, burning plastic.

AMETHYST

Amethyst is a purple quartz, much prized by BC collectors until huge amounts were shipped in from Ontario and Brazil, so that today amethyst doesn't get the respect it used to. Still, finding amethyst in BC is a challenge, and well worth the effort, since the material can be beautiful both in the rough (as clusters of crystals) and when cut as a February birth stone.

Like quartz, it has a hardness of 7, making it suitable for jewelry. The deep purple (possibly manganese) is considered the best. Amethyst has a long and distinguished history, dating back as a prized stone to Phoenician times. The Romans believed that amethyst kept the wearer sober, although the literature is not specific as to whether this meant the wearer constantly refused a drink, or was capable of holding it when he accepted!

Amethyst-lined geodes occur at Little River Camp near Squilax, at Pillar Lake south of Chase, on the Green Mountain Road near Penticton, and near Cherry Creek. Amethyst druzes are found at Scottie Creek north of Cache Creek, and on the highway just east of Terrace.

ANALCITE

Analcite (or analcime) is a trapezohedrion or cubic crystal found in basaltic vugs. Usually white with a greasy appearance. Fragile but quite hard (H = 5).

ANDALUSITE

The *chiastolite* variety is common in the black schist of the hills near Armstrong. Crystals as large as a centimetre have been found in the Jordan River valley, near Sooke, Vancouver Island. See *Volume 1* for details.

A silica compound, often found in slate as a product of metamorphism, the crystals are thick prisms in gray, brown or opaque. One variation, *chiastolite*, forms a crystal cross. Transparent crystals are rare. SG = 3.2, hardness = 7.5. Named after Andalusia in Spain.

ANHYDRITE

See *Gypsum*.

ANKERITE

A calcium-iron carbonate that varies in colour from white through gray to yellow and brown, ankerite crystals have a pearly lustre and a brittle, well-defined rhombohedron habit. Found in dolomite in compact form, and in siderite. Hardness less than 4, SG = 3.1.

APATITE

Nothing to do with dieting; apatite gets its name from the Greek "to deceive", because it was often confused with other minerals. Occurs in veins with quartz, feldspar and iron ores. Hexagonal crystals, white, green, brown, yellow, even violet. Streaks white. It is used as the standard for 5 on the Mohs hardness scale. SG = 3.2. A thin chip colours a gas flame orange.

APLITE

A felsic, igneous rock having quartz, alkaline feldspar and mica, sometimes with marked veining (as at the Hope Slide) or other texture. Common in intrusive masses, often at contact zones.

APOPHYLLITE

A complex silica, apophyllite forms beautiful tetragonal crystals, and is found in basalts and tufas in association with *stilbite*. Colour varies from yellow to pale green. Not really suitable for jewelry since it has a hardness of only 4.5 – 5 (SG = 2.3), it makes an interesting collector's piece with its perfect basal cleavage and clean lines.

ARAGONITE

Aragonite is a type of hard (3.5 – 4), dense (SG = 2.9) calcite, and occurs in many different forms. For instance, oyster pearls are made out of aragonite, as is the bare skeleton of a coral. Found as orthorhombic crystals, varying in colour from white, to pink and even blue in caves and around hot vents.

ARGENTITE

The sulfide of silver, and an important silver ore. Found in massive or cubic crystal form. Colour silvery when fresh, black or gray when tarnished. H = 2.5, SG = 7.3. Often found in association with lead and zinc deposits.

ARGILLITE

Argillite (pronounced *are*-jil-ite) is a fine-grained shale that cleaves in thin slabs, and was the "slate" that so many kids of a few generations ago carried to school. It is common throughout the world, and can contain fossils, oil or even copper. In its dry state, it is hard, but when first quarried, it is soft and easily workable. It is this workability that has made the Chuck Creek Quarry on the Queen Charlotte Islands so famous, as it is from this site that the Haida Indians have taken material for their dark stone carvings.

The mineral is reserved exclusively for the Haida, and cannot be removed from the Queen Charlottes in unworked form. The carvers bury it in the ground to keep it moist and workable until such times as they need a piece. Found also on the Sea-to-Sky Highway north of Horseshoe Bay.

ARSENOPYRITE

An iron-arsenic sulfide with a white/silvery metallic colour, often with pink tints. When hit with a hammer, it gives off a garlic odour (arsenic) as opposed to sulfur smell (pyrite). Prismatic crystals. Quite hard (H = 5.5), it is heavy (SG = 6), and is the principal ore of arsenic.

ASBESTOS

Asbestos is a variety of *serpentine* in the *chrysotile* group of minerals, having no cleavage, a hardness varying from 2.5 – 4, and unmistakable fibres that are elastic enough to be woven, having a silky lustre. The longer the fibre, the more valuable the mineral, since (despite its questionable health record) asbestos still serves as a valuable additive to many manufactured products where heat resistance or strengthening are required. One of the largest deposits in the world is at (surprise!) Asbestos, Quebec.

It is usually found in thin veins filling cracks, and can be identified easily because nothing else is as fibrous. The fibres can be divided into almost invisible strands, and vary in length from about 1 cm to 8 cm.

AXINITE

Axinite occurs commonly in altered calcareous rocks, where it can be either massive (large lumps with very fine grain), or crystalline, in any colour varying from violet and pink to yellow and brown. Transparent crystals (triclinic) are the gemstone tourmaline, having a hardness of 7.

BARITE

Sometimes found in limestone cavities, hydrothermal veins, or in sulfides, barite is a variable mineral that can form attractive thick rhombic crystals in a variety of colours, or as rosettes as *desert rose*, much prized by collectors. Crystals as long as a metre have been found in England. Soft (H = 2.5 – 3.5) but quite dense at 4.5, it often has a pearly or glassy lustre, and streaks white. It is the main source of barium, which unlucky patients get to drink before being X-rayed. Also used in the paint industry as a pigment.

Facetable yellow crystals over 10 cm long have been found in veins of fluorite at the Rock Candy Mine on Kennedy Creek, north of Grand Forks.

BASALT

Basalt is the product of extrusive volcanic lava flows that spread out and cool rapidly to form dark, massive, fine-grained rocks, made up mostly of *pyroxene* and *plagioclase feldspar*. *Olivine* can also be present. Much of the

Western and Central divisions of the province have extensive basalt covers. In colour, it varies from dark gray with a greenish tinge, to black, although in the dry Interior, it can be covered in a pale gray or even white crust. On the coast in the rain belt, the iron can sometimes leach out, giving the matrix a rusty look. Underwater, it cools quickly, forming *pillow basalt* which looks, as the name implies, like a pillow or the top of a mushroom. The upper surface of a basalt flow can sometimes be filled with gas bubbles, forming a porous variety called *scoria*. These holes can later be filled with agate or calcite, making interesting samples.

Basalt can also be found as a dark band of rock forming a dyke or sill (there's a famous vertical one on the right hand side of the Stawamus Chief, the huge rock wall overhanging the town of Squamish. It's famous because there is, believe it or not, a rock climb that follows the entire length of this huge dyke!), or as hexagonal columns, such as at Green Lake, or Highway #99 en route to Whistler.

BERYL

An ore of beryllium, a minor metal, beryl is alloyed with copper, or used in nuclear research. Transparent beryl crystals are the stuff of dreams: aquamarine, heliodor and emerald, depending on colour (blue, yellow or green). All are highly prized gemstones. Hardness usually 7.5 – 8, SG = 3.6.

Most beryls in BC are found in pegmatites. Although occurrences are numerous, beryls are sadly not very common. Beryls of the Logjam Creek, Horseranch Range and Dortatelle Creek in the Cassiar area are small, opaque, poorly formed crystals of bluish green colour. A few well-formed pale bluish green beryls have been seen at Fort Graham in the Buttle Range. Beryls have been identified at the Bonanza mica mine near Tete Jaune Cache. Pegmatite dykes on Mount Begbie also contain beryls.

Pegmatite dykes and loose blocks are abundant in the Kootenay District. Most beryls are very pale, near white with occasional blue-green crystals occurring in the Angus, Porcupine, White, Skookumchuk and Hellroaring Creek areas. Recently pockets of pegmatite containing yellow to yellow-green to aqua coloured beryls have been found in the Slocan Valley.

BLOODSTONE

Bloodstone is a variety of *jasper*, and is usually a dark green with red spots of iron oxide, which gives it its name. The more spotty, generally, the more it is prized. Bloodstone is often used in men's signet rings, or as March birthstone rings. It has a hardness of 7 and poor cleavage, making it ideal for jewelry such as cabochons.

BORNITE

A copper-iron sulfide, usually massive, it is soft (H = 3) with poor cleavage and a gray-black streak. A valuable copper ore, its surface oxidizes upon exposure to air to form *peacock rock*, with iridescent blue, green and purple shades. SG = 5.7, rare crystals are cubic or rhombohedric. Often found with malachite.

BOURNONITE

A lead-copper sulfide rich in antimony, and a main source of lead and copper. Commonly found with galena and sphalerite. Tabular or prismatic crystals having a metallic lustre, are soft (H = 2.5 – 3). Reportedly found at Gold Bridge.

CALCITE

Calcite can take many forms, such as *microcrystalline* (limestones), *saccharoidal* (marbles), *fibrous* (satin spars) and *concretionary* (stalactites and stalagmites). It is soft (H = 3) with a density of 2.7, has perfect rhombohedral cleavage, and is basically calcium carbonate.

Collectors prize calcite when found in crystal form. In BC, there are several types: *aragonite* is a harder (4) and denser (2.9) variety with no cleavage; *chalk* is a white, soft form, usually full of tiny sea animal shells; *dogtooth spar* is a common form with sharply pointed crystals; *Iceland spar* is a transparent crystal which has the property of bending light in two directions, so that when looking through a slab of it, everything below appears double; *Mexican onyx* is not true onyx, but a calcite with swirls and lines that resembles onyx (onyx has a hardness of 6.5 while calcite is 3); *travertine* is a massive, fine-grained form deposited in caves; *tufa* is a porous white form of travertine.

CARNELIAN

Carnelian is a clear red, red-brown or orange *chalcedony*, having a hardness of 7.

CASSITERITE

Tin is a metal used a great deal in foodstuffs, where a thin layer of it coats the iron canister, preventing the iron from rusting and spoiling the contents. Nearly all tin comes from the ore *cassiterite* (tin oxide), which is almost 80% tin. The ore is brown or black but streaks pale, with a glassy lustre. Sometimes forms crystals, but more often occurs as *wood tin* which looks like a fibrous mass, or as crusts or veins in pegmatites. H = 6 – 7, quite dense with an SG of about 7.

CHABAZITE

Chabazite is a *zeolite*, often found in association with *stilbite*. It forms large rhombohedral crystals that are almost cubic, usually pale or pink with a glassy lustre, transparent or translucent. With a hardness of 4 – 5 and a SG of 2.1, a cluster of chabazite crystals is a real find.

CHALCEDONY

Pronounced "kal-*sydney*", it is a major part of the quartz family, since it covers a wide variety of waxy, fine-grained translucent stones of interest to the rockhound. It forms in cracks and seams in volcanics and is widely distributed in BC and throughout Canada.

Some of the types of chalcedony found in BC are: *agate*, a variegated chalcedony; *carnelian*, which is translucent red or orange; *chrysoprase*, a nickel-stained apple-green chalcedony; *onyx*, which is an agate having coloured bands; *plasma*, a faintly translucent chalcedony with white or yellow dots; *sard*, a deep smooth brown colour; *sardonyx*, which is a combination of sard and onyx in the form of flat layers of brown and white.

CHALCOPYRITE

Chalcopyrite is a commonly mined copper ore. It is often a brassy, almost golden, colour with a hardness of 3.5 – 4, and a SG of 4.2. It streaks greenish black and is very brittle. It may form small tetrahedral-like crystals (rare), but is generally found in massive form. Sometimes found with other copper minerals such as *malachite*, or with *pyrite*, making an attractive base for the fool's gold (pyrite) crystals.

CHERT

Chert is generally a tan/brown chalcedony (silica), but may be greenish or dark gray. Hard, it chips with a conchoidal fracture like flint or obsidian, and was used for early tools.

CHRYSOCOLLA

Found with other copper minerals, green chrysocolla is a copper-silicate with a hardness of 2 – 4, and a density of 2. Crystals are very rare. It is valued primarily for its attractive green colour, similar to *azurite* and *malachite*, and is found in thin veins, or occasionally, in grape-like (*botryoidal*) clusters. The Highland Valley area near Logan Lake has produced some fine material.

CINNABAR

The major ore of mercury, this mercuric sulfide is associated with low temperature hydrothermal veins and volcanic deposits. Found in granular reddish masses with free mercury droplets in the voids, its weight (SG = 8) and softness (H = 2.5) are recognizable properties.

CONCRETIONS

Concretions are found all over the province, and are known variously as "mud balls" and "clay balls". They are believed to be formed by calcite and silica depositing out of groundwaters, forming layer upon layer of material, like an onion. They come in every imaginable shape and size (1 cm to 30 cm diameter), and can look like teardrops, donuts, bowls or even human figures. Found mostly in clay beds alongside rivers, or in soft sandstone beaches, where, being harder than the surrounding rock, they remain when the beach weathers out. Being clay, many dissolve with time in water, but they look great on a shelf, and are the whimsical pride of many rockhounds.

CORUNDUM
Corundum materials are all alumina (Al_2O_3), and are difficult to identify, except that they are very hard (9). The crystals form rhombohedrally, are heavy (SG = 5.2), fragile, have no cleavage and are found in volcanic lavas, pegmatites and hydrothermal vents. There are two varieties.

The black/gray types are found along the Fraser River but are difficult to identify, except by hardness. Corundum and magnetite, when crushed, gives us *emery*, which is used as an industrial abrasive. Corundums are found in metamorphic rocks, such as gneisses and schists. Both hosts are known to exist at Kinbasket Lake, Kootenay Lake and in the Vernon and Prince Rupert areas.

The other type varies in form from clear (sapphire) through red (ruby) to blue (sapphire again). You can quickly figure out that corundum of the coloured variety is rather valuable. Recent discoveries in the Slocan area suggest the province may yet produce world class stones. Gem-quality sapphire pebbles of light green colour have been found in the Pend Oreille River. Tiny granular rubies have been found in some of the tributary creeks of the Tulameen River.

CYANITE
See *Kyanite*.

DALLASITE
Dallasite was named for Dallas Road, Victoria, which runs along the southern tip of that city. While not exclusive to that area, it is the provincial capital's "personal" stone in many ways. A volcanic *breccia*, it is a blend of green-brown basalt penetrated by white quartz.

DIAMOND
There are reports of microscopic diamond crystals in chromite found on Olivine Mountain, near Tulameen and from Scottie Creek and Bonaparte River near Ashcroft.

DIOPSIDE
A light green or brown pyroxene (silicate), diopside is found in igneous rocks such as dykes and sills. Like most pyroxenes, it cleaves into cubic fragments fairly easily. Diopside is often found in metamorphosed dolomite marbles. Hardness of between 5 and 6, and an SG of 3.4.

EPIDOTE

With its apple-green colour, epidote has a complex chemistry. Generally found as thin stringers in metamorphic rocks, sometimes granular and occasionally crystalline (prismatic or fibrous). Found in quartz at Kelsey Bay, Kennedy Lake on Vancouver Island (see *Volume 1* for details), and in the Whistler Valley.

FELDSPAR

Feldspars constitute the world's most abundant group of minerals, with many forms. They are found in nearly all igneous and metamorphic rocks. In granites, for example, which are made up of quartz, mica/hornblende and feldspar, it is the feldspar that gives the granite its characteristic colour of white, gold or pink, since it makes up as much as 60% of the mix. Next time you walk past a bank or public building faced with granite, take a look at the feldspars.

Feldspars gems include moonstone, sunstone, amazonite, and labradorite. There are 100 million t of feldspar reserves in 22 documented occurrences in BC. All these deposits are commercial grade, and to date gem quality materials have not been reported.

FERRIERITE

Ferrierite is a form of *zeolite*, and so is related to the feldspars, with chemically bonded water added. Found west of Kamloops.

FLUORITE

Very fine cubic crystals have been found lining cavities as large as a metre across, at the Rock Candy Mine near Grand Forks. Green is the most common colour, but purple and colourless varieties also occur. Other less noted areas are at Whiteman Creek Scuzzy Creek, Lumby, Hellroaring Creek, and the Liard River Hot Springs. Calcium fluoride, H = 4.

FOSSIL WOOD

See *Petrified wood.*

GALENA

Galena is the main source of mined lead (PbS), and has been smelted since before Roman times. It's usually found in veins in carbonate rocks, together with sphalerite (zinc), copper and silver, so the ore is valuable for several reasons.

Galena is a heavy (SG = 7.5), brittle silver-gray ore which is sometimes forms as beautiful cubic crystals, having perfect cleavage. These crystals, incidentally, were used in very early radios ("cat's whiskers" or "crystal sets"). Galena streaks gray, and has a hardness of 2.5.

GARNET

Of the many types of garnets, only two varieties are reported to exist in BC, *almandite* and *andradite*. Perfect, clear-red almandite crystals up to 3 cm in diameter occur in mica schist along the Stikine River. Andradite garnet, not suitable for cutting, has been found on Texada Island (in the Strait of Georgia).

In a recent study, 16 garnet occurrences in seven general areas were recorded:

Southern Shuswap – Nelson area
Shuswap Lake – Vernon – Okanagan area
Revelstoke – Frenchman Camp – Big Bend area
Canoe River – Valemount – Mica Creek area
Aiken Lake – Mesilinka River area
Hope – Yale – Harrison Lake – Lytton area
Prince Rupert – Skeena River – Douglas Channel area.

Often a deep red, hard gemstone, garnet is sometimes called "the poor man's ruby". It is common in many igneous and metamorphic rocks. Garnets are a family with similar characteristics. In BC creeks, crystals are abundant. Unfortunately, they are usually about the size of a pinhead! With 12 or 24 sides, they appear symmetrical and rather like a ball unless examined under a magnifying lens, when their smooth faces are obvious. With a hardness of 7, they are found in schists, gneiss and marbles, and sometimes in lavas and granites. They are often crushed and used as *garnet paper*, like sand paper.

Members of the garnet clan are: *almandite*, the common red garnet found in metamorphics; *grossularite* which may be white or green (the name refers to the Latin name for gooseberry) and usually has traces of chromite; *pyrope*, the precious garnet variety known sometimes as "cape ruby", and which is (of course) rare; *spessartite*, a yellow to red garnet with iron that occurs in granites and pegmatites; and *uvarovite* is found in serpentines, and is usually green.

One of the main reasons for mentioning garnets is that in other important areas in the world, garnets are found in *kimberlite pipes*, a geological form of igneous intrusive that can contain diamonds. While kimberlites are hard to find, and not every kimberlite has garnets, and not every kimberlite with garnets has diamonds, still ... you can see where we're heading. To date, no diamonds have been found in the province, but BC is huge, and the opportunities vast. Finding a kimberlite could really cheer you up. The new Ekati Mine in the NWT (1998) is centred on two diamondiferous kimberlite pipes.

GOLD

What can you say about gold that hasn't already been said? Heavy, malleable, slow to tarnish, and rare, gold has been the cause of more human disruption, effort, valour and failure than all other minerals rolled into one.

It is soft (H = 2.5 to 3) and is sometimes alloyed with copper to harden it and make it go further. As an alloy, it loses that deep rancid butter colour and becomes paler, like margarine. Pure gold is 24 karats; 14-karat gold is 14/24ths gold, or about 60% pure.

Gold is found in quartz veins, sometimes with pyrite (fool's gold). Being very dense (SG = 19.3), it works its way into rivers and creeks and is deposited in deep cracks and fissures from where you can pan it as *colour*, *flake* or *nugget*.

It would not be untrue to say that the discovery of gold in the 1850s is what created the province of British Columbia, and even today there are new gold mines being opened. But by and large, the move has been away from the placer deposits in streams and rivers, to hard rock mining, which is the realm of "the big boys". For more information, see Chapter 7.

GROSSULARITE

Grossularite is a type of white/green garnet, and can be confused with jade since it has similar colour and hardness. The surest way to tell the two apart is to look at a break—jade has a fibrous break, while grossularite is granular or crystalline—the difference being most obvious under a X10 lens.

To make things confusing, grossularite is sometimes called "garnet jade" or "Washington jade" or "Oregon jade" (from those respective states). There are various names for different colours, too: *amethystzontes* is purplish red; *essonite* is cinnamon; *jacinthe* is reddish orange; *landerite* is pink or rose; *succinate* is yellow-amber. Grossularite luminesces strongly under ultraviolet light. See also *Garnet*.

GYPSUM

Gypsum is the basis for the huge industry of plaster, plasterboard, rock lath and other building materials. The ancients used to dry gypsum in kilns, then grind it to a powder; today we call this *plaster of Paris*. When water is re-added, it sets hard again. A fine-grained, translucent form (*alabaster*) is a popular medium for sculptors.

Gypsum is calcium sulfate, sometimes having impurities that colour its whiteness. With a hardness of just 2, and an SG of 2.3, it has a pearly lustre, and streaks white. *Selenite* is crystalline gypsum, found in limestones cavities; the crystals can grow to a metre in length. *Anhydrite* is gypsum without water; crystals are rare. It is harder (3 – 3.5) and denser (SG = 2.9) than gypsum.

HEMATITE OR HAEMATITE

Hematite is an iron oxide ore, having about 70% iron, which explains its weight (SG = 5). It is an important source of iron. Hardness varies from 1 – 6, depending on the ore's chemistry. When tumbled, hematite takes on a smooth, shiny metallic lustre that is unmistakable, and popular in jewelry. The name comes from its curious property of streaking cherry red, due to iron oxides present. The Greeks thought it was blood, and called it "haema" (blood) stone.

HEULANDITE

This zeolite, with a complex chemistry, may be found in small quantities as globular or granular (usually white) crystals in lava cavities. Confirmed samples at Douglas Lake, southeast of Kamloops.

HYALITE

Non-precious form of white opal.

IDOCRASE

Formerly called *vesuvianite*, idocrase is a glassy, transparent to translucent mineral found in metamorphosed limestone. Formed as a crystal, or massive, it is hard (6), with an SG of 3.3, and the green variety (*California jade*) is often offered as a jade substitute.

An apple-green, fine-grained, massive idocrase is found southeast of Skihist Mountain near Lytton. Some of the material is translucent and may be gem quality.

ILMENITE

An iron-titanium oxide, hard and heavy, and generally brown or black in colour. Found often in schists and gneisses, it is weakly magnetic when cool, but becomes more so when heated. A source of titanium (used in high-tech metals), large concentrations have been found in marine sands.

IOLITE

A magnesium aluminum silicate with a hardness of 7, iolite is blue-gray gem that exhibits *pleochroism*, where it exhibits two or even three different colours, depending on the angle of viewing. Recent discoveries in matrix in the Slocan Valley.

JADE

The term jade is somewhat imprecise, since it is applied to the aggregates of two different minerals. The one, a variety of amphibole, is called *nephrite*, while the other, a pyroxene, is called *jadeite*. Nephrite is found in BC, China and New Zealand (to name a few of the more famous locales), where it has a long history of use as a tool and ornament. The nearest source of jadeite is in Washington state; the most famous source is the "imperial jade" found since the late 1780s in Burma.

Nephrite is defined as a tough, fine-grained *tremolite* or *actinolite*, breaking with a splintery fracture and having a glistening lustre. Polished nephrite is translucent (you can see through thin sections, but not thick ones). Contrary to popular opinion, jade comes in every colour under the sun from black to white and everything in between, although BC material tends to be green, gray or near black.

JASPER

Jasper is common throughout BC, and comes in such bewildering varieties there's always something new to see. Because it is a quartz (with a hardness of 7, SG of 2.6), it polishes and wears well in jewelry.

Jasper is a *cryptocrystalline quartz*, meaning it is made of tiny crystals. It is commonly found in smooth red or yellow masses, or with other crystals and chunks in it, when it is known as *breccia* (pronounced "brech-ee-a"). It has been found with fossil shells in it (*turritella jasper*), or with little eye-like dots as *orbicular*. It can have patterns in it as *picture jasper*; dark green with red spots as *bloodstone*; or it can replace wood to form *jasperized wood*.

KYANITE

Kyanite, or cyanite, is an aluminum silicate found generally in schists and gneisses. The crystals are knife-like and long, and can be white to blue-gray, or even black. With an SG of 3.6, it has an unusual hardness—between 4 and 5 along the crystal axis, but 7 across it. It is used to make *mullite* in refractory porcelain and brick. Bladed specimens up to 10 cm in length found north of Revelstoke.

LAZULITE

Found in azure blue masses, its distinctive colour, vitreous lustre and indistinct cleavage make lazulite easy to recognize, although it can look like lazurite or sodalite. With a hardness of 5.5 – 6 and an SG of 3.1 – 3.4, it's found in pegmatites, quartz veins or quartzite.

LIMESTONE

Most limestones were formed as sedimentary deposits by animal and plant life, to form what is essentially calcite ($CaCO_3$). They vary in colour, form and texture, depending on their origin. In this era of greenhouse gases and global warming, it is interesting that there appears to be a relationship between the carbon dioxide in the air, the sea and the limestone rocks. The cliffs of the Grand Canyon are good examples of limestone. *Marls* are limestones with lots of clay. With magnesium, we get a *dolomite limestone*. It's the main ingredient of cement, so is an important economic mineral.

MAGNESITE

Generally found in massive or granular form, magnesite is magnesium carbonate and is mined for magnesium, a valuable additive to metal, and used in the aerospace industry. There are large deposits in Washington and California. Hardness of 4, and SG of 3.0.

MAGNETITE

An important iron mineral (Fe_3O_4), magnetite is the only black ore that can be picked with a magnet, and so is easy to identify. (Pyrrhotite, which is also magnetic, is yellow/gold.) It is quite hard at 6, with an SG of 5.2, containing 72% iron by weight.

MALACHITE

Malachite is often found with *azurite*; both are copper carbonates. Malachite forms smooth, irregular masses of beautiful green swirls, or grows as acicular crystals, and is much favoured for jewelry, boxes, pyramids and other ornaments. It has a hardness of 4 and an SG of 3.7 – 4.

MARBLE

Marble is a recrystallized limestone, usually white, but can be tinted almost any colour due to impurities. Limestones altered by trickling water are often called "marble", but to be a real marble, the stone must have undergone metamorphosis of heat and pressure. Marble seldom shows banding characteristic of schists and slates. It is used extensively in building.

MARCASITE

Has the same chemistry as iron pyrite (fool's gold), and is often called *white pyrite* although it is more brittle and somewhat lighter than true pyrites. It forms in radiating or cockscomb crustations in peat or clay, and streaks gray-brown. Tends to be very crumbly, with poor cleavage. Oxidizes quickly in air, forming white flakes of melanterite. SG = 4.3.

MOLYBDENITE

Usually found in veins or pegmatites, this sulfide is very soft (H = 1.5), has a metallic lustre, and streaks gray-blue. Occurs as flecks or tabular crystals. Molybdenum is an essential additive in high strength steels.

MUSCOVITE

Muscovite is a pale, almost colourless mica, named after Muscovy where it was used as a glass substitute. Common in granites and pegmatites, it has a hardness of 2.2, SG of 2.8, and nearly perfect cleavage, where it appears as flaky platelets.

NATROLITE

This member of the zeolite group forms as slender/acicular prismatic crystals. It is usually an uninteresting white colour (although sometimes colourless, gray, yellowish or reddish), and is more of interest to specimen collectors. It is reported occurring in the Ice River area east of Golden.

NEPHRITE

Commercial quantities of quality nephrite occur in the province, extending from the northern provincial boundary southeastward to the lower region of the Fraser River. Found as small to very large boulders, some weighing more than 15 tonnes (one specimen was estimated to weigh 80 tonnes). The best quality (in terms of colour and absence of internal fractures) comes from the Dease Lake area (central to northern BC). Known sources of nephrite yielding commercial quantities are currently mined in the Atlin Lake, McDame, Dease Lake, Wheaton Creek – Turnagain River and Mount Ogden – Fort St. James areas.

Because of its historical significance and popularity, jade has many substitutes. Serpentine is a common alternate. Known as *Korea jade* or *Soochow jade*, it can be identified by its lack of hardness or different density. Bowenite, willemsite and some forms of idocrase (*California jade*) are more difficult to detect. Green grossular garnet from South Africa passes under the trade name *Transvaal jade*, but is not as hard as nephrite. Pectolite from Alaska has similarly been called jade, but is attacked by warm hydrochloric acid, which jade is not. *Muttonfat jade*, a white material commonly found in the lower Fraser River, is actually a quartzite having blue dumortierite and fine sillimanite needles included.

Nephrite has a hardness of 6.5, slightly harder than steel. This is a useful field test to sort out the "keepers" from the "leavers". But since nephrite often has other material blended into it, notably at the surface, be careful you are not testing the softer rind.

Nephrite is made up of interlocking fibrous minerals, visible at the microscopic level only, so is difficult or even impossible to break. In the rockhound dialect, "it's *tough*". Even a small boulder will resist breakage, when attacked by an 8 lb sledgehammer. Of course, hitting a jade sample with an 8 lb hammer to prove it's really jade is somewhat counterproductive, because when it does finally break, it will be so fractured internally as to be pretty valueless! For this reason, blasting jade is a waste of time and money.

The other field test for nephrite is checking for translucency at a thin edge. Very thin slices are almost transparent. See also *Jade*.

OBSIDIAN

Obsidian, pumice and rhyolite are chemically the same; the difference is in their cooling. Obsidian (sometimes called *volcanic glass*) is a classic extrusive lava that chills quickly, allowing no crystal separation. It is black and glassy, and breaks conchoidally (shell-like cusps). Along with flint, it has been used by primitive cultures for millennia for tools, arrowheads and ornaments (hardness = 6). In Canada, obsidian was actively traded between Natives of the West Coast and prairies long before colonization.

Varieties of obsidian are *snowflake obsidian*, which has small white crystals of devitrified glass in the black matrix; *Apache tears*, which are translucent round nodules of obsidian found when the main mass has been altered; and *rainbow obsidian*, which has a beautiful play of colours.

When collecting obsidian, it's important to wrap it very well, as it can cut its way through newspaper and damage surrounding specimens. It is a very popular rock with collectors, and is used widely in jewelry.

Black obsidian occurs in varying sizes north of Anahim Lake, on Anahim Peak and Ilgachuz Mountains.

OLIVINE (PERIDOT)

Olivine belongs to a group of minerals that rarely form crystals. Magnesium is always a key ingredient, and olivines constitute a major rock-building group. The gem form is apple-green peridot. Timothy Mountain near Lac La Hache produces volcanic bombs from which excellent dark green stones weighing as much as 10 carats have been obtained. Peridot grains large enough to cut small gems have been produced at Lightning Peak in the Monashee Mountains, and at Boss Mountain east of Williams Lake.

OPAL

Formed by silica (quartz) with between 3% and 9% water, opals are an enigma. They come in many colours and tints, have a glassy or waxy lustre, and have no chemical structure (they are *amorphous*). There are two types of opal: *precious* and *semi-precious*. Some varieties (notably from Australia) have a striking play of colours called *opalescence*, making them highly desirable.

Opal is porous and easily stained, so avoid immersion in dirty water. For this reason, beware of most brilliantly "coloured" opal, which is in fact dyed stone. Opal loses water easily, and should be immersed from time to time to avoid cracking. Opal should not be exposed to sudden temperature changes either; the stresses can split the material.

Opal can look like quartz, but has a hardness of 5.2 – 6.5 (use a hardened file), so can readily be distinguished. It has an SG of about 2. It is found in both igneous and sedimentaries, and often replaces the material in petrified wood, making fine natural sculptures of *opalized wood*. When handling opal, be careful—it is as fragile as it is beautiful.

Common opal is widespread in volcanic rocks, being milky, green, yellow or brick red with a glassy, translucent look; *hyalite* is a white variety found encrusting rocks or filling small veins; *geyserite*, as its name implies, is found near hot springs, and is usually white and opaque; *tripolite* is formed from microscopic shells of diatoms, and is chalky, fine-grained and hard enough to scratch glass.

Common opal occurs in seams of rock outcroppings north of Princeton, and also in tertiary rocks at Savona Mountain, Agate Mountain, Horse Fly River, Fourmile Creek and at Slocan Lake. Good quality hyalite is found near Hihum Lake and the Bonaparte River. Fire opal has been found along the banks of Deadman Creek northwest of Kamloops. Well-grained opalized wood in black, brown, white and green hues is reported along Barnes Creek near Ashcroft. Precious opal occurs only in a few locations in BC, notably near Vernon.

The Eagle Creek deposits near Burns Lake have been set aside for rockhounds. Milky coloured opals with only small portions displaying a red and green play of colour have been found on an unnamed mountain west of Penticton.

Commercial mining, fee digging and site tours of precious opal in the Vernon area is popular (Okanagan Opal Inc). See Chapter 10: Addresses.

PASTELITE

Pastelite is an agate breccia and, as its name implies, ranges in colour through the whole spectrum. Being an agate, it is hard (7) and makes attractive cabochons and medallions.

PEGMATITE

An important igneous material, pegmatites often include well-defined crystals of quartz, feldspar and mica (muscovite, biotite, lepidolite), and may contain tourmaline, beryl, topaz, zircon or other rare minerals. These are therefore rocks of economic importance. Typically recognized by their pale colour and well-defined quartz and mica crystals, there are numerous outcrops around the province.

PENTLANDITE

The main ore of nickel, pentlandite occurs in pyrrhotite and is similar to it. Semi-hard at 3.5 – 4, SG = 5, with a metallic lustre and no cleavage, it is magnetic and streaks bronze-brown. The world's largest deposits are found at Sudbury, ON. Found also at the BC Nickel mine north of Hope.

PERIDOT

Also known as *olivine* or *chrysolite*, peridot is a valuable member of a group of magnesium silicates. Peridot is found where igneous rocks are rich in magnesium and poor in quartz, such as the darker basic rocks like diorites and gabbros. Mostly green, with a hardness of 6.5 – 7 and an SG of 3.3, clear peridot is cut as a gem stone, and is prized for its fresh, apple-green colour. Crystals are rare.

PERLITE

A lustrous, pearly gray volcanic glass, often with clusters of concentric cracks, like an onion. Sometimes has a central core of uncracked obsidian. Found at Blackdome Mountain south of the Gang Ranch near Clinton.

PETRIFIED WOOD

Many people think petrified wood is "wood that has dried out in a desert and been replaced by sand". Not so. It must first be buried; then the wood fibres must be slowly replaced by liquid minerals which eventually harden, taking the shape of the original fibres; finally, the now petrified wood must be exposed again by erosion.

Petrified wood (from the Greek word *petra*, a stone) is fairly easy to recognize, since it looks like wood, although there are some schists that look very bark-like. The value of a piece depends to a great degree on the detail of replacement, and the mineral that did the replacing. Opal and agate are popular, since they are often spectacular in colour, but calcite, dolomite or pyrite are all known to make up petrified wood specimens.

Complete tree stumps may be found off the Campbell Range Road near Monte Lake and at Loughborough Inlet north of Powell River. Other specimens have been located up the Deadman River Valley west of Kamloops; the Hat Valley near Cache Creek; west of Princeton; on Willis Creek south of Princeton; at Cheslatta Falls near Vanderhoof; and at the Perry Ranch east of Cache Creek.

PLATINUM

Native platinum and the mineral *cooperite* (PtS) are found in dark extrusive igneous rocks (called *basic* or *ultra-basic* rocks). Platinum, sometimes called "white gold", was definitely the noble metal's ugly sister—in South America the Spanish threw it away when it was found along with gold and silver! It is only in this century that its value as an inert (non-reactive) metal was appreciated. Because it doesn't oxidize or react willingly with anything, it's used widely in laboratories for ultra-pure containers, as a catalyst in industrial chemistry, and to a lesser degree in jewelry.

Like gold, it is malleable, with a density of 14 – 19 depending on purity, but is gray/silver in colour. Hardness of 4 – 4.5, it streaks gray. Crystals (isometric) are very rare (typically 2 mm across) and extremely valuable. Usually found as grains or small nuggets in placer deposits, like gold; because of its SG, it can be panned like gold. The Tulameen River produced a limited amount in the 19th century.

PORPHYRY

A porphyry is any igneous intrusive or extrusive where the rock has a texture of at least 25% coarse grains or crystals (called *phenocrysts)*. Thus a granite having at least a quarter of its matrix made up of phenocrysts would be called a *granite porphyry*. Similarly, we could find a *basalt porphyry* or a *syenite porphyry*. The *gabbro porphyries* of Vancouver Island are known as "flowerstone", because the feldspar phenocrysts look like white daisies on a dark (gabbro) background. Very thin feldspar phenocrysts are called "mouse track" porphyry.

PREHNITE

Found in cavities and veins of basic volcanic rocks, in impure metamorphic limestones, and in some igneous rock veins. Forms as barrel-shaped clusters, green, white or gray. H = 6.5. Fine material suitable for cabochons is found at the Le Roi Mine near Rossland.

PYRITE

Pyrite (FeS_2) or iron pyrite is often called "fool's gold" because of its gleaming gold colour, but gold seldom forms crystals, and pyrite has much greater hardness (H = 6 – 7). With an SG of just 5 compared to gold's 19, pyrite won't fool you for long. Still, a large cluster of pyrite cubes makes an attractive collector's piece, and it is often found with gold in quartz. A freshly broken specimen smells strongly of sulfur (bad eggs).

PYROLUSITE

Usually found as fibrous or earthy masses, this oxide of manganese can vary in hardness from soft and crumbly to H = 6.5 in crystals, which are rare. Has a greasy feel; streaks black; SG about 5. Pyrolusite is an important ore of manganese. Forms fernlike dendrites in cracks and moss agates.

PYROPHYLLITE

A very soft (H = 1 – 2) silicate, crystals are rare. Usually yellow, white or pale green, it has a greasy feel and pearly lustre. Difficult to distinguish from talc, except chemically.

PYRRHOTITE

An iron sulfide that frequently has surplus sulfur to the extent that a new break will smell strongly of bad eggs. Usually golden/bronze, with an SG of 4.6 and a hardness of 4. Streaks gray-black, and is often magnetic.

QUARTZ

Quartz is a crystalline silica, often clear when pure. The main constituent of glass. Cleaves conchoidally. A common mineral in BC, occuring in many types of rock formation. Fine deposits of agate are found throughout the province. There is a great variety ranging from fine blue agate, moss agate, banded agate and eye agate, to red agate resembling Mexican agate (locations are too numerous to mention). Along with agates other forms of chalcedony are found, including onyx, jasper and petrified wood.

REALGAR

Realgar is an arsenic-sulfur compound that forms in low temperature veins as a crust, grain or fleck, or as massive deposits. It is usually red, soft (H = 2), with an SG of 3.5. Crystals are rare. Realgar slowly breaks down if exposed to light, turning into *orpiment* (As_2S_3).

RODINGITE
See *Serpentine*.

RHODOCHROSITE
A pink manganese carbonate that is quite soft (H = 4), it is found most often in veins or crusts, except for a spectacular deposit in Argentina. Much used as an ornamental stone, and in jewelry, and has perfect rhombohedral cleavage. SG about 3.5.

RHODONITE
A manganese silicate, rhodonite has a hardness of about 6, and is much used in jewelry and ornaments because of its pale to hot pink colouring, often with strands of black in the matrix. Prismatic cleavage. Crystals are large and flattened. Derived from the Greek *rhodon*, meaning a rose. In the rough it frequently has a crust of black manganese oxide hiding its inner colours. Sometimes mined for its manganese content.

Most rhodonite deposits in BC are in the form of lenses occurring with bedded chert or jasper. Quality rose-pink material occurs on Salt Spring Island and near Lake Cowichan on Vancouver Island (Hill 60 and Mount Franklin: see *Volume I* for details). Other rhodonite bearing sedimentary rock formations are the Shoemaker Formation near Keremeos; the Cache Group from Tsitsutl Mountain (near Fort St James) extending to Williams Lake; the Fennell Formation (Clearwater to Barriere); the Cassiar area; Kaslo to Slocan area; fine pink material with black patterns from the Bella Coola area; and very wide deposits up to a metre thick of pale pink from the Queen Charlotte Islands.

RHYOLITE
Rhyolite is a light coloured, acidic, extrusive igneous rock having the same composition as granite, but, being extrusive, it has cooled more rapidly, so is fine-grained. When more than 25% of it is quartz phenocrysts, it is called *rhyolite porphyry*. Colour is white to pink to gray, although iron can stain it red in places. Many rhyolites are porous, and can absorb mineral-rich solutions that infiltrate the rock, causing attractive banding. When the infiltration hardens the base material, it is called *wonderstone*, and can be made into unusual jewelry similar to picture jasper.

SARD
See *Carnelian*.

SARDONYX
Sardonyx is a form of banded chalcedony (*onyx*) with even, parallel bands of black and white, or brown and white.

SCHEELITE

Scheelite is an important tungsten ore that is found in quartz veins or at the contact of igneous rock and limestone. Colour is variable, but usually light. Hardness of 5, SG = 6, with a glassy, sometimes transparent lustre. Streaks white. Good cleavage, tetragonal crystals. Fluoresces in short wave ultraviolet light.

SELENITE

See *Gypsum*.

SERPENTINE

A magnesium silicate with water, serpentine may also have small amounts of iron or nickel present. The fibrous form is *asbestos*. Varies in colour from creamy white through green to black. Hardness varies from 2.5 to 4, S.G. = 2.6. Usually has a greasy lustre and feel.

SHATTUCKITE

This rare hydrous silicate of copper closely resembles blue azurite, and quality samples are used in a similar manner. Crystals are rare. Usually found in irregular masses of spherules with tiny crystals radiating from a central point. This distinguishes it from azurite. SG = 3.8, hardness variable 3.5 – 4. Usually associated with azurite, malachite and chrysocolla.

SIDERITE

Siderite is an iron carbonate, but the iron content is low at 48%. However, because it is sulfur-free and often has associated manganese, it is mined. Rhombohedral crystals are common; sometimes found as botryoidal clusters. Found in hydrothermal vents, quartz vugs, associated with galena and sphalerite. Colour yellow, brown or gray. Hardness about 4, SG = 3.8. Streaks white. Pearly lustre.

SILLIMANITE

This aluminum silicate is usually silky/fibrous in shape with long, slender crystals, having a pearly luster. Hard (6) and heavy with an uneven fracture. Found in metamorphic rocks, and used in the refractory industry.

SILVER

Second only to gold in history as a noble metal, silver can be found in large, twisting, branching masses as silver sulfide—*argentite* (from the Latin "argentum" meaning silver or money). Shiny when clean, silver tarnishes fairly easily. Argentite may be massive, or can form cubic crystals; hardness 2.5, SG of 7.3, with a metallic lustre. Often found together with lead, zinc and other rare minerals.

SKARN

A dark metamorphic rock containing calcite, pyroxene, garnet and sulfides. Often the host rock for minerals containing copper, iron, manganese and molybdenum. Generally formed when limestone is intruded by an igneous source.

SOAPSTONE

Soapstone is basically talc and colouring. It is ideal for carving, is the preferred medium of the arctic Inuit, and is much in demand worldwide. It can be found in many colours, although a mottled brown is common. Green soapstone is prized. Easy to identify, soapstone feels slippery to touch and is soft enough to be scratched with a fingernail.

SODALITE

Sodalite is a bright marine-blue silicate, with an SG of 2.3 and a hardness of 6, making it popular as a semi-precious stone. The sodalite capital of Canada is Bancroft, ON, but there is quite a bit in BC too, although most of it to date has been found in national parks, where collecting is prohibited. Seldom found as a crystal. The blue can sometimes be tinged with green.

Blue cutting-grade sodalite found as float in the Ice River near Kicking Horse Pass between Field and Golden provides material for carvings, cabochons and decorative objects. Also found north of Golden near Mount Mather.

SPHALERITE

A zinc sulfide, often with iron or lead inclusions, having a metallic black sheen. Streaks yellow-brown. An important zinc ore.

SPINEL

As a gemstone, spinel was confused for centuries with ruby, being very hard (H = 8). The Black Prince's huge "ruby" in the English Crown Jewels turned out, with modern testing, to be a spinel. Brown, green and blue have been found, depending on elements present. Non-gem spinel is found in association with marly dolomites. SG varies from 3.5 – 4.1.

STEATITE

Formed by hydrothermal alteration in which magnesium-rich minerals are altered to talc. Steatite is the massive, cryptocrystalline form of talc.

STIBNITE

Stibnite is the sulfide of antimony, found with pyrite, galena or arsenic minerals, usually in low temperature veins. Long thin steel-gray crystals are quite common, sometimes bent. Soft (H = 2) with perfect lengthwise cleavage. SG = 4.6. Antimony is used in low friction metal alloys, pewter, and in batteries.

STILBITE

Stilbite is a *zeolite* that forms in wheat-sheaf-like crystals of white to yellow to reddish brown. Hardness 3.5 – 4, SG of 2.1. Often found in lavas, filling cavities and veins.

TALC

This hydrous magnesium silicate never occurs in distinct crystals, but instead in scaly aggregates of white, gray or brown. Has a greasy feel. Very soft (H = 1) with perfect cleavage. Can be worked with hand tools as *soapstone*, and is commonly found with schists. Used in paper, rubber, paint and, of course, in cosmetics as talcum powder.

THOMPSONITE

This is one of the *zeolite* family, found in metamorphics, lining vugs and veins. Usually blue and botryoidal (like a bunch of grapes). Because of its softness (only 2.5 – 3), it is not jewelry material, but favoured as a collector's piece.

THUNDEREGGS

While Oregon state is famous for its thundereggs, these unusual forms of agate, jasper or opal are found as far north as central BC. Ranging in size from a centimetre to as much as a metre, thundereggs appear from the outside as a nodule of warty rhyolite that looks anything but interesting. But cut it in half, and a stunning void filled with startling patterns of chalcedony appear, each unique and much in demand by collectors. Many thundereggs have an axis of symmetry, meaning that if you cut along that plane, the left and right hand pieces will closely mirror each other. To guess this axis, look for a knob on the outside which has a dip directly opposite on the nodule—that's your best bet for a mirror set of eggs.

A variation on the agate-filled thunderegg is found north of the Lillooet area (Fountain Valley). There, a mixture of calcite and agate materials are found within nodules that have a surface that is much rougher than the usual Oregon variety. The calcite generally fluoresces brilliant green in ultraviolet light. Thunderegg beds are reported between Lillooet and Blackdome Mountain west of Clinton.

TONALITE

An intrusive igneous rock having plagioclase, hornblende, biotite and more than 10% quartz. Usually a medium gray colour with dark clusters of minerals. Common throughout British Columbia.

TOURMALINE

Tourmaline is a complex aluminum silicate that is found with mica and feldspar in granite rocks and pegmatites. It forms long, needle-like crystals with striated sides and distinctive triangular ends. In BC it is often black (*schorl*) due to iron impurities, and has little value. Elsewhere, bi-coloured crystals are found with one part of the crystal being green, the other rose, red or orange (called "colour zoning"); these are known as *watermelon tourmaline*. Streaks white; hardness of 7, SG of 3, with a vitreous lustre.

Only a few occurrences have been reported in BC. Pegmatites at the headwaters of Skookumchuck Creek and St. Mary Lake north of Cranbrook, the Slocan Valley north of Castlegar, and Midge Creek west of Kootenay Lake have reported coloured tourmaline crystals.

Pegmatite dykes on Mica Mountain, south of Tete Jaune Cache, and Mount Begbie, south of Revelstoke, contain black, green and red tourmaline.

TRAVERTINE

Travertine is a massive, non-crystalline form of *calcite*, often found in caves. Opaque, often coloured with impurities. Forms as *tufa* (spongy limestone). H = 3.

TUFF

Tuff is volcanic ash, often having a variety of small and large angular fragments. May be layered like sedimentary rocks, although it is of igneous origin. Large deposits have been found considerable distances from volcanoes. Colour usually pale gray or brown. Sometimes used as a cheap construction stone.

TURQUOISE

Turquoise is a secondary mineral formed in dry regions from the alteration of aluminum-rich rocks. It is a waxy, vitreous mass that varies in colour from blue-green to light green, and has been highly prized from ancient times for jewelry. Having a hardness between 5 and 6, it is distinguishable from "me-too" copies such as chrysocolla (H = 2 – 4) and variscite (H = 3.5 – 4.5).

Much valued by the native North Americans, turquoise and silver jewelry is popular and commands high prices. But beware of imitations—even turquoise is dyed to appear more blue, plus a lot of what looks like turquoise, isn't!

URANINITE

Uraninite is a steel black, opaque, uranium compound with a hardness of 5.5 and a density of 9 – 9.5. In BC, usually found in sand. Cubic form is rarely found. Radioactive.

VESUVIANITE

See *Idocrase*.

WOLLASTONITE

Wollastonite usually occurs as fibrous or radiating gray masses with a pearly luster. SG of 4.5 with perfect cleavage. Forms at high temperature due to the reaction of silica (SiO_2) and calcite ($CaCO_3$, usually in the form of fairly pure limestone or marble). Used in the manufacture of refractories.

YALAKOMITE

Local name given to material from Yalakom River north of Lillooet—usually an altered, brecciated serpentine cut by magnesite veins. Takes a good polish. Also found around the Pinchi Lake mercury mine.

ZEOLITE

Widely distributed, zeolites are chemically related to *feldspars*, with the addition of water. When heated in a flame, zeolites boil and bubble—hence their name, which means "boiling stone". There are about 25 in the group, and they are found in lavas, filling cracks, veins and cavities. Three of the more common found in BC are: *chabazite*, having rhombohedral (almost cubic) crystals; *ferrierite*, which display sunburst formations of yellow or pale brown crystals; *stilbite*, having pearly, wheat-sheaf-like masses of twinned crystals in white, yellow or brown. All three are pale, soft (H = 3.5 – 5) minerals of low density (SG = 2.1).

ZIRCON

Zircon ($ZrSiO_4$) is common in acidic igneous rocks and their derivatives, but fairly rare as a transparent gemstone. Found as small brown tetragonal crystals with a hardness of 7.5 and an SG of 4.7. Zircon is heat-treated in large quantities to improve colour; its brilliance can be mistaken for diamond. However, zircon is strongly doubly refractive, while diamond is not, and is also brittle, and prone to chipping.

CHAPTER 7: GOLD!

Gold, man's first follie.

– Pliny, 79 A.D.

Gold has some important qualities beyond its warm yellow colour and metallic lustre. For a start, it is very rare; it has been estimated that the world's total supply would only occupy a cube having 15 m sides (about 65,000 t). You should be aware that gold accumulates too—very little gets lost once it's found (despite all the stories about wrecks on the Spanish Main, and Blackbeard's treasure). Gold tends to be recycled and re-used over and over again, especially in times of strife, so that the ring on your finger could well contain gold worked by the Incas, or early Chinese, or Egyptians.

Gold is the most malleable of metals and can be hammered into a foil a thousand times thinner than a sheet of paper—so thin, in fact, that light can pass though it. For example, it serves as a coating on astronaut visors to shield harmful rays. Gold is also extremely ductile, meaning that a piece the size of a golf ball can be drawn into a wire so fine that it could stretch from Vancouver to the Alberta border (600 km).

These properties, combined with gold's great corrosion resistance, have made the metal vital in many high technology processes such as electronics, aerospace and medicine. Gold has always been in demand in the arts, in weaving, ceramics, sculpture, pottery and of course in jewelry. Finally, gold has a value as exchange (money). You may know that the person who put England (and ultimately, the world) on the Gold Standard was the same man who invented calculus—Sir Isaac Newton. After leaving Cambridge University, where he was Master of Trinity College, he was made director of the Royal Mint. There, he set out to stabilize the pound sterling, at a time when the importance of international trade was first becoming apparent.

Gold has gripped the mind of man the way no other mineral ever has. In the first century B.C., Diodorus Siculus wrote, "Nature herself makes it clear that the production of gold is laborious, the guarding of it difficult, the zest for it great, and its use balanced between pleasure and pain". Hardly surprising that Shakespeare wrote of "saint-seducing gold" in Romeo and Juliet!

Canada's earliest gold mine was founded in 1847 in Quebec. The Klondike Gold Rush began in 1896, and the largest nugget ever found there weighed a hefty 2.64 kg (that's 5.8 lb)! But that bonanza was nothing compared to the largest ever found in North America, at Carson Hill, California, where a 72.8 kg monster (160 lb) was discovered. However, if you really want to tell a tale of rags to riches, consider the 214 kg (470lb) beauty picked up at Hill End in New South Wales, Australia. You wish ...

7.1 RECOGNIZING GOLD

There are two common types of gold found in the province of British Columbia: quartz gold and placer gold. Gold has also been found sometimes with copper deposits, and in skarns. To the two major sources, it's possible we should add "fool's gold" (iron pyrite). Quartz gold is bonded to the quartz, requires big bucks and even bigger machinery to hack, crunch, separate and smelt, so is of less interest to us here. Placer gold, on the other hand, involves panning in rivers and old stream beds to find gravity-fed gold, that looks like gold, smell likes gold, tastes like gold, and by golly, it is gold. The only way you can be fooled is, obviously, by fool's gold. But the differences are obvious:

Property	Gold	Pyrite
Hardness	2.5 to 3	6 – 7
Specific gravity	19.3	5.0
Malleability	Bends easily	Brittle, shatters
Colour	Rich yellow	Pale brass
Surface texture	Matt, lumpy	Flat crystal faces

7.2 PANNING FOR GOLD

There are some excellent books dealing with this subject; there isn't enough space in a field guide like this to cover all the subtleties. We will stick to the basics. A gold pan is a cheap investment and can be bought at many outfitters or hardware stores. Choose a plastic one—it's easier for a beginner, as it requires no maintenance (doesn't rust), light, stays warm in cold rivers (doesn't freeze your fingers as much), and allows you to see the gold better. Dark green is the best contrast; black is OK.

If you're new to the game, it's a good idea to get some practice before you head out. Get a few ball-bearing sized pieces of lead (cut up a piece of lead sheet, or get hold of some lead shot). Fill your pan level to the brim with gravel and sand (easily found at the beach or in some stony gardens), and add the lead shot.

Have running water available (a garden tap is fine). Fill the pan with water.

Break up the lumps of soil so the result is a muddy mess (nobody promised you'd get rich AND stay clean!), and then, holding the pan on either side, shake the pan horizontally from side to side or in a circular motion, so that the gravels and soils are thoroughly swirled around. This is the most important part of the panning process. What it does is liquify the slurry in your pan, so the heavy objects can sink through the slop to the bottom. With any luck, your gold (er, lead) will do just that.

After about 20 seconds of vigorous circular motion, you'll notice that the pebbles have floated to the top of the slop (yes, pebbles can float, but only on denser muds and gravels). That's a sure sign you're doing it right. If the stones rise, the gold has sunk.

Scrape all the loose stones off the top, refill with water, and repeat until most of the bigger, lighter stones have risen to the top. Refill with water again, and tip the pan away from you, still holding on with a hand on either side. If your pan has riffles (little grooves on one side of the pan's sloping surface), these should be away from you.

Now swirl the pan in a horizontal, rotating motion again, so that each time you swirl, a small amount of the gravel and grit slips over the far edge of the pan, together with some water. Refill from the tap, if necessary; it's important to keep the pan moist so that any gold settles in the lowest point of the pan, below the lip that is spilling. Gradually continue to reduce the contents of the pan, swishing around and around until only a skim of sand and gravel remains in the bottom curve of the pan.

Tip level, and examine closely; your lead shot should still be in the pan. If it's not, you're either not shaking hard enough at the start, or are panning too vigorously during the concentrating stage. Try again, until you get every piece.

7.3 WHERE TO LOOK

Here are the three Golden Rules for finding gold:
1. Look for gold where gold has been found before. The chances of you finding a new deposit are considerably less than the chances of winning the lottery.
2. Gold, being very heavy, often settles into the deepest cracks. Hunt where the river slows down: on gravel bars, in tree roots or under boulders.
3. On some streams, gold settles close to the bedrock. On others, it doesn't. Remove the upper loose rocks and loose gravel. Dig down, watching for layers, either in the form of colour change or gravel size. Pan a sample from each layer. When you get a hit, note the layer's properties, and try to stay in that layer as you widen your search.

Remember that creeks and rivers change their courses, so be on the lookout for old stream beds; they are often where the real pay dirt is! Old river beds (and young ones) can also get covered with a layer of hard clay (often blue gray in colour) that looks like bedrock, but isn't. The real bedrock may be further down.

Back in the Gold Rush days, the story goes that Billy Barker (of Barkerville fame) and buddies couldn't get a stake on Williams Creek where all the action was. So they headed to below the gorge to try their luck, although the area had already been gone over thoroughly, with disappointing results. Digging down, at the gravel layer they found the usual streak of dull, dark gold. Unlike the sourdoughs on the upper reaches of the river, they kept going down—40 feet, then 50 feet. Barker was the laughing stock of the Cariboo, but he refused to give up. At 52 feet they hit the real bedrock, and with it, the most incredible pay streak. The rest is history—a single pan yielded $5 (gold was $20 an ounce), and a foot of ground turned up an incredible $1,000. By the end of 1862, almost $2 million worth of gold had come from the Cariboo fields, much of it from Williams Creek. A year later, there were almost 4,000 people living in "Barkerville", where the year before there had been nothing!

And Billy Barker? He was an old man at 45, but a rich one. He married a pretty young lady, who managed to spend his entire fortune before leaving him. He died, broke and lonely, in a Victoria flophouse. There's probably a lesson here, but I'm not sure what it is.

When panning a river, gold tends to travel in straight lines, and to cut corners where the river bends. Avoid panning where the river is fast-flowing; it's likely the gold will be carried on by. Pan the soil taken from overturned tree roots or river banks. Moss is a great trapper of gold, too. Some of the best finds have been in these unlikely places.

Stay out of potholes—it's true that gold will drop into them and concentrate, but the pounding water plus the rolling action of the gravels will turn any gold to flour in a single spring flood. Stick to fast-flowing rivers that change their speeds; once they are on the flat, they are too slow to carry gold very far.

Finally, be aware that despite all the evidence to the contrary, you are not the first! A century ago, men made of stern stuff moved mountains with shovels and sweat, and believe me, they didn't leave much unworked! In particular, the patient Chinese were known to work an area with a thoroughness that was amazing.

On the other hand, every winter exposes new surfaces, brings new material down into the creeks, and opens up new possibilities. And isn't that what it's all about?

7.4 EQUIPMENT

Gold panning requires pretty much the same stuff as rockhounding, but there are a few differences. In addition to a shovel, pick and prybar (and a pan, of course), you should take along a pair of tweezers for lifting gold out of narrow cracks, a stiff brush or paintbrush (for sweeping gravels out of same), a magnet (to confirm magnetite—a good sign, since it's associated with gold-bearing gravels), and a plastic bottle (a clear film container is OK, although a screw cap is better) filled with water, for storing the nuggets, flakes and flour. Waterproof gloves and boots will allow you to work freezing streams long after the rest of the party have chilled out.

It's often a good idea to pan your gravels down to the concentrate stage (a skim at the bottom of the pan), and then to save it in a large plastic jar with a screw cap, to be panned carefully later, when there's more time, fewer distractions, warmer water, no bugs and better light.

The problem of how to get gold "flour" out of the pan and into your collector's bottle when you only have huge fingers or tweezers, and tiny flakes, is easily solved with a matchstick. Dip the match's blank end in water to wet it, and then touch the flour. Surprise! The flour sticks to it. Now immerse your stick in the water of your collector's bottle, and the gold will drop off.

7.5 WEIGHTS AND MEASURES

The weighing of gold goes back to times before the invention of the avoirdupois pound (which Canada used to use) or the kilogram (popularized by Napoleon I). Gold was, and still is, weighed in troy ounces. Instead of there being 16 ounces to the pound as you'd expect, with the troy sytem, there are only 14.583. So, when you buy a Maple leaf or Kruger Rand, you are getting slightly more than an "ordinary" ounce of gold. That's because a troy ounce is really 20 pennyweights, and each pennyweight is made up of 24 grains. In times gone by, a *grain* was probably the weight of an average kernel of wheat. Confused yet? In the metric age, gold is now often sold in grams. There are 28.35 grams to the avoirdupois ounce, or 31.1 to the troy ounce.

Pure gold is 24 karats, but is too soft for most jewelry work, so it is alloyed with other metals, notably copper. When the mixture is 75% gold and 25% copper, for example, the gold is said to be 24 x 75/100 = 18 karat gold. Expensive gem settings are usually done in 18–22 karat gold, while economy stones are set in 10–12 karat gold.

CHAPTER 8: OTHER TREASURES

8.1 FOSSILS

It has been said that collecting fossils requires a different kind of mind from collecting minerals and gemstones. The latter speak for themselves with their colours, their shapes and their properties. Not so fossils. On the face of it, a fossil is a pretty ordinary thing to look at—the shape is simple, often indistinct, the colouring is boring, and the properties ho-hum. Yet fossils hold some people's attention like nothing else does, because to hold a fossil in your hand is to glimpse, however dimly, the immensity of time, and the history of life. No doubt about it, fossils appeal to the intellect.

Fossils are most abundant in sedimentary rocks such as shale, sandstone and limestone. They are hard to recognize in metamorphics, and are generally absent (for obvious reasons!) in igneous. If you can find an unaltered bed of sedimentaries, you've got the opportunity to find fossils lying where they lived and died millions of years ago. To be preserved, they had to be covered quickly and fossilized slowly.

8.1.1 Collecting fossils

What can you take? Fossils are now protected under the Heritage Conservation Act. To acquire title to fossils on Crown Lands, you have to apply to your nearest regional office of BC Lands. In theory, this applies to all fossils. In practice, common fossils are seldom assessed. But if you turn up fossils while digging, you are required to notify the Archaeology Branch of BC Lands in Victoria. They may assign someone to check out your find.

Fossils in limestone may be found in sedimentary strata within a day's drive of the city of Vancouver. Here are some of the oldest rocks within the vicinity, going back to the Paleozoic era, notably the Devonian era (360 million to 410 million years ago). At that time, the area was covered by sea and subject to sporadic vulcanism.

Most of the fossil-bearing limestones exhibit crinoid stems and corals. On the south end of Texada Island, Paleozoic crinoids are common in the limestones, while on the western margin of the Cascade Mountains (Chilliwack River, Slesse Creek), crinoid stems are also found. There are productive sites in abandoned lime quarries in the Rosedale–Chilliwack areas too, notably near the Agassiz bridge over the Fraser River.

Upper Jurassic and Lower Cretaceous shell beds are found extensively around the south end of Harrison Lake, notably on the west side around Twenty Mile Creek, where *buchia* and *belemnites* are prolific. Of the same era, but further east, ammonites, corals and belemnites are found throughout Manning Provincial Park, where they may be admired, but not collected.

8.2 METEORITES

Meteorites are rocks that have fallen from outer space. As a result, they can be found anywhere, and vary in size from a pin head to several tonnes. Large ones have left huge craters as witness of their awesome impact. For instance, the crater near Manicouagan in northern Quebec measures over 100 km across.

Most meteorites are probably from *asteroids*, and as such, give us valuable information on the geology beyond our little planet. There are three types: *stony*, *iron* and *stony-iron*. The stonies (*aerolites*) consist mostly of silicates, and are hard to recognize since they look pretty much like any other rock, to the casual observer. They are usually more or less round in shape and have a fine-grained texture inside.

The irons (*siderites*) contain metallic iron compounds and are slightly to strongly magnetic. They may also have cobalt, copper and, surprisingly often, diamonds! They are easier to recognize as they have a fused crust which is dimpled, as though pushed in by thumbs, caused by the heat of atmospheric entry. They, too, exhibit a dull brown to black surface, but may have a light interior. Meteorites can be mistaken for weathered rocks or metal slag, but weathered rocks lack the fused look, and slag has a low SG, whereas the density of meteorites is generally 7.5, with a hardness between 4 and 5.

The stony-irons (*siderolites*) are an equal mixture of silicate material and nickel-iron.

Meteorites aren't something you actually look for; rather, you just happen to recognize one while you're hunting for something else. Very few meteorites have ever been found in BC. Not, we suspect, because there aren't any, but because the terrain is so difficult. By contrast, the prairies have produced quite a few, which tells you something about the Alberta–Manitoba topography. The National Meteorite Collection at the Geological Survey of Canada in Ottawa pays a reward for meteorites. Check Chapter 10 for the address.

The largest siderite on record is the Hoba Iron, which weighs about 60 t, and lies where it was found in 1920, in Namibia, Africa. It probably weighed a lot more when it arrived, but has lost weight due to erosion. The Ahnighito Iron weighs 36 t, and was transported by Admiral Peary in 1897 from south of Thule, Greenland, to the Hayden Planetarium in New York, NY. By comparison, the largest aerolite to date is the Norton Achondrite, weighing just under a tonne, found in 1948 in Norton, KS. The Great Mosque in Mecca, the centre of the Muslim faith, is built around the Black Stone of Islam, which is believed to be a meteorite of considerable size.

Where are most meteorites found? Since they fall randomly onto the planet, 73% fall into the oceans and are lost. The rest may be found by accident. While we see them falling often enough, unless you have a camera with its shutter open at the critical moment, the precise trajectory cannot be calculated. On the rare occasions when this has occurred, it was still very difficult to find evidence of a meteorite actually striking the ground.

While there have been a number of publicized meteorite–civilization impacts (crashing through cars or houses), the only proven case of death-by-meteorite was a dog in India.

If you guessed that the largest country in the world (Russia) produced the most meteorites in the world, you'd be logical, but wrong. In the 1980s, scientists discovered that Antarctica is home to many hundreds. Why? Antarctica is a huge sheet of ice, over 3,000 m high in the centre, which acts like a set of giant conveyor belts, grinding very slowly to the coast, where fierce winds scour away the ice. Anything landing on the upland surfaces (meteorites, dust, pollution) is carried inexorably toward the sea, where it is exposed, to await collection.

Tektites are small, bottle-green to black siliceous glass bodies that resemble obsidian (volcanic glass), but differ chemically from terrestrial glasses. They have been found shaped like buttons, teardrops, dumbbells, pears and spindles, with their surfaces characteristically pitted due to rapid cooling. Tektites are actually chunks of earth that were thrown into the atmosphere during a meteorite collision. Tremendous heat of impact caused them to fuse and cool rapidly. Most commercially available tektites are found in China, Czech Republic and the south-central USA.

8.3 JADE

Jade gets its name from a corruption of the Spanish name *piedra de ijade*, meaning "stone of the loins". When Cortes ventured into Central America, one of the many wonders he discovered was that the Mayas used jade to cure kidney disorders. In fact, like the Chinese and Maori cultures, Montezuma's civilization had based its whole culture on jade, and the story goes that after his first meeting with Cortes, Montezuma was supposed to have said, "Thank the gods they are only after the gold and silver. They don't know about jade."

Piedra de ijade was translated into French as "*pierre de l'ejade*", but somehow ended up as "*le jade*". When the mineral was being classified using the traditional Greek style of the 18th century, it was called *lapis nephriticus*, literally, "stone of the kidneys," just like the original Spanish. That's how we get "*nephrite*".

8.3.1 What is jade?

Jade is the provincial stone of BC, and worthy of the honour. However, to confuse things, jade is the name given to two different minerals that are really mineral *aggregates*. The type of *actinolite* found in BC (and in lesser amounts in China and New Zealand) is *nephrite* and its toughness, hardness (6.5) and translucent colouring are what has made it so desirable for centuries, notably in China, where it has been at the centre of a culture going back at least 4,000 years as a tool, weapon and art form. So, if anyone tells you that BC jade isn't *real* jade, tell them it's the same stuff the Chinese craftsmen have been carving with such elegance for millennia, thank you.

The other form of jade is *jadeite* (hardness of 6.5 – 7). It belongs to the *pyroxene* group, and first appeared in 1784 from Burma. A little has been found in the state of Washington. Jadeite is also the stone of choice in early Central American cultures (such as the Mayan and Aztec empires). Jadeite is today considered more valuable than nephrite, possibly because of its greater rarity. However, from a collector's point of view, the two aggregates are almost indistinguishable (nephrite has an SG of about 3.0, jadeite of 3.2).

Jade comes in just about every colour, from black to white, although that intense green is what most people think about when you mention jade. Along the Fraser River there is a variety of nephrite known as *chicken guts jade* because of contorted swirls in the colour patterns, if you can imagine pale green guts. *Mutton fat jade* is also found in the river; however it is not a nephrite, but a blend of quartzite, sillimanite and sometimes dumortierite.

For the sake of simplicity, and to conform with the generally accepted usage, the words "jade" and "nephrite" are used interchangeably when speaking about BC deposits.

8.3.2 The history of jade in BC

Nearly all jade deposits found in Canada come from BC (with just a few occurrences in the Yukon). The first Canadian reference to jade seems to have been made by Sir John Richardson in 1851. G.M. Dawson commented in 1887 of the use of jade by the Salish people along the Fraser and Thompson rivers, and noted that *in situ* deposits were known. Archaeological investigations have dated jade artifacts in southern BC to 3,000 B.C. Adzes, decorative material and blades have been found in Lillooet and near New Westminster.

Early Chinese placer miners recognized the material (1860–1900), and shipped unknown quantities back to their homeland by the simple method of filling the coffins of their deceased compatriots with the prized mineral, thereby avoiding export duties on the material, and proving conclusively that you *can* take it with you.

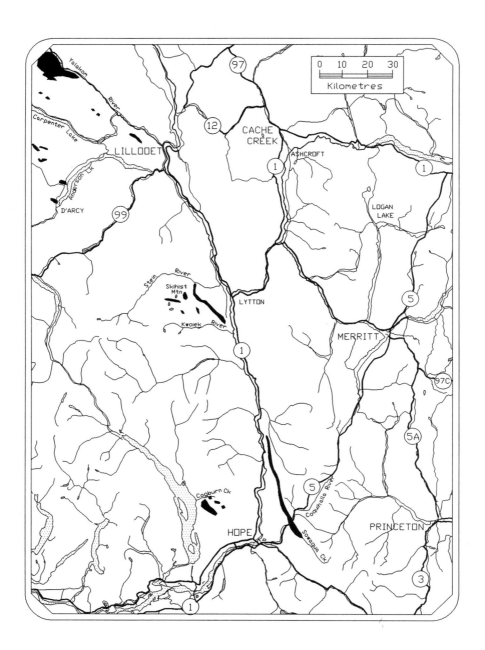

Although the deposits in the Fraser Canyon and higher up on the Yalakom River were known in the late 1800s, the sources proved erratic and marginal, so it was not until 1938, when nephrite was discovered in Wheaton Creek near Cassiar, that a substantial lode allowed the development of an industry. Still, it was only in the mid-1970s that Cassiar displaced Lillooet as the jade capital of the province. Even today, 10-tonne boulders turn up periodically along the Bridge and Yalakom River water courses.

Other jade discoveries have followed, on Mount Ogden, near Provencher Lake, and elsewhere. In 1965 a significant deposit was uncovered in the Dease Lake area, which is still being developed today. In 1967 a sharp observer realized that nephrite was being stripped off the asbestos site at Cassiar and sent to the dump! But not for long.

8.3.3   Jade prospecting methods

Hunting for jade in BC is usually done along gravel bars at low water. Know your river! BC Hydro has a habit of changing the flows at unexpected times.

Jade is heavy and fibrous, so it tends to collect less mud than other rocks. If washing off the silt on a stone reveals a depth of green colour, the next test is to chip off a sliver (gently, remembering that (a) nephrite is very hard, and (b) a shattered rock is worthless!). The sliver must be translucent. When held up to the light, if there's no glow though the edges, drop it and continue. If, on the other hand, it passes that test, the next check is to scratch it with a knife. The knife shouldn't scratch it (jade has a hardness of 6.5, a knife has a hardness of 6). If it passes this test, you can start getting excited, and it's time to start getting back to the workshop to put it through a slabbing saw. When polished, jade has a vitreous lustre that is unmistakable.

Another method of jade prospecting can be done after a fire has swept through an area: a characteristic white powder covers any exposed nephrite surface after high heat. This makes it noticeably different from other boulders in the neighbourhood. (The powder is likely a form of talc deposit, precipitated from the serpentine rind.) The "powder check" method is best done in densely forested areas, where there has been intense heat; creek fires are seldom hot enough.

In the late 1960s, when sizeable jade boulders were still a novelty, Harry Street extracted a one-and-a-half-tonner from Noel Creek near Gold Bridge, west of Lillooet. The find caused a sensation in the press, and after cleaning the boulder sold at the New York Exhibition for over $30,000, then a small fortune. A second boulder was subsequently found some distance downstream of where Noel Creek enters Cadwallader Creek. The bridge engineers had placed a pile on it some years earlier! Needless to say, this boulder was replaced with something cheaper. In 1970 a 23-tonne boulder from the Mount Ogden area was exhibited outside the BC Pavilion at Expo 70 in Osaka, Japan. In 1990 a 13-tonner from Jade West's northern BC properties was carved by Italian sculptors into the world's largest jade Buddha, for a monastery in Thailand. How did the good abbot finance such an expensive undertaking? He had all the jade chips collected and, after being blessed, they were sold to the faithful. This simple ploy raised the necessary funds comfortably.

Closer to home, in 1967 a 6-ton jade boulder from the Bridge River was bought by the O'Keefe Brewing Company and donated to Simon Fraser University. Dr. Allan Cunningham, head of the history department at the then new university, conceived of the idea of the jade boulder to symbolize the evergreen forests and waters of the province. The boulder was officially unveiled by Premier W.A.C. Bennett at the garden entrance of the campus. However, after construction was complete, it was moved to the pool of the Academic Quadrangle—the centrepoint of the university—where a large reflecting pond is surrounded by a grassy knoll. At the time of the donation, it was rumoured that O'Keefe had paid $1,000 for the boulder. It was widely reported "to be worth $100,000". This would have been high, as it meant a value in excess of $7 per pound, which was excessive, even for the Swinging '60s.

Nephrite from the Bridge River–Fraser River area is highly variable, even within the same boulder. Vivid hues are rare, with predominant colours being dark green, grayish green, olive and yellow-green. Some material is so dark that it appears black, but true black has not been found.

There are lots of fake jades. In fact, you could say the world is awash with the stuff. Green quartz, albite, diopside, aventurine, vesuvianite, chrysoprase, chrysolite and bowenite are all popular substitutes—buyer beware.

8.4 AGATE

Agate is just one of many forms of cryptocrystalline quartz (that's microcrystal quartz to you) that is sometimes known by its other name of *chalcedony*. Since the material has been collected for centuries, it has many local names, one of which is "agate". The Romans and Greeks appreciated its fine grain and used it for signet rings, and set it in brooches and hairclips. Agate snuff boxes were very "in" when Louis the Sun King was on the French throne, and Faberge, jeweller to the Czars, used chalcedony in many of his elaborate creations.

8.4.1   What is agate?

While chemically identical, agate is physically different from crystal quartz. It is composed of slender, fibre-like crystals, so small that even high-powered microscopes cannot easily detect the individual crystals. Recent discoveries have shown that there are gaps between these tiny crystals, which are filled with water. This may explain why chalcedony has a lower refractive index (1.53 compared to 1.55) and specific gravity (2.6 compared to 2.65) than quartz crystal.

One of agate's attractions is that, like snowflakes, no two are the same. Different trace minerals (iron and other metals particularly) give agate its distinctive colour bands, hardening out at different temperatures as the strata cool and form. However, over 99% of any agate is still silica (SiO_2). In the past few decades there have been some major advances in "enhancing" agate — in other words, dying it. Heating will sometimes change the original colours, but in the absence of colour (or plain gray), artists have learned to use everything from molasses mixtures to various acids. The liquids are taken up by the minute cracks and voids in the material, and will often colour one band in the agate while leaving the adjacent band undyed.

Lab experiments reveal that agate forms quite near the earth's surface, under only moderate temperature and pressure, and is often associated with amorphous silica (opal), which commonly converts to chalcedony if heated above about 100°C.

While almost half the earth's crust is made of silica, it is still quite rare to find the conditions which allow agates to grow successfully. The current belief is that even solid rocks are full of fine pores, through which water and/or silica can percolate, concentrating in pockets, vugs and other holes, to form agate.

8.4.2   Hunting for agate

What every agate hunter needs to know about hunting agate, is that it's easy if you have the right equipment. Countless books (like this one) will tell you WHERE to look, but few reveal the secret of HOW to look. Well, the mystery is finally revealed ... what you need is the Miracle Agate Detector (MAD). Yes, such a thing exists! Not only has it been rigorously tested over countless years in the field, but you can make one too. Actually, you probably own one already.

Either a small squirt bottle or a larger garden spray gun will do the trick. Filled with water, it allows you to look at the wet surfaces of whole talus slopes with little effort and great effectiveness! On hot days, when the scree slopes are baking under a summer sun, the effect lasts less than a minute before the agates blur again into the background, but you will nevertheless outperform all your co-hunters, using the amazing Miracle Agate Detector!

Another trick worth mentioning is that, when working in the early morning or late evening, try to work facing the sun. Agates that are almost invisible down-sun, stand out like polished glass when looking into the light.

Agate is widely distributed throughout the province, indeed throughout the continent. Most pebble pups cut their rockhound teeth learning to hunt for agate, yet few people know that possibly the largest agate ever discovered in North America came from BC. In 1961 two enterprising guides, who owned a rockshop in Vernon, found an agate giant weighing a staggering 755 kg, while out scouting for a club field trip. Snow conditions and soft ground prevented them from moving it immediately, and they had to wait an agonizing month before being able to return and "acquire" it. With considerable effort, it was brought to Vernon, BC. Its location is not known today.

8.4.3 Thundereggs

Thundereggs are a special form of agate, having a roughly spherical coarse outer skin or rind, which hides an agate-filled centre. Some also contain calcite, which fluoresces electric green under ultraviolet light. Eastern Oregon is famous for thundereggs; indeed, the thunderegg is the state mineral. But BC has some fine material too, with new sites being found from time to time.

Hunting for thundereggs is pretty straightforward, since they are more or less round and stand out from everything else in the area. In BC they vary from the size of a cherry to that of a grapefruit. Being hard, they don't willingly break open, and many a beautiful inside has been destroyed by an over-zealous rockhound who couldn't wait to get back to his saw before opening his finds!

When deciding to cut, notice that most thundereggs aren't truly spherical, but are usually egg- or pear-shaped. The larger dome was generally at the top of the original vug when it filled with chalcedony. To get the best cross-section, it is recommended that you cut along the line of the core (if pear-shaped), to get two matching halves.

If you don't own a diamond saw, soak a length of string in kerosene (not gasoline), tie it around the thunderegg, and light it. When the flames burn off, quickly drop the egg into cold water. This often introduces a fine, circumferential crack. Tap lightly with a hammer to split apart.

8.5 OTHER MATERIAL

Over the years, a lot of people have hunted for Indian artifacts and neo-historical materials, such as arrowheads, axes and so forth. If at all possible, avoid doing this. There are many reasons, not the least is that perceptions have changed, and today the collecting of these artifacts is perceived to be an affront to the First Nations peoples, much as a Norwegian would object to having Viking berms excavated.

But there is a much more fundamental reason to avoid doing this, and that is the matter of the resource. Early sites are few and far between, and the material to be found is extremely rare. Amateur archaeologists can be likened to the grave robbers of ancient Egypt—grabbing whatever sparkles and leaving a chaotic mess behind which, many years later, makes the serious archaeologist's job almost impossible. Real archaeology is painstakingly slow and delicate. The layers in which items lie buried is of critical importance to estimating dates and building up a composite of the culture. Rockhounds, digging cheerfully into a Fraser River bank, looking for "stuff", unknowingly destroy what little historical record there is.

For the sake of the future, leave the archaeological past for the professionals. And if you do own rare artifacts, make sure they end up, sooner or later, in a museum or university, where they can contribute to our overall understanding. Seeing a rare West Coast jade adze used as a garage doorstopper is not something to make a person feel proud.

CHAPTER 9: PROSPECTING SITES

The thrill is in the finding, but the fun is in the hunting.

Charles Southworth, amateur paleontologist, 1880–1969

There are a variety of maps available, starting with the 1:250,000, which is all right for general information but lacks a lot of key detail about minor creek names and slope types (peaks usually appear deceptively smooth on 1:250,000, until you get there and find soaring cliffs everywhere).

The 1:50,000 maps have better detail, but you need a lot more of them to cover a specific area, and as they are getting close to $10 a piece, you can blow a lot of money quickly. Further, you should consider Hudson's Law of Maps, which says "the point of interest is located at the corner of four adjacent maps", thereby necessitating you buy all of them.

On the other hand, consider the humble map. It costs less than ten bucks, yet the knowledge contained on that single piece of paper can save you hours, sometimes days, of pain, effort and frustration. When seen in that light, a survey map must be one of the last great government bargains.

The BC Forest Service puts out an excellent series of simple maps at a scale of between 1:100,000 and 1:250,000, depending on the area. These show roads, lakes, rivers and camp sites, but not contours. However, they are free, and serve as a useful basis upon which to navigate.

Finally, there are now books that have suites of maps, usually in a limited number of colours, and are a bargain. The brothers Mussio produce a series of five books at 1:100,000 that cover the southwest of the province— see Chapter 12.

HOW TO READ A SITE DESCRIPTION

Many of the sites reported in this guide are described more fully in MINFILE, a computer data set of mineral records in the province. If you are serious about finding out more about mineral localities, or armchair prospecting without the hassle of bugs or freezing rain, and computers don't scare you, then you can download everything you ever wanted to know about mineral sites in the province. And it's free! You can log into:

http://www.ei.gov.bc.ca/geosmin/minfile/minfile.htm

Of course, you can't carry a computer around with you in the field, nor can you light fires with it, or roll cigarettes in it, or clean up behind the dog with it, which are the advantages of a fieldguide. But to make it easy for you to switch between the computer program and this guide, many of the conventions have been kept the same. When downloading the field data, you will need to know which map sheets to load. This book covers some or all of mapsheets 092 G, H, I, J, O and P.

THE MINFILE NUMBER

This is found at the top of each site description (eg: 092HNE137). The Geological Survey Branch of the BC government has a unique computer file number for most mineral sites in the province. Wherever possible, this is shown so you can reference sites more precisely when visiting your local Gold Commissioner's Office or District Geologist's Office (see Chapter 10 for addresses).

The first four digits serve as the map number in the 1:250,000 series, so that, for example, the MINFILE number 092G 094 means you will find the site on the federal or provincial map number 092G (which happens to be the Vancouver area).

Sometimes there are two blanks after the first four digits, as in 092G 094; other times, these spaces have two letters, as in 092HNW076. This tells you that the mineral site is on map 092H, in the northwest (NW) quadrant. You can often buy 1:100,000 maps of these areas, that give you greater detail. In this case, ask for map 092HNW (which happens to cover Yale).

The final three digits identify each unique site. Within an area, the sites are listed by increasing number. There is no logic in how they were originally numbered, so that two adjacent sites may have quite different numbers. If there is no MINFILE number given, then the site is not in the government database.

Crown Publications in Victoria (see Chapter 10 again) sells an inexpensive MINFILE blueprint map (no pretty multi-colours) with all the mineral sites shown in place. Cost in 1999 was just $7, and the map is extremely useful for people who are serious about exploring an area fully.

SITE NAME(S)

This is listed below the MINFILE number. Often, sites have been worked for many years under various names. The name line gives the most common or historically relevant names to identify a specific site.

STATUS
The level of development of a mineral site is described as being in one of five stages:

Showing: there is little mineralization, or very little exploration has taken place to prove larger bodies.

Prospect: some limited work has been done (survey work or trenching); may have a track to it.

Developed Prospect: site has been developed so there is a reasonably detailed estimate of its value (likely a few drill holes, bulk test samples and a rough road).

Producer: either Open Pit or Underground, from which ore is currently being mined for commercial gain. Usually closed to all but the most creative rockhound.

Past Producer: no longer being mined, but there is usually good access, and interesting trenches, dumps or other features. Beware of old shafts and adits!

LATITUDE, LONGITUDE
Allows you to pin-point a site using the latitude and longitude coordinates, expressed in degrees, minutes, seconds format. With the arrival of cheap Global Positioning System (GPS) receivers, you can suddenly afford to know exactly where you are in latitude, longitude and altitude, to within 100 metres, sometimes even better than this. If you are serious about rockhounding, and going beyond the ordinary weekend trip, a GPS will save you a lot of time, and bushwacking, and devil's club, and mosquitoes, and ... you get the picture. The only warning is that GPS receivers do not work well in forests or narrow canyons, where the view to the sky is limited or blocked. In those circumstances, a good map, compass and common sense are the best way to find your position.

UTM NORTHING, EASTING
The Universal Transverse Mercator (UTM) is the alternate coordinate system used world wide, and appears as pale print at the edge of most colour maps of the province. It is easier to locate a site using UTM, if you are used to the system, because the spacing is the same everywhere, and is metric. Because UTM assumes a "cylindrical" world which can be projected onto flat maps, there is some overlap, but it is minimal.

ELEVATION
The estimated height in metres above sea level. (If you think in feet, multiply this number by 3.3.) The elevation reading is useful in mountainous terrains, since it gives you a contour to follow to pin-point the site, if the latitude and longitude readings appear unreliable.

COMMENTS

Listed comments may tell you something about how to get there, or what is of interest once you do.

COMMODITIES

Indicates the site's end product. For example, the location may show galena, but the commodity would be lead. Similarly, chalcopyrite ore means the commodity is copper. Commodities are listed in decreasing order of importance, based on economic significance to the mining industry. You, on the other hand, may value secondary commodities more. For example, where a site lists copper, lead, zinc, you may find that all three are in massive chalcopyrite and galena, making them of little interest to a rockhound. On the other hand, the Associated Minerals (see below) offer great finds.

SIGNIFICANT MINERALS

Gives you a list of what to look for in ore bodies, primary minerals, etc.

ASSOCIATED MINERALS

Secondary minerals that may or may not require detailed care to find.

9.1. GREATER VANCOUVER AREA

At first glance the downtown area of the City of Vancouver may appear to be a dull spot for rockhounding. At least two glaciations have left erratics and till in thick layers. A brittle layer of clay offers up some poor quality fossils (mostly univalves and tubeworms), while the underlying coal contains some amber. Amateur paleontologist Peter Thorne has spent 50 years checking the newly dug foundations of buildings in the area, and has found some remarkable material, including fish fossils.

Notwithstanding these discoveries, the cities of Vancouver, Burnaby, New Westminster, Port Moody, Delta, Surrey, Langley and Abbotsford are built on flat ground (when compared to everything else around them). This area is the mouth of a major river, so it is not surprising that its geology is a bit dull. The basic rule is: If it's flat (or flattish), then it's sand, silt, glacial till, river gravel or peat bog. There's not a lot to get excited about within the city limits.

There are exceptions: The seawalls around Stanley Park and Kitsilano Beach show sandstones and shales, as does Burnaby Mountain (Simon Fraser University). Up the Fraser Valley, you must go as far as Grant Hill (across from Fort Langley) or Silverdale Hill (north of Mission) to find similar non-glacial material. There are limestone deposits in the Chilliwack River valley. The southside of that river, immediately west of where Slesse Creek joins it, and further south in the USA, host fossil corals (coenites) which form branches in either white or black, depending on the fossilization process.

The north shore of Burrard Inlet is different. Coast intrusives (granites, granodiorites and diorites) survive where recent glaciers (prior to 10 million years ago) failed to gouge. Most are a blend of quartz diorite, although the base rocks at the Mount Seymour ski area, and much of Bowen and Gambier islands in Howe Sound, are primarily andesites (another plutonic intrusive). Lighthouse Park shows good examples of glacially scoured granodiorites.

9.1.1 PLACES TO VISIT

Stanley Park

The seawall runs around the seashore, passing underneath sandstones (which worried the foundation engineers of the Lions Gate Bridge). Close to Siwash Rock, an igneous intrusive dyke of andesite is seen as a 20 m cliff — the same as Siwash Rock. The top of the cliff shows columnar pillars. Within sight of Siwash Rock, dark brown concretions are visible in the sandstone. These are not remote boulders, but formed due to seepage of iron oxide, which "cemented" the material together.

The boulders offshore are glacial till, brought down from hither and yon by slowly grinding ice.

Highway #99

Start at kilometre 0, at the Horseshoe Bay ferry turnoff.

Km 2 to 3.5: These metamorphosed sedimentaries and volcanics are the oldest rocks in the Vancouver area (greater than 185 million years), and are cut by granite and diorite intrusions. Light feldspar-rich gneisses alternate with dark amphibolites.

Km 4.6: The rock cut at the north end of Schlufield Creek exhibits breccia (fragments of granitic rock, gneiss and amphibolite) within quartz diorite.

Km 10 to 12: Lions Bay is built on the alluvial fans of two steep creeks. In the past, flash floods have caused considerable damage: In 1983, five homes and both highway bridges were taken out.

Km 14: The bridge at M Creek was swept away by a boulder torrent one night in 1981, and nine people died when they drove their cars into the black void.

Km 16: Argillite in a Gambier Group area of rocks has been used for carving. Ammonites have also been found here.

Km 19: At the pull-out for the Pacific Great Eastern Railway, cross the highway to the outside and view a large anticline (folded rock).

Km 31: Britannia Beach used to be Britannia Mine (1905–74), and was one of the most successful mines in BC. Visit the BC Museum of Mining. The host rock is visible in places; it is a schist with faint blue and green copper stains. In 1915 a rock slide took out a bunkhouse, killing 50 people.

Km 34: The famous rock climbing area around the Stawamus Chief (east of Squamish on Highway #99) is granodiorite, with a west face almost 700 m high. There is a distinct black dyke, 2 m wide, running up the right hand wall, which is a hornblende diorite. Much of the area is polished smooth by the passage of ice.

Km 39: Mount Garibaldi is the remains of a volcanic cone which erupted as recently as 9,600 years ago. Lava flows are found on the north side of

Mamquam River (east of Squamish). Turn off onto Guildford Road which leads to Mamquam Forest Road. Some 10 km off Highway #99, volcanics are visible in the roadcuts.

Km 64: Turn off Highway #99 and cross the river and rail tracks before driving 1.5 km up west side of valley on unpaved road. Basalt columns above the road and views across the valley to the Barrier make this a worthwhile side-trip. The volcanic plugs of Black Tusk to northeast and Garibaldi to the southeast show recent vulcanism. To the right of the Barrier, Table Mountain shows lava flows.

9.2. GEORGIA STRAIT

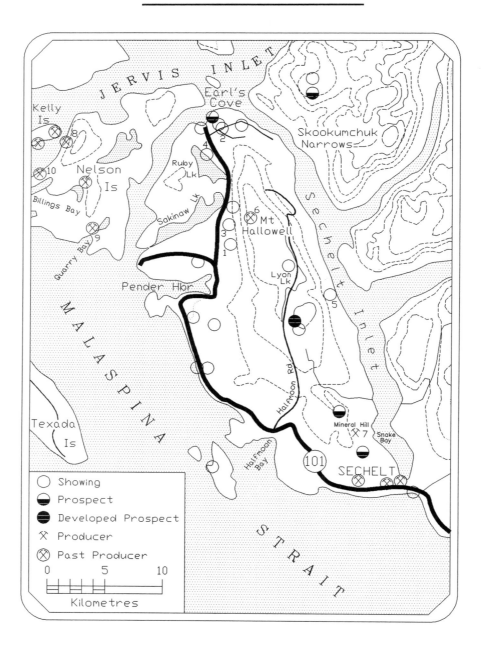

9.2.1 THE SECHELT PENINSULA

The area is noted for its Upper Triassic limestones and dolomites, which host skarn-type minerals. The Mineral Hill deposit just NW of the town of Sechelt contains almost 300,000 t of wollastonite, with local limestone and garnet. Associated with this, the Sechelt Carbonate deposit to the NW has been estimated to contain over 3 million t of dolomite.

A series of mineral showings in the road cuts of Highway #101 make the drive from Sechelt to the ferry terminal at Earl's Cove interesting, if you make the time to stop and hound around.

---

1. MINFILE NUMBER: 092GNW033
NAME(S): DAY

Low grade polymetallic mineralization is exposed along Highway #101, 4.3 km NNE of the head of Pender Harbour on the Sechelt Peninsula. At the Day showing, a silicified shear zone up to 24 m wide strikes NNE for 210 m in granodiorite and quartz monzonite. The shear zone is mineralized with minor amounts of pyrite, chalcopyrite, molybdenite and sphalerite as disseminations and fracture-fillings.

---

2. MINFILE NUMBER: 092GNW050
NAME(S): NORTH LAKE

The showing outcrops along Highway #101, 300 m NE of the W end of North Lake on Sechelt Peninsula. A road cut along the highway reveals a vein hosted in granodiorite for an exposed length of 30 m. The vein varies up to 27 cm in width. Other minor tension veins are found in the granodiorite along the NW side of the main vein over a distance of 20 m. The veins are comprised of marcasite in a gangue of quartz.

---

3. MINFILE NUMBER: 092GNW059
NAME(S): EDDY

At the Eddy showing, pyrite and chalcopyrite mineralization is exposed over a 60 m by 60 m area along a road cut 100 m E of Highway #101, 5.8 km NNE of the head of Pender Harbour. The mineralization is hosted in basalts and andesites.

4. MINFILE NUMBER: 092GNW060
NAME(S): BACON, RUBY LAKE

Copper mineralization is exposed for 250 m along Highway 101, on the E side of Ruby Lake. Pyrite, pyrrhotite and chalcopyrite occur as fracture in-fillings along conjugate joints and as blebs in the roof pendant rocks.

5. MINFILE NUMBER: 092GNW032
NAME(S): WAR

Widespread low grade copper-molybdenum mineralization is exposed just E of Lyon Lake at Lyon Lake Rec Site, 14.5 km N of Halfmoon Bay on Halfmoon FS Road. A zone of sulphide mineralization is developed over a 1700 m by 850 m area. Pyrite occurs with minor molybdenite and chalcopyrite as fracture fillings, disseminations and blebs in volcanics, sediments and quartz veinlets.

6. MINFILE NUMBER: 092GNW011
NAME(S): CAMBRIAN CHIEFTAIN

Status:	Past producer, open pit, underground		
Latitude:	49 40 54	Northing:	5503430
Longitude:	123 56 17	Easting:	432320
Elevation:	985 m		
Comments:	Main workings are on Upper Sheep Creek. Access is now difficult, as the Hallowell FS Road is washed out, but that is the only way in. Leave Highway #101 10 km N of Pender Harbour. The mine is 7 km up steep terrain, on the S side of Mt Hallowell.		
Commodities:	Copper, silver, zinc, gold		

MINERALS

Significant:	Chalcopyrite, pyrite, pyrrhotite, magnetite, sphalerite, hematite
Associated:	Garnet, epidote

High-grade copper ore was mined periodically from an open pit; underground workings located on S side of Mount Hallowell. A zone of discontinuous garnet and epidote-rich skarn alteration strikes NNE for 550 m, within thinly bedded limestone, chert and massive greenstone. The zone varies up to 30 m in width. Chalcopyrite, pyrite, magnetite and sphalerite occur along fractures and as disseminations in the garnet-epidote skarn. Copper mineralization is most intense in the northern 150 m of the zone, where chalcopyrite forms massive bands and pods up to 0.9 m thick, accompanied by minor pyrite, sphalerite and magnetite. Over 1400 t were mined intermittently from 1949–63.

---

7.   MINFILE: 092GNW052
NAME(S): MINERAL HILL, SNAKE BAY

Status:	Producer, open pit	Northing:	5484871
Latitude:	49 30 56	Easting:	440904
Longitude:	123 48 59	Elevation:	268 m
Comments:	1.5 km W of Snake Bay.		
Commodities:	Limestone, wollastonite		

MINERALS

Significant:	Calcite, wollastonite, garnet
Associated:	Diopside, epidote, quartz, tremolite, pyrite, chalcopyrite, sphalerite

The Mineral Hill deposit is located 1.5 km W of Snake Bay. A wollastonite deposit is hosted within a roof pendant and is comprised mostly of limestone and banded skarn. Thinly bedded, light and dark gray limestone outcrops in the N half of the roof pendant. It is locally massive and coarse-grained, and occasionally contaminated by layers containing calcite, garnet, quartz and wollastonite. The limestone is reported to be 90% pure.

Variably striped, maroon, green, yellowish white and brown to black skarn, containing diopside, epidote and wollastonite (with rare pyrite, chalcopyrite and sphalerite), outcrops throughout most of the roof pendant. It, and the enclosing diorite, are intruded by greenish black dykes that strike W.

Wollastonite is found near the E end of the roof pendant, over most of its length, where it occurs in three forms: (i) in layers up to 8 cm thick, alternating with garnet in banded skarn, (ii) as a very fine replacement of siliceous layers in limestone, that comprise up to 35% of the rock, and (iii) in thinly laminated calcium silicate rock, comprised of layers of coarse crystalline, light brown wollastonite, alternating with layers of dense, green wollastonite, tremolite and other calcium silicates, excluding garnet.

Nelson Island

For those with a sailboat, and who enjoy the subtle colours of marbles and granites, then Nelson Island, en route to Jervis Inlet, makes an interesting stop-over. Historically, this island has supplied building stone for many of Vancouver's older buildings, when a bank wasn't a real bank unless it was built with lots of marble interiors and granite exteriors. Nowadays, of course, banks just look like ATMs (although they do stay open all night).

8. MINFILE NUMBER: 092F 100
NAME(S): NELSON ISLAND

Status: Past producer, open pit, underground
Commodities: Dolomite, limestone

The deposit is generally comprised of fine to coarse-grained, white to light bluish, high-calcium limestone. The NE side of the band contains silicious blue limestone and dolomite. Thin lenses of white dolomite are scattered throughout the rest of the deposit. Located on the W side of Telescope Passage, leading from Blind Bay to Jervis Inlet.

9. MINFILE NUMBER: 092F 189
NAME(S): QUARRY BAY, NELSON ISLAND

Status: Past producer, open pit
Commodities: Granite

Four quarries occur in granodiorite on Quarry Bay at the S tip of Nelson Island. The granodiorite is light gray, uniform and has a medium-grained texture. Black blades of biotite and occasional hornblende crystals contrast with the light gray feldspar and quartz matrix.

The quarries have been operated intermittently since the mid-1800s, providing stone for a number of buildings and monuments in Vancouver, Victoria, New Westminster and Nanaimo. The stone has also been exported to Australia, California and Hawaii, under the trade name "Nelson Island Gray".

10. MINFILE NUMBER: 092F 196
NAME(S): KELLY ISLAND, GRANITE ISLAND

Status: Past producer, open pit
Commodities: Granite

Jurassic granodiorite was mined in five quarries at the turn of the century on the SW end of Kelly Island (formerly Granite Island), near Billings Bay on the W side of Nelson Island. The largest of the quarries is 110 m long and has a face 12 m high. There are potential reserves at all five quarries.

9.2.2 TEXADA ISLAND

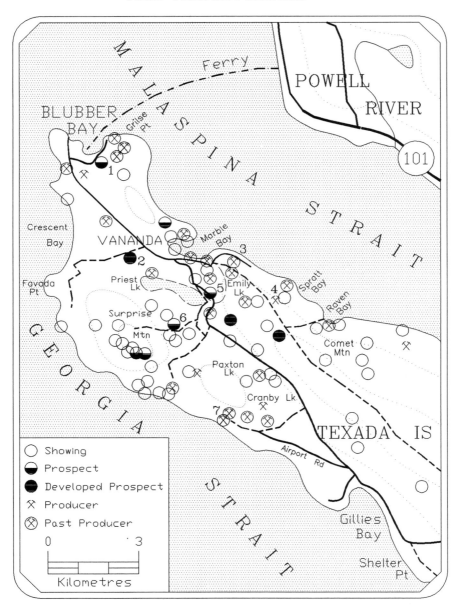

Texada Island, reached by a 35-minute ferry ride from Powell River on the Sunshine Coast, overlies the contact between the Wrangellia and North American plates. Like Quadra Island to the N (see *Volume I*), Texada is highly mineralized. Since 1896, polymetallic skarns have produced over 10 million t of magnetite iron ore, 35 thousand t of copper, 40 t of silver and 3.3 t of gold.

Other quarries produced huge amounts of high-calcium limestone for the manufacture of cement and lime. Some of the West Coast's best flowerstone porphyry is found around Surprise Mtn in the NW of the island. Beach-combing further S at Shelter Point or Gillies Bay may also produce fine flowerstone material. Banded black and white limestone is found at Imperial Quarries. Crinoid fossils of the Paleozoic era are found in the marble/limestone deposits at the southern end of the island. In the late 1800s, Van Anda boasted the only opera house north of San Francisco.

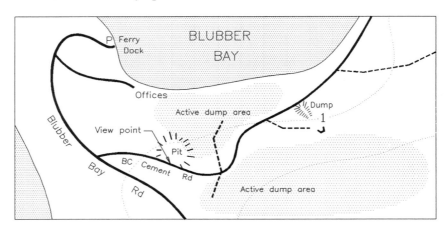

1. MINFILE NUMBER: 092F 266
NAME(S): PARIS

Status:	Prospect	Northing:	5516360
Latitude:	49 47 26	Easting:	384135
Longitude:	124 36 35	Elevation:	40 m

Comments: Bulldozed-over shaft, just E of Blubber Creek, on the BC Cement Rd halfway around the bay. The upper and lower cement workings are close.

Commodities: Copper, gold, silver, zinc

MINERALS
Significant: Magnetite, chalcopyrite, pyrrhotite, pyrite, sphalerite

The area is underlain by limestone intruded by small diorite dykes. A distinct (white), E-trending, quartz-porphyry dyke transects the prospect. Skarn zones comprised in part of garnet, pyroxene and actinolite are developed at the limestone/diorite contacts. They contain massive magnetite with disseminations and stringers of chalcopyrite, pyrrhotite, pyrite and sphalerite. A few shallow shafts have been sunk on some of the magnetite lenses. The property is noted for its production of flake gold specimens.

2. **MINFILE NUMBER: 092F 364**
   NAME(S): BOLIVAR

Status:	Developed prospect	Northing:	5513040
Latitude:	49 45 39	Easting:	385550
Longitude:	124 35 21	Elevation:	60 m
Comments:	Pit is on S side of the golf course (unpaved) road, just 500 m off the main (paved) island road, 5 km S of Blubber Bay.		
Commodities:	Gold, silver, copper, zinc		

MINERALS

Significant:	Gold, chalcopyrite, sphalerite
Associated:	Graphite, pyrite, pyrrhotite, quartz

The Bolivar occurrence area is underlain by limestone in contact with basalt. An irregular wedge, thinning to the NW, of siliceous skarnified rock roughly parallels the limestone/basalt contact. Some disseminated pyrite and minor chalcopyrite occurs within this, and along the contact with the basalt and limestone. The basalts are thick bedded, epidotized and cut by quartz veins. These range from 1 cm to 50 cm in width, and commonly contain pyrite and lesser amounts of pyrrhotite and chalcopyrite.

The limestone is mainly fine-grained, gray and cut by numerous basaltic dykes. Local zones within the limestone show varied intensity of recrystallization to marble. Black carbonaceous (graphitic) material occurs in pockets. Native gold occurs as streaks and disseminations along subparallel graphitic slips in a sheeted zone of variably recrystallized limestone. Pyrite is also present but is most abundant in the carbonaceous material. The gold-bearing zone is 40 m long, 3 m wide and 15 m deep.

3. **MINFILE NUMBER: 092F 105**
   NAME(S): LITTLE BILLIE

Status:	Past producer, underground		
Latitude:	49 45 31	Northing:	5512710
Longitude:	124 32 44	Easting:	388680
Elevation:	30 m		
Comments:	Old shaft and dump are visible above the road after the last house on Gracemere/Olive St, along the sea shore SE of Van Anda, about 1 km from centre of village.		
Commodities:	Gold, copper, wollastonite, silver, molybdenum, zinc, lead, tungsten, bismuth		

MINERALS

Significant:	Chalcopyrite, bornite, wollastonite, molybdenite, sphalerite, galena, scheelite, silver, hessite, petzite, wehrlite, pyrrhotite
Associated:	Quartz, pyrite, magnetite

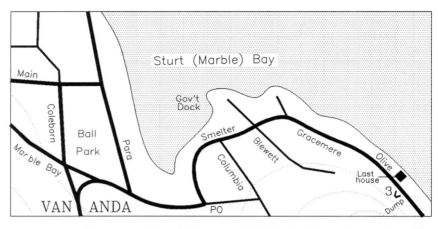

The Little Billie mine is located just outside Van Anda on the coast road. Historic work at the mine included moderate underground development. Two types of skarn ore are recognized. The first is a gangue of coarse granular brown garnet and abundant magnetite, loosely held together, and the second is a gangue of green garnet, wollastonite and diopside which is dense and hard. The main ore minerals are chalcopyrite and bornite, with variable but minor amounts of molybdenite, pyrite, magnetite and sphalerite. Bornite sometimes occurs as coarse crystals intergrown with garnet, and the higher gold values are commonly found with the higher copper concentrations. Chalcopyrite and bornite are mixed with bladed wollastonite. Although chalcopyrite and bornite occur together in both the green and brown garnet (andradite) skarn bodies, the chalcopyrite favours the brown garnet-magnetite bodies and the bornite favours the green garnet- wollastonite-diopside bodies.

---

4.   MINFILE NUMBER: 092F 394
NAME(S): IMPERIAL LIMESTONE

Status:	Producer, open pit	Northing:	5510746
Latitude:	49 44 28	Easting:	390020
Longitude:	124 31 35	Elevation:	140 m

Comments: Located 2 km S of Van Anda village. From the post office, take Copper Queen Rd and Alladin Rd to reach Wall St (to Central Rd).

Commodities: Limestone, silver, lead, copper, gold, aggregate building stone

MINERALS

Significant: Calcite, sulphide

Limestone has been quarried since 1951, from near the E edge of a 13 km long belt of Quatsino Formation limestone, up to 3 km wide, that covers the N end of the island. It is mined from a 100 m thick bed of high calcium limestone. Several steeply dipping faults are exposed in the quarry, and a few hundred metres to the SW, the limestone contacts basaltic flows.

The deposit consists of irregular masses of white limestone in black limestone, with gradational and sharp contacts separating the two types. Both types are fine-grained. The deposit was initially quarried by Don McKay 1951–58. Imperial Limestone acquired the property in 1959, and has continued to the present day. From 1952–87, over 4.5 million t of limestone have been quarried. Most is barged to Seattle.

Recent sampling by quarry personnel of sulfide mineralization at the edge of the quarry, returned values in zinc, silver, lead, copper and gold. The showing, known as MOLLY SKARN (092F 522), is E of the Imperial quarry and 800 m W of Spratt Bay. It lies close to the contact between limestone and basalt. Minor iron skarn occurs and is comprised of magnetite and chalcopyrite with high cobalt values. A Ministry of Mines sample from a shaft at the showing identified erythrite (bright red crusts, when freshly exposed) in small quantities.

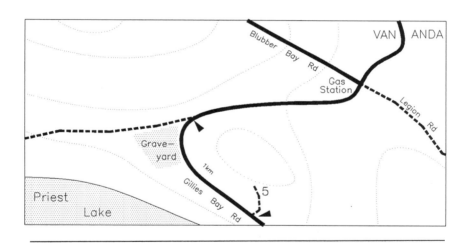

5. MINFILE NUMBER: 092F 516
NAME(S):YEW

Status:	Developed prospect	Northing:	5511300
Latitude:	49 44 45	Easting:	387910
Longitude:	124 33 21	Elevation:	87 m
Comments:	Trenches and pit 1 km S of Van Anda graveyard (which is on the main island road to Gillies Bay). A 50 m track leads E to site.		
Commodities:	Gold, copper, silver		

MINERALS
Significant: Pyrite, magnetite, pyrrhotite, chalcopyrite, bornite, gold

At the Yew occurrence, stratigraphy is comprised of three rock units: (a) a lower, thick series of green-gray basalt flows overlain by (b) a thin, white-gray fine-grained limestone that rapidly thins and thickens over short distances (c) an amygdaloidal basalt breccia. White zeolites, epidote, pyrite, quartz and chlorite comprise vesicle fillings within the basalts.

Pyrite, magnetite, pyrrhotite, minor chalcopyrite and trace bornite replace limestone at the lower contact of the limestone bed. The mineralized zone is flat-lying, close to surface, thin and tabular, and ranges from 40 cm to 1.8 m in thickness. A second zone comprising garnet-epidote skarn within basalt occurs below the massive mineralization and contains visible native gold.

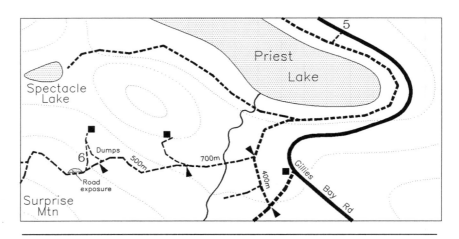

6. MINFILE NUMBER: 092F 359
NAME(S): GEM

Status:	Prospect	Northing:	5510210
Latitude:	49 44 08	Easting:	386560
Longitude:	124 34 27	Elevation:	152 m

Comments: Shaft located between Priest Lake and Surprise Mtn. The dump is currently being re-processed. Phone (604)486-7564 for permission to visit. The major interest to hobbyists is the host material, which is the famous Texada flowerstone (gabbro/basalt porphyry). The dump has large amounts, plus the road some 200 m beyond (W) cuts more material.

Commodities: Gold, silver, lead, copper

MINERALS

Significant: Pyrite, gold, galena, chalcopyrite
Associated: Porphyry, quartz, calcite, pyrrhotite, arsenopyrite

The Gem occurrence is underlain by amygdaloidal basalt, close to the intersection of the Kirk Lake and Holly faults. A fault zone in basalt hosts steeply dipping quartz veinlets and an occasional massive vein with some calcite. The zone ranges in width from 0.6 m to 1.2 m. Mineralization consists of pyrite, local native gold, galena, occasional chalcopyrite and minor pyrrhotite and arsenopyrite. High but erratic gold with minor silver values occurs along the length of the vein system. Past development included shafts and drifting on two levels. Although production records report 2 t of ore mined, the workings at the site indicate considerably more took place.

---

7.   MINFILE NUMBER: 092F 106
NAME(S): PRESCOTT–TEXADA MINES

Status:	Past producer, open pit, underground		
Latitude:	49 42 12	Northing:	5506575
Longitude:	124 32 57	Easting:	388300
Elevation:	50 m		
Comments:	Numerous mines and pits, now merged into one. Best access is via the Airport Rd from just N of Gillies Bay. The site was still active in 1999.		
Commodities:	Iron, copper, silver, gold, zinc, magnetite		

MINERALS

Significant: Magnetite, chalcopyrite, pyrite, pyrrhotite, arsenopyrite, sphalerite

Magnetite skarn mineralization at the mine comprises an irregular lens or group of lenses, occurring with reddish brown garnet, pyroxene (hedenbergite-diopside), epidote, amphibole (actinolite), minor calcite and sporadic chalcopyrite, pyrite and pyrrhotite. Traces of arsenopyrite and rare sphalerite are also observed.

The initial discoveries of the four main iron skarn deposits were the Prescott, Yellow Kid (092F 258), Paxton (092F 107) and Lake (092F 259). From 1885–1908, some 26,000 t of magnetite ore were reported to be shipped. Sporadic activity continued until 1916; at that time the workings at the Prescott mine included a large quarry, shaft, an adit connected to the shaft and four working levels above the adit.

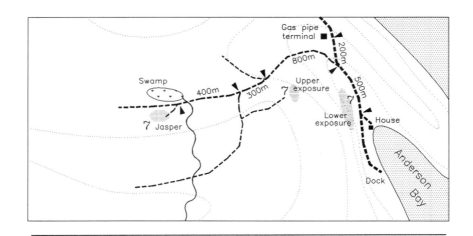

8.   **MINFILE NUMBER: 092F 088**
     NAME(S): ANDERSON BAY

Status:	Past producer, open pit	Northing:	5485310
Latitude:	49 31 00	Easting:	417300
Longitude:	124 08 33	Elevation:	150 m

Comments: An example of the pink fossiliferous marble may be seen at the Texada Inn reception desk, Van Anda. Access to Anderson Bay from the N end of the island is long, sinuous and rough, but well signed. Most of the way it follows the new gas pipeline. Follow "Anderson Bay" or "Anderson Main" signs. The lower quarry is visible through the trees from the only house in the area. Access to the upper zone is via a forest road which leaves the main road 500 m up from the bay.

Commodities: Limestone, marble

MINERALS
Significant: Carbonate, calcite, marble, dolomite
Associated: Jasper, fossils

The deposit is located just NW of Anderson Bay near the S tip of Texada Island. Marble was produced from several quarries until 1917. A 30 m to 60 m thick limestone bed extends N for 1.7 km, and is sometimes overlain by basaltic flows, and underlain by mafic breccias, gray argillites and volcanics. The limestone bed pinches out to the S, and is truncated to the N by a fault. It comprises coarse- to fine-grained, white to reddish brown, fossiliferous limestone. The lower 10 m to 15 m consist of white to pink crinoidal limestone, that grade upward into 10 m to 15 m of banded pink to red crinoidal limestone, containing some jasper. This is overlain by red and green tuffaceous limestone. Dolomite and high calcium beds are found in the upper portion of the deposit. Lenticular masses of fine-grained pink dolomite veined with white calcite occur near the N end of the deposit. Beyond this, a band of jasper is found next to a small swamp area (100 m by 50 m). Bulldozer tracks climb 100 m S to a small rise, where the brick-red material is exposed.

Two small quarries were opened on the marble deposit in the early 1900s. Nootka Quarries operated a quarry 400 m NW of the head of Anderson Bay. By 1916, 100 t of marble had been produced for ornamental stone. Red marble from this site was likely used in the columns and panelling throughout the rotunda in the Legislative Buildings, Victoria.

9.3. HOWE SOUND – WHISTLER VALLEY

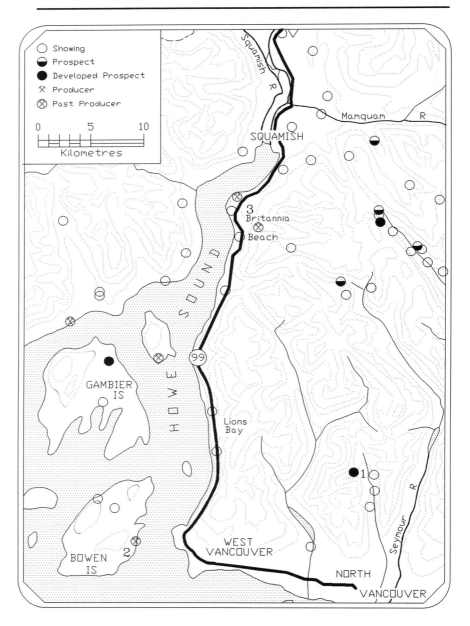

9.3.1 HOWE SOUND

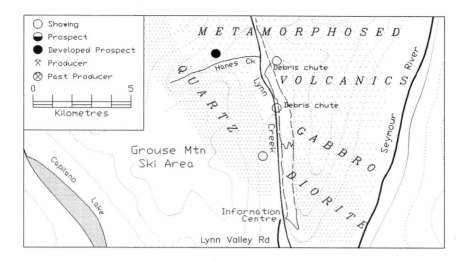

The area is part of the Coast tectonic belt, and is comprised mostly of plutonic rocks of the Tertiary and Jurassic ages. Historically, volcanic massive sulfides and veins, such as the highly productive Britannia Mine, have made important economic contributions to the development of the city of Vancouver. On Gambier Island (in Howe Sound), a huge copper-molybdenum porphyry is estimated to contain over 200 million t of ore.

---

1.   MINFILE NUMBER: 092GSW003
NAME(S): LYNN CREEK

Status:	Developed prospect	Northing:	5474053
Latitude:	49 25 16	Easting:	495567
Longitude:	123 03 40	Elevation:	700 m
Comments:	Located on N side of Hayes Creek.		
Commodities:	Zinc, silver, lead		

MINERALS

Significant: Sphalerite, pyrrhotite, galena, chalcopyrite, pyrite, cubanite, marcasite, hematite

Associated: Quartz

The area of the Lynn Creek zinc property is underlain by diorite which hosts a metamorphic pendant of volcanic and sedimentary rocks. Mineralization occurs in two areas, about 500 m apart and 350 m vertically. Access is subject to regulations of the North Vancouver Water District. In both places, the mineralization consists mainly of massive dark sphalerite, with smaller amounts of pyrrhotite, galena, chalcopyrite, pyrite, cubanite, marcasite and hematite. Gangue minerals include vuggy, coarse quartz, garnet and other skarn minerals. Silver values varied up to 68 gm/t. Zinc values average about 9%.

---

2. MINFILE NUMBER: 092GSW004
NAME(S): BOWENA, SNUG COVE

Status:	Past producer, underground		
Latitude:	49 21 42	Northing:	5467495
Longitude:	123 19 48	Easting:	476037
Elevation:	100 m		
Comments:	Old adit, located on the SE of Bowen Island, between Snug Cove and Seymour Bay.		
Commodities:	Gold, copper, silver		

MINERALS
Significant: Chalcopyrite, pyrrhotite, magnetite, pyrite

The property is located close to shore, just N of Apodaca Provincial Park on Bowen Island. It is underlain by dark green andesites, white to light gray and purple cherty tuffs with minor quartzite, porphyry and limestone. Minor pyrrhotite and pyrite are common throughout much of the rock. Copper mineralization is present in zones, occurring in silicified and brecciated shear zones and in one area with massive magnetite and pyrrhotite.

Production recorded amounted to 54 t of ore, shipped in 1907.

---

3. MINFILE NUMBER: 092GNW003
NAME(S): BRITANNIA MINE

Status:	Past producer, open pit, underground		
Latitude:	49 36 41	Northing:	5495200
Longitude:	123 08 23	Easting:	489900
Elevation:	1067 m		
Comments:	A major economic force for half a century in the Lower Mainland. The mine museum is well worth a visit. For mine tours and opening hours, call (604)688-8735. Closed for the winter.		
Commodities:	Copper, zinc, lead, silver, gold, cadmium		

MINERALS
Significant: Chalcopyrite, sphalerite, galena, tennantite, tetrahedrite, pyrrhotite, argentite, gold
Associated: Quartz, muscovite, chlorite, anhydrite, siderite, carbonate, silica, barite

The sulfide orebodies of Britannia are highly diverse mixtures of sulfides, altered host rocks, and discrete veins. The main mineralogy is simple and fairly constant. Pyrite is by far the most abundant mineral, with less chalcopyrite and sphalerite, and minor erratically distributed galena, tennantite, tetrahedrite and pyrrhotite. The main non-metallic minerals include quartz and muscovite (chlorite), anhydrite and siderite.

Past work consisted of extensive underground and surface development. From 1905–77, the Britannia orebodies yielded over 50 million t of ore, grading 1.1% copper, 0.65% zinc, 6.8 gm/t silver and 0.6 gm/t gold.

Just 2 km N of Britannia Beach, and 250 m S of Murrin Provincial Park, the showing VENUS (092GNW022) is located between the shoreline and Highway #99. Underlain by granodiorites, old trenches expose chalcopyrite and molybdenite fillings in quartz porphyry.

9.3.2 WHISTLER AREA

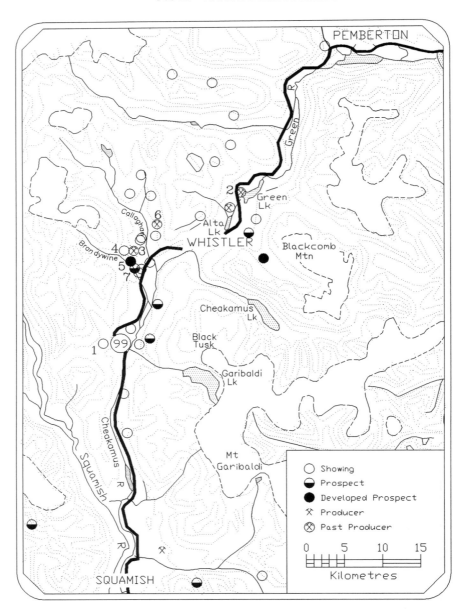

When you look at the valley containing Whistler Village today, it's hard to realize that as late as the 1970s there were still active mines in the area. Plutonic rocks are common with local faults trending parallel to the Coast Mountains. The region had its day: over 5 t of gold and 26 t of silver were extracted from the NORTHAIR site alone. Today, golf courses provide a better return on investment.

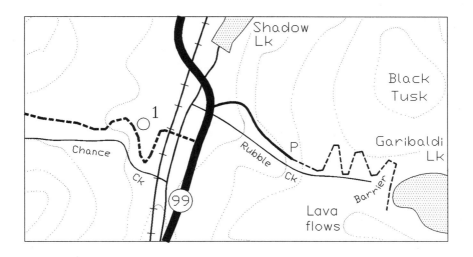

---

1. **NAME(S): TRICOUNI**

Status:	Producer, open pit	Northing:	5535250
Latitude:	49 58 10	Easting:	488645
Longitude:	123 09 30	Elevation:	500 m

Comments: Almost opposite the Garibaldi Lake parking area (on R), turn W (L) to cross the Cheakamus River. Cross the railway and turn S where an unpaved road starts to climb. At 1.5 km, well-formed basalt columns appear above the road. These are currently quarried as landscape material at Whistler Village. Higher up the road, the view E shows a panoramic view of the Garibaldi group (SE) and Black Tusk (NE), both old volcanic plugs, dating from 20 million years ago with flows as recent as the last ice age (10,000 Ya). Directly across the valley (E) the eroding Barrier shows where Garibaldi Lake, having no river outlet, leaks out through the cobbles to form Rubble Creek.

---

2. **MINFILE NUMBER: 092JSE015**
   NAME(S): IRON KING, COUGAR

Status:	Past producer, open pit	Northing:	5553236
Latitude:	50 08 00	Easting:	501548
Longitude:	122 58 42	Elevation:	820 m
Comments:	Iron		

MINERALS

Significant: Limonite

The Iron King bog iron deposits, mined 1918–44 where the Whistler Secondary School now stands, are located about 2 km N of Alta Lake, near Whistler. The geology of the region consists of pyritic tuff preserved within plutonic rocks. Weathering of the pyritic tuffs is a likely source of the iron. In 1944, 5,500 t of ore were mined and 2,500 t of iron were recovered, indicating between 40% to 50% iron.

---

3.   MINFILE NUMBER: 092JW 001
NAME(S): TEDI

Status:	Past producer, open pit	Northing:	5547750
Latitude:	50 05 02	Easting:	489800
Longitude:	123 08 33	Elevation:	975 m
Comments:	Silver, gold, lead, zinc, copper		

MINERALS

Significant:	Pyrite, sphalerite, galena, chalcopyrite

The Tedi deposit is situated between Brandywine and Callaghan creeks. Andesitic and volcanic rocks are intruded by felsite dykes. Mineralization consists of pyrite, sphalerite, galena and chalcopyrite, which occur both as narrow (less than 5 cm wide) veins and as massive bands which parallel foliation. Mineralization within the hosting andesite and diorite is discontinuous.

The Tedi pit was mined in conjunction with the Silver Tunnel deposit (092JW 003) in 1977, and recorded production from 1970–78. A total of 10,000 t of ore were mined, yielding 700 kg silver, 343 kg gold, 13 t copper, 165 t lead and 160 t zinc.

---

4.   MINFILE NUMBER: 092JW 006
NAME(S): STAN

The STAN showing (092JW 006) is located 500 m due W of TEDI. Skarn mineralization is reported to consist of pyrite, chalcopyrite, bornite, sphalerite, pyrrhotite and malachite in greenstone.

---

5.   MINFILE NUMBER: 092JW 003
NAME(S): SILVER TUNNEL

Status:	Developed prospect	Northing:	5545989
Latitude:	50 04 05	Easting:	489464
Longitude:	123 08 50	Elevation:	762 m
Comments:	Gold, silver, lead, zinc, copper		

MINERALS

Significant:	Pyrite, chalcopyrite, sphalerite, galena, ruby, silver, tetrahedrite
Associated:	Quartz, carbonate

The Silver Tunnel deposit is situated up Brandywine Creek en route to Brandywine Meadows (ski touring). Andesitic volcanic rocks are in contact with diorite, granodiorite and quartz monzonite. A series of felsite dykes intrude the volcanic and plutonic rocks. Mineralization occurs as bands, narrow veins and fracture fillings in felsite, which is locally sheared and crushed, as well as in the andesite and diorite. Both modes of mineralization are erratic and discontinuous.

The deposit experienced brief underground production in conjunction with the TEDI pit during 1977.

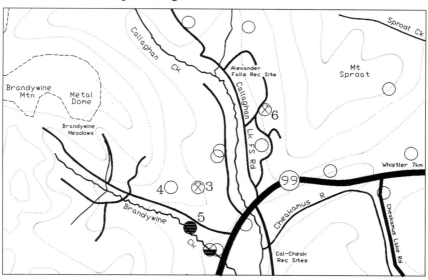

6.   MINFILE NUMBER: 092JW 012
NAME(S): NORTHAIR

Status:	Past producer, underground		
Latitude:	50 06 53	Northing:	5551175
Longitude:	123 06 08	Easting:	492700
Elevation:	853 m		
Comments:	Portal on the W slope of Mt Sproat, 1 km E of Callaghan Creek, off the Callaghan Lake Road.		
Commodities:	Gold, silver, lead, zinc, copper, cadmium		

MINERALS

Significant:	Pyrite, galena, sphalerite, chalcopyrite, tetrahedrite, argentite, pyrargyrite, electrum, gold, stromeyerite
Associated:	Quartz, calcite

The Northair mine is located in volcanic and sedimentary rocks within the southern Coast Plutonic complex. Host rocks are andesitic pyroclastic breccia and lapilli tuffs. The ore deposits are comprised of three or four tabular zones, up to 7 m wide and approximately 1200 m long. Veins of pyrite, galena and sphalerite are common; often they are irregular sulfide pods and lenses, separated by barren, brecciated host rock. Production ran from 1974–82. The site is noted for its quartz crystal clusters.

---

7.   MINFILE NUMBER: 092JW 021
NAME(S): BRANDYWINE NO. I ADIT

Status:	Prospect	Northing:	5544999
Latitude:	50 03 33	Easting:	490356
Longitude:	123 08 05	Elevation:	580 m

Commodities: Gold, silver, zinc, lead, copper

MINERALS
Significant: Pyrite, sphalerite, galena, chalcopyrite
Associated: Quartz

The Brandywine Adit (Quartz Tunnel) is situated on the S side of Brandywine Creek, approximately 3 km NW of Brandywine Falls. A 1 m wide mineralized fissure cuts a diorite body, containing narrow bands and stringers of quartz which are mineralized with streaks of pyrite, sphalerite, galena and occasional chalcopyrite. Diorite wallrock enclosing the quartz stringers is pyritic and contains local streaks of sphalerite. The fissure walls are locally coated with pyrolusite.

9.3.3 ANDERSON LAKE

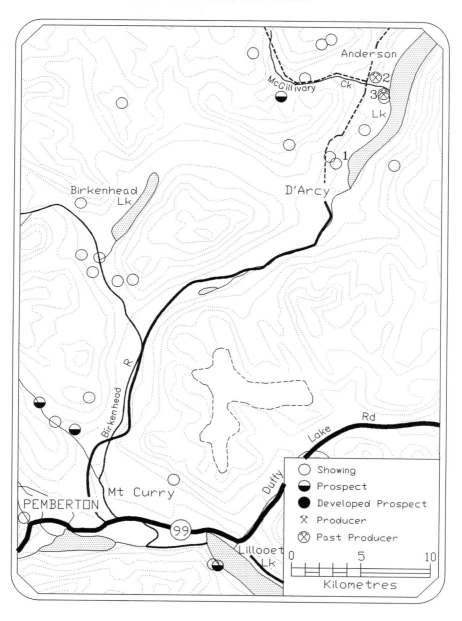

1. **MINFILE NUMBER: 092JNE119**
    NAME(S): D'ARCY NEPHRITE

Status:	Showing	Northing:	5601391
Latitude:	50 33 55	Easting:	536396
Longitude:	122 29 10	Elevation:	630 m

    Comments: The D'Arcy Road heads N up Birkenhead River from Mount Currie, and ends at Anderson Lake. Site is about 1.5 km NW of D'Arcy, just off the powerline road. Tremolite occurs as "shreds" and prismatic grains.

    Commodities: Jade, nephrite

    MINERALS
    Significant: Nephrite
    Associated: Tremolite, chromite, diopside

The deposit is just off the powerline at a point where the road, having run uphill, abruptly turns E. Nephrite is found in small lenses within serpentinite on N side of road, at the contact with andesite. The widest band is 50 cm in a zone trending NW for 150 m. The grade is not high; it is termed "semi-nephrite" and contains much shredded tremolite. Fractured chromite grains within the nephrite are partly replaced by chlorite. Clinozoisite is present in the alteration zone and minor amounts of prismatic tremolite and diopside are present.

2. **MINFILE NUMBER: 092JNE079**
    NAME(S): BRETT, MCGILLIVRAY CREEK

Status:	Past producer, underground		
Latitude:	50 37 30	Northing:	5608052
Longitude:	122 26 45	Easting:	539199
Elevation:	780 m		

    Comments: Access is difficult. Best by boat up Anderson Lake from D'Arcy.

    Commodities: Gold, silver, copper, zinc, lead

    MINERALS
    Significant: Gold, pyrite, arsenopyrite, chalcopyrite, sphalerite, galena
    Associated: Quartz, ankerite

The mine was in production in the early 1900s, and again in 1962. The total ore extracted was 9,000 t, which yielded 21 kg of gold. The mine was worked on several elevations, but most of the production came from the "49er" level.

The deposit consists of an irregular, ribboned quartz-ankerite vein, averaging 4 m to 7 m in width. Pyrite is the main sulfide in the vein, with some intersections showing arsenopyrite, chalcopyrite, sphalerite and sparse galena. Alteration minerals include sericite, mariposite, calcite and ankerite.

---

3. **MINFILE NUMBER: 092JNE110**
    NAME(S): LUCKY JANE, LAKE SHORE

Status:	Past producer, underground	Northing:	5606825
Latitude:	50 36 50	Easting:	540290
Longitude:	122 25 50	Elevation:	360 m
Comments:	Remote access. Best from SW corner of Anderson Lake (Pemberton, Mount Curry and D'Arcy).		
Commodities:	Talc, fluorite		

MINERALS

Significant:	Talc, fluorite, apatite
Associated:	Magnetite, actinolite

Located on the W side of Anderson Lake, on the Pacific Eastern Railway about 800 m S of McGillivray Creek. All the workings, including several short tunnels (longest is 30 m), are close to the railway tracks. The deposit was worked from 1917–35, and produced about 450 t of talc. The mineral occurs in bands up to 3 m wide, or as narrow veins which pinch and swell, following erratic paths within shears in the metasediments and greenstone. The talc is light greenish gray to dark green, highly sheared, soft, fissile and intensely slickensided. Impurities such as pyrite, magnetite, limonite and actinolite occur.

The granite intrusion to the S of the talc deposit hosts many small, angular cavities and contains fluorite and apatite as accessory minerals.

9.3.4 LILLOOET LAKE

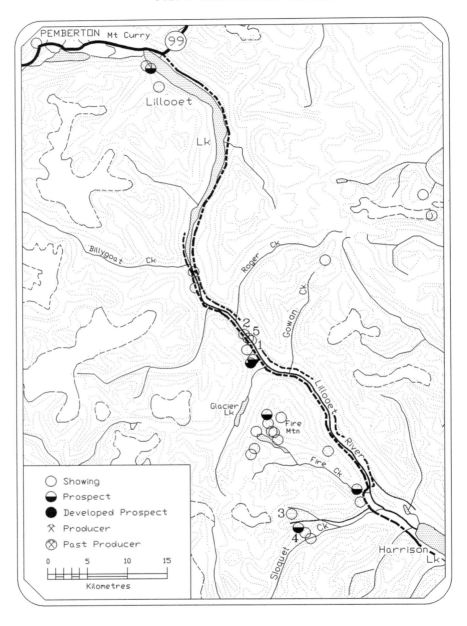

I.   MINFILE NUMBER: 092GNE013
NAME(S): MONTE CRISTO

Status:	Showing	Northing:	5534620
Latitude:	49 57 52	Easting:	540825
Longitude:	122 25 51	Elevation:	143 m
Comments:	Metals found as sub-micron sized particles.		
Commodities:	Gold, platinum		

MINERALS
Significant: Gold, platinum

Precious metal bearing alluvial sands underlie a 400 m to 800 m wide section of the Lillooet River valley, 31 km NW of the N end of Harrison Lake. These post-Pleistocene sands contain gold and platinum in sub-micron sized particles.

---

2.   MINFILE NUMBER: 092GNE019
NAME(S): CHILCO

Status:	Showing	Northing:	5535500
Latitude:	49 58 21	Easting:	539890
Longitude:	122 26 37		

The CHILCO showing is located 32.5 km NW of the N end of Harrison Lake. Precious metal bearing sands cover a 400 m to 800 m wide section of the Lillooet River valley, to depths in excess of 40 m, similar to MONTE CRISTO.

---

3.   MINFILE NUMBER: 092GNE027
NAME(S): SLO

Status:	Showing	Northing:	5511800
Latitude:	49 45 32	Easting:	546130
Longitude:	122 21 34	Elevation:	1113 m
Comments:	Road is washed out (4WD only) and grown-in.		
Commodities:	Gold, silver, lead, zinc, copper		

MINERALS
Significant: Pyrite, galena, chalcopyrite, sphalerite

Gossanous cliffs outcrop for 1.3 km along the S side of the N tributary of North Sloquet Creek (Simpson Creek), 16 km W of the N end of Harrison Lake. The showing is hosted in a nearly flat sequence of felsic ash and lapilli tuffs. Mineralization is confined largely to the felsic tuffs, which contain up to 40% pyrite, occurring as blebs, stringers, 1 cm to 3 cm clasts, and as pods up to 30 cm in diameter. Traces of galena, chalcopyrite and sphalerite are also evident.

Other mineralization (092GNE038, QUET) occurs in outcrops for 1 km along the S side of North Sloquet Creek, and is exposed over a large area. Mineralization consists of sphalerite, galena and chalcopyrite occurring as disseminations in the tuff and in an extensive quartz vein stockwork.

---

4.   NAME(S): SLOQUET CREEK HOT SPRINGS

Found on the S arm of Sloquet Creek. Hiking trail crosses N Sloquet Creek, and follows the true left bank of Sloquet Creek for 3 km. The hot springs seep from a bank of a creek a few metres up from Sloquet Creek. The water is clear with a sulfur odour and taste, and flows at 150 l/min. The temperature ranges from 59°C to 68°C, with a ph of 8.9 (alkaline). Much algae grows in the stream outlet.

---

5.   NAME(S): SKOOKUMCHUCK HOT SPRINGS

Other hot springs exist further N on the Goldrush Trail at SKOOKUMCHUCK HOT SPRINGS. They are on a private lot along the Lillooet River, 3 km N along the road from Skookumchuck Indian Reserve 4. They percolate from old river gravels below the road along the Lillooet River. The water is clear, with a sulfur smell and a weak sulfur taste, and flows at the rate of 60 l/min. The temperature is 54°C, and the ph is 8.0. Gas bubbles up from the bottom of the pool.

9.4. FRASER VALLEY

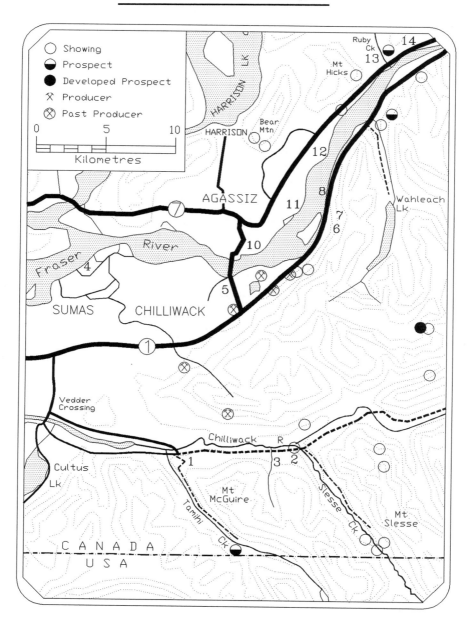

9.4.1 CHILLIWACK – HOPE

CHILLIWACK RIVER

1. Exit Highway #1 S onto Vedder Road in Chilliwack. Drive 5 km to Vedder Crossing and take Chilliwack Lake Road E, that runs on N side of river. Red-tinged obsidian is reported 10 km upstream from Vedder Crossing at Tamihi Creek, in an area of rhyolite.

2. Upstream, the Chilliwack River runs through Permian rocks. Marine fossils are found in gray limestone on the SW side of the junction of Chilliwack River and Slesse Creek (20 km from Vedder Crossing). Heading ten minutes up (S) Slesse Creek, the first stream to enter from the right (W) has boulders of crinoidal (sea-lily) limestone. Crinoid stems appear as stacked-up calcite disks about 2 cm in diameter. There are also limestone outcrops about a km NE of the Slesse Creek junction, on the N side of the Chilliwack River.

3. Another less common fossil found in the area is a *fusulinid*, present in limy shales in Nursery Creek, 1 km W of Slesse Creek.

FRASER RIVER

There are many sites along the lower Fraser River which offer access to the banks and bars. Agate, jade, jasper, rhodonite, quartzite and picture stone are just some of the minerals to be found there. Best times are in the spring and fall slack water periods. Watch the water level; it can change rapidly.

Bridal Falls Restaurant on Highway #1, E of Chilliwack (look for the turnoff to Agassiz, or the large dinosaur logo) has a museum-class display of rocks and minerals, collected over two generations by the Killer family (the owners). Some imported material is for sale. Check out the interesting boulders in the parking lot. 53560 Bridal Falls Road, Rosedale, phone (604)794-3003 for details.

Garnets: The area between Harrison Lake and Yale, and S to Chilliwack, contains numerous creeks that drain garniferous deposits. Ruby Creek (E of Agassiz), Cogburn Creek at Bear Creek camp, Garnet Creek on Old Settler Mountain, Butler Creek, Zofka Ridge (W of Yale), Emory Creek (W of Yale) and America Creek (W of Yale) all contain varying amounts of pink and red garnet material up to 5 mm in size. Use a gold pan to find the garnets.

---

4. **NAME(S): MINTO LANDING**

Latitude:	49 12 20	Northing:	5450600
Longitude:	121 56 55	Easting:	576600

Drive N out of Chilliwack on Young North. Some good agate suitable for tumbling has been found here, plus some jasper.

5. NAME(S): ROSEDALE–AGASSIZ BRIDGE

Latitude:	49 12 17	Northing:	5450700
Longitude:	121 46 40	Easting:	589000

Both upstream and downstream of the bridge on the N side, agates and jade have been found.

6. NAME(S): CRYSTAL CREEK

Latitude:	49 14 00	Northing:	5454000
Longitude:	121 39 45	Easting:	597400

Driving E, leave Highway #1 just beyond the Wahleach Power Station build-ing, which stands right on the RH side of the highway. Park at the gate, and walk up 300 m uphill to meet the road under the powerlines along the hill. Cross the hydro-pipe via the wooden bridge. After 300 m heading W you cross a small creek. It is possible to bushwack upstream, but easier to con-tinue 200 m W and take old track uphill. When you reach a gate (open) cut E down into creek to first waterfall. Small (but clear) quartz crystals have been found in the creek bed at the base of the third waterfall upstream. It's about a 60-minute hike to reach the site from the parking area.

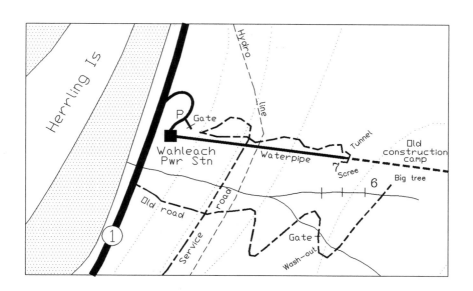

7. NAME(S): WAHLEACH POWER STATION

Latitude:	49 14 05	Northing:	5454200
Longitude:	121 40 00	Easting:	597070

As for CRYSTAL CREEK (above). Leave Highway #1 at Wahleach Power Station. Above the building, follow the hydro-pipe to where it exits the tunnel from Wahleach (Jones) Lake behind Four Brothers Mountain. What looks like a mine dump (the tailings from the tunnel) has small quartz crystals (some up to 8 cm reported) and an unknown crystal, possibly epidote. This site has been heavily worked.

8. MINFILE NUMBER: 092HSW118
NAME(S): CHEAM VIEW

Latitude:	49 15 30	Northing:	5456800
Longitude:	121 40 30	Easting:	596400

About 5 km beyond (NE) of Wahleach Power Station (which is right on Highway #1), opposite Seabird Island.

9. MINFILE NUMBER: 092HSW117
NAME(S): HOPE

Latitude:	49 23 00	Northing:	5471000
Longitude:	121 27 00	Easting:	612500

Park at golf club and take trail out to the bar.

10. MINFILE NUMBER: 092HSW119
NAME(S): AGASSIZ BAR

Latitude:	49 13 00	Northing:	5452100
Longitude:	121 44 00	Easting:	592200

Cross the Agassiz bridge, turn R onto the dyke to the second crossroad. Turn R and follow road out to the bar. Only possible very early in the year, otherwise only by boat. To get to the island W (downstream) of the bridge, approach from Highway #1, turn R and go down under the bridge. Turn L and after about 400 m, a trail leads R over a dam to the island.

11. MINFILE NUMBER: 092HSW130
NAME(S): SEABIRD ISLAND

Latitude:	49 15 00	Northing:	5455900
Longitude:	121 41 10	Easting:	595600

Popular location for many years. Head E on Highway #7 from Agassiz about 3 km. The bars have been well-worked, but still yield fine agates, jasper, quartzite and some jade.

12. MINFILE NUMBER: 092HSW115
NAME(S): WAHLEACH BAR

Latitude:	49 18 10	Northing:	5461800
Longitude:	121 40 00	Easting:	597000

About 12 km NE of Agassiz bridge on Highway #7, or 1.5 km before Granite Bluff. Walk over railway line to bar.

13. NAME(S): RUBY CREEK

Latitude:	49 21 07	Northing:	5456300
Longitude:	121 36 25	Easting:	601200

Park at Ruby Creek bridge on Highway #7 and walk down the creek bed to the bar. As its name suggests, the creek is full of garnet, but crystals are seldom larger than a pinhead. Some serpentine is found, and is reported to have its source less than a km up the creek "at a big log jam". Veins of dark gray-green material are found in the W bank.

14. NAME(S): JOHNSTON SLOUGH

Latitude:	49 21 30	Northing:	5468100
Longitude:	121 31 30	Easting:	607100

About 0.5 km E of Granite Bluff. Cross tracks down to river.

15. NAME(S): KATZ BAR

Latitude:	49 22 00	Northing:	5469100
Longitude:	121 32 15	Easting:	606200

About 5 km beyond (NE) of Ruby Creek, cross the railway opposite a church and drive down to the bar.

16. MINFILE NUMBER: 092HSW120
NAME(S): BEAVIS BAR

Latitude:	49 22 45	Northing:	5470520
Longitude:	121 28 00	Easting:	611280

Drive through Hope, cross the Fraser, and turn W onto Highway #7. Take first L at blinking light; drive to bar.

17. NAME(S): PIPE LINE BAR

Latitude:	49 22 30	Northing:	5470000
Longitude:	121 31 00	Easting:	607660

Opposite Flood (close to Silverhope Creek). Approach from Highway #7.

9.4.2 HARRISON HOT SPRINGS AREA

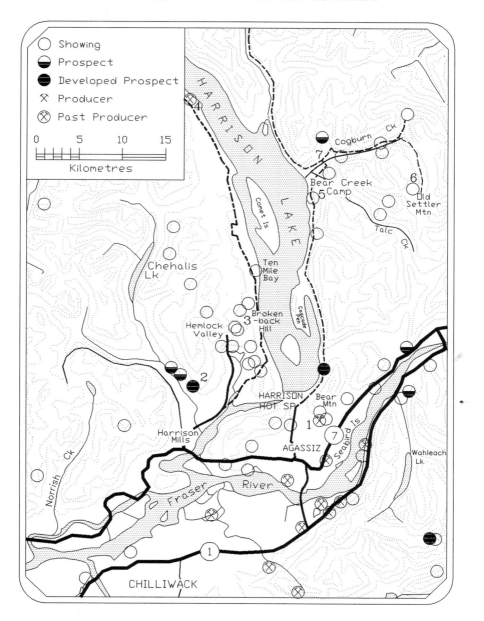

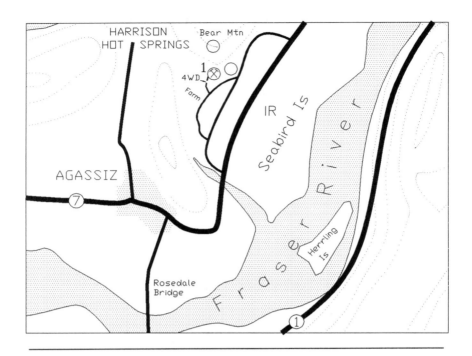

I.   MINFILE NUMBER: 092HSW008
NAME(S): EMPRESS

Status:	Past producer, open pit	Northing:	5459393
Latitude:	49 16 57	Easting:	590911
Longitude:	121 45 00	Elevation:	500 m

Comments: Located on S slopes of Bear Mtn, N of Seabird Island. Turn off Highway #7 at Seabird Island sign, and drive Detention Camp Rd 3 km to where a treed ridge reaches down from Bear Mtn to the road. An unpaved 4WD track climbs the ridge I km to the site, which is close to the hydro lines.

Commodities: Copper, molybdenum, silver

MINERALS
Significant: Chalcopyrite, molybdenite, pyrite, bornite, magnetite

The property is located along the contact between the limestone and a granodiorite intrusion. A limestone cliff is visible above. Mineralization occurs in the metamorphosed limestone and along the granodiorite-limestone contact. The garnet-wollastonite skarn hosts chalcopyrite with some bornite, molybdenite, pyrite and magnetite. Considerable development work was done on the property from 1915–17.

West side of Harrison Lake

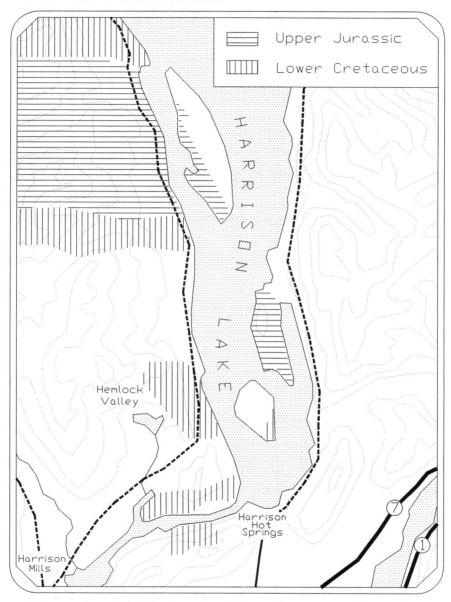

The area is underlain by Jurassic and Lower Cretaceous sedimentaries. Fossils (especially ammonites) are widespread in the SW corner of the lake, as well as on the SW side of Cascade Peninsula on the E side of the lake. The Harrison Lake Shear Zone runs N–S along the lake, generally dividing the sedimentaries on the W from the metamorphics and volcanics on the E.

Access is via Highway #7 on N side of Fraser River. Turn N at Harrison Mills (just W of Harrison River). Take Morris Valley Road to Hemlock Valley ski area. At 8 km, bear right on Harrison Lake Rd. The paving ends about 11 km from Highway #7, near the Weaver Creek Spawning Grounds. The road (Harrison West FS Rd) is variable. Beyond Wood Lake Rec Site (28 km from Highway #7—see next two sites) it becomes 4WD.

About 36 km from Harrison Mills, fossil shells (belemnites and bivalves) start to occur along the road for 30 km as it cuts through Upper Jurassic and Lower Cretaceous strata until 20 Mile Creek (opposite the N end of Long Island). Sites are plentiful. Just S of marker 27 km a large slab shows *belemnites* (cigar-shaped mollusks). Another particularly rich outcrop occurs 200 m S of marker 28 km. Both the local boulders and the cliff are thick with *buchia* shells (resembling clams).

The northern limit of these Lower Cretaceous fossils is 20 Mile Creek. Fossils are found down the W side of Long Island and on the N and S ends of Cascade Peninsula on the E side of Harrison Lake. Upper Jurassic fossils are found at the S end of the lake and on the S and E sides of Echo Island.

---

2.   MINFILE NUMBER: 092HSW013
NAME(S): SENECA

Status:	Developed prospect/Open Pit		
Latitude:	49 19 02	Northing:	5463038
Longitude:	121 56 37	Easting:	576776
Elevation:	274 m		
Comments:	Located on E side of the Chehalis River, about 8 km N of Harrison Mills.		
Commodities:	Zinc, copper, silver, gold, lead		

MINERALS

Significant:	Sphalerite, chalcopyrite, pyrite, galena, barite, tetrahedrite
Associated:	Barite, pyrite, quartz

The area is underlain by a complex interbedded pile of volcanics that are pyritized to varying degrees over much of the area. Locally, narrow quartz-pyrite stringers are mineralized with pyrite, sphalerite, chalcopyrite and minor galena. The main showing is a massive sulfide deposit hosted by felsic volcanics. In 1962, about 260 t of ore was shipped from a small open pit.

3.   NAME(S): BROKENBACK HILL

Status:	Showing	Northing:	5471000
Latitude:	49 23 15	Easting:	583500
Longitude:	121 50 40	Elevation:	120 m

Comments: Located on the W shore of Harrison Lake, opposite Cascade Peninsula (on E side). Access by boat allows the rockhound to cruise the shoreline, which has numerous showings. Otherwise, take W Harrison Lake FS Rd. Extensive fossil beds on N side of Brokenback Hill, and in roadcut, mostly of the bivalve *buchia* are found. The ammonite *cardiaceras*, and *cephalopods* are also been found. At an overgrown quarry, a small area contains the ammonite *dumortiera*.

Further N on the FS Rd, along the 8 km between the Sunrise Lake turn-off and 20 Mile Creek (which flows into Harrison Lake opposite the N tip of Long Island), there are extensive fossil deposits alongside the road and in adjacent cuttings. Twenty Mile Creek appears to be the northern Cretaceous era limit. There is a particularly dense area of *buchia* shells and *belemnites* just S of the 28 km marker (some 9 km N of Walian Creek, which flows into Harrison Lake at the S end of Long Island).

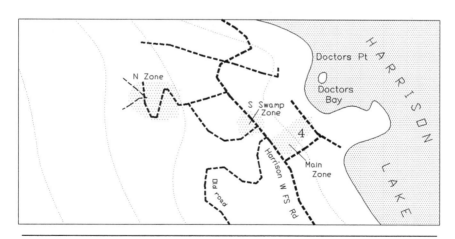

4.   MINFILE NUMBER: 092HNW071
NAME(S): DOCTORS POINT

Status:	Developed prospect	Northing:	5500100
Latitude:	49 39 04	Easting:	573020
Longitude:	121 59 18	Elevation:	122 m

Comments: About 30 km N of Ten Mile Bay on W side of Harrison Lake. Harrison West FS Rd can be 4WD only.

Commodities: Gold, silver, lead, zinc, copper

MINERALS

Significant: Pyrite, arsenopyrite, galena, sphalerite, chalcopyrite, tetrahedrite

Associated: Quartz, scorodite, anglesite, schultenite, jarosite, malachite

Look for Kayama Petroglyph sign, located at Doctors Bay. Site is 250 m up-slope W of Doctors Bay, on the Harrison West FS Road. The occurrence is close to the Harrison Lake shear zone. Gold-silver mineralization is hosted in narrow, gently dipping, vuggy quartz-sulfide veins, found in 12 separate localities, underlain by either diorite or hornfelsic rocks. On surface these veins vary from 1 cm to over 1 m wide. Pyrite and arsenopyrite are the most abundant sulfides, with traces of galena and sphalerite.

East side of Harrison Lake

Harrison Lake is essentially a landlocked fiord. Although surrounded by mountains, its surface is just 10 m above sea level, while the lake bottom is 200 m below sea level. Unpaved roads above both shores now allow an approach along either side.

Access to the E side of the lake is by a paved road that leaves Harrison Hot Springs from the E end of town, leading to Sasquatch Park. A gravel road continues beyond. Stop at Rainbow Falls to see heavily folded talcose schists in the river bed. Great views of lake from road, which at times is high above the water. The prominent Cascadia Peninsula is best accessed by boat, and is reported to have a continuation of the fossil beds found at Brokenback Hill. Sites at the N and S ends of the peninsula.

---

5.   **MINFILE NUMBER: 092HNW064**
     NAME(S): HOPE

Status:	Showing	Northing:	5485425
Latitude:	49 31 00	Easting:	590480
Longitude:	121 45 00	Elevation:	150 m

As you reach the booming grounds at Bear Creek Camp from the S, look up-slope. A 100 m cutting leads nowhere, exposing vertically bedded shales with a slippery, greasy covering. Narrow seams of graphite are present within carbonaceous slates.

6. MINFILE NUMBER: 092HNW063
NAME(S): OLD SETTLER MOUNTAIN

Status:	Showing	Northing:	5487403
Latitude:	49 32 00	Easting:	597685
Longitude:	121 39 00	Elevation:	150 m

Some 3 km beyond Cogburn Beach Recreation Site, turn SE up Talc Creek to W slopes of Old Settler Mountain. Schistose talc is found in serpentine. Some kyanite has been noted in metamorphic rocks between Garnet Creek to the SE and Old Settler Mountain.

7. MINFILE NUMBER: 092HNW073
NAME(S): COGBURN CREEK

Status:	Showing	Northing:	5491098
Latitude:	49 34 00	Easting:	597016
Longitude:	121 39 30	Elevation:	1450 m

If the road up Cogburn Creek is too dusty or too busy with logging trucks, try panning for garnets at the bridge. Every pan reveals a residue of "pink sand" which, under the loupe, turns into facetted almandite garnets.

Locally, the schists and gneisses contain abundant kyanite, sillimanite, andalusite and garnet. In the area between Hope, Yale and Harrison Lake, the Settler Schist outcrops. North of Cogburn Creek it contains up to 23% kyanite and may reach 1.5 cm in length, and yeild a few percent of coarse sillimanite in prisms in excess of 4 cm long.

9.5. FRASER RIVER

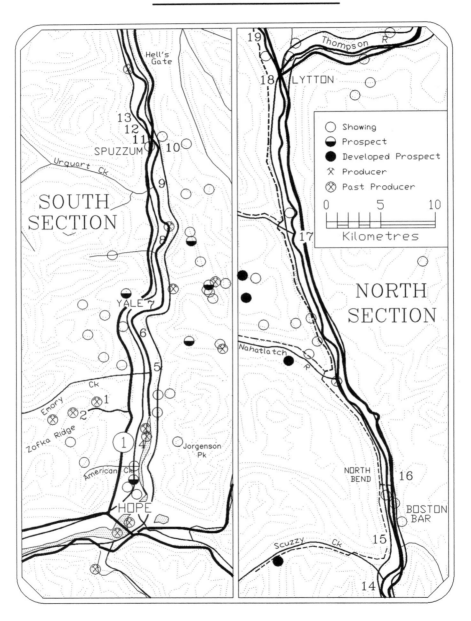

9.5.1 THE FRASER RIVER CANYON

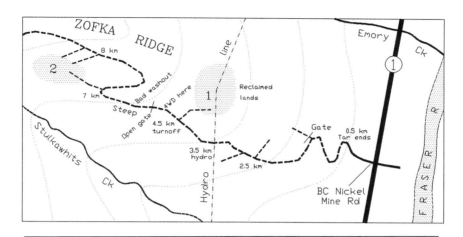

I. MINFILE NUMBER: 092HSW125
NAME(S): CHOATE, GIANT NICKEL

Status:	Past Producer	Northing:	5482136
Latitude:	49 29 02	Easting:	609855
Longitude:	121 29 00	Elevation:	750 m

Comments: Turnoff marked on Highway #1 about 2 km S of Emory Creek as "BC Nickel Mine Rd". First 500 m paved. First 4.5 km drivable in 2WD to extensive dumps, which are level and seeded (area popular with off-road bikes). Washouts above this point require 4WD to reach PRIDE OF EMORY (092HSW004) mine at 8 km.

Commodities: Chromium, nickel, copper

MINERALS
Significant: Pyrrhotite, pentlandite, chromite, magnetite, chalcopyrite
Associated: Olivine, enstatite, hypersthene

The complex hosting the Giant Nickel Mine mineralized zones comprises diorite, quartz diorites and ultrabasic rocks, which intrude schists and earlier intrusives. The older rocks are found NW and SW of the ultramafic complex, and form an irregular stock-like mass about 3 km across. The NE half consists of barren pyroxenites and peridotites which contain little or no hornblende. The SW half is a highly variable, hornblende-rich assemblage of peridotites and pyroxenites which are mineralized and contain some 17 ore bodies associated with the mine.

Mineralization occurs as pipe-like concentrations of enstatite, olivine and hypersthene containing pyrrhotite, pentlandite, chalcopyrite and magnetite, with lesser amounts of chromite and cobalt minerals. In the deposits where the sulfides are relatively massive and comprise about 50% of the rock, there is four times as much pyrrhotite as pentlandite. Chalcopyrite, magnetite and chromite each make up about 3% of the rock.

Magnetite and chromite occur as the principal metallic minerals in several places within nickeliferous bodies along Stulkawhits Creek near Choate. Both magnetite and chromite occur as small crystals or as rounded grains, scattered throughout the sulfide bodies and the hornblende-pyroxenite. Both occasionally occur within the silicate minerals.

---

2. MINFILE NUMBER: 092HSW004
NAME(S): PRIDE OF EMORY

Status:	Past producer, open pit, underground		
Latitude:	49 28 30	Northing:	5481105
Longitude:	121 30 46	Easting:	607742
Elevation:	1100 m		

Comments: Located near the headwaters of Stulkawhits Creek. Numerous nickel orebodies extend for 3 km along Zofka Ridge. One of the few nickel-bearing production areas in the province. Access is beyond CHOATE. Washouts above this point require 4WD to mine at 8 km from Highway #1. A gate at 6 km is currently unlocked. Abandoned site.

Commodities: Nickel, copper, cobalt, gold, silver, chromium, platinum, palladium, zinc

MINERALS

Significant: Pyrrhotite, pentlandite, chalcopyrite, magnetite, pyrite, sphalerite, chromite, linnaeite, morenosite

Associated: Olivine, orthopyroxene, millerite, magnetite

The Pride of Emory mine operated from 1958–74, and is presently undergoing re-evaluation. Ore is associated with pipe-like concentrations of enstatite, olivine and hypersthene containing, in order of abundance, pyrrhotite, pentlandite, chalcopyrite, magnetite, pyrite and sphalerite, with lesser amounts of chromite and cobalt minerals which include linnaeite and morenosite. Over 4 million t of ore were mined from this property. Nickel and copper were the prime metallic products, with the ore grading 0.8% nickel and 0.3% copper, with cobalt as a by-product. However, chrome oxide, platinum, gold and silver are also present.

Sillimanite crystals up to 5 cm in length can be found along Zofka Ridge, or panned in Emory Creek. A dirty brown, heavily pitted material is chromium manganese silicate. Further S, pink garnets are common in America Creek (W of the Fraser River) and in the creeks draining Jorgenson Park on the E side of the Fraser.

Fraser River Bars

"I came to the Fraser River a skeptic, but have returned winter after winter, for reasons I am just beginning to understand.

There is ... a feeling of wonder, that the river could have carried so many stones, from so many different places, and laid them out all rounded and packed in sand as though on a giant sorting table ...

I'm convinced that there is some great mathematical truth hidden in the manner in which the stones have been distributed. There is such a balance between abundance and scarcity."
– Anonymous, *The Canadian Rockhound*, April 1966

Early prospectors headed up the Fraser River canyon in the 1860s with little more than a dream, a shovel and a willingness to test their luck on an unknown frontier. Just 140 years later it seems hard to imagine how vast and uncharted all this area was back then.

The Fraser River from Chilliwack through Hope and up to Lillooet is a great source of rough material. Unlike other sites in this book, the bars are re-stocked every winter and summer, so there is always something new to find. Gold, jade, rhodonite, serpentine, agate, thulite, idocrase, sillimanite, nickel silicate, porphyry, magnesite and jasper fetch up on the gravel bars after the summer melt and winter run-off. Best times to hunt are early spring and late fall, when water levels are lowest. But be careful, the river can change level quickly. And be aware that some of the bars are staked, while others are open to the public. Still others are on Indian Reserve land. Always check at the local First Nations band office if you are uncertain about access. You can also get information from Mineral Titles, Mineral Development Office, Vancouver at (604)660-2672.

The same applies to the Yalakom and Bridge rivers N and W of Lillooet. Some areas may be staked, or lie on Indian Reservation land. Check with the New Westminster Mining Division (southern areas) at (604)660-8666 or Lillooet Mining Division (northern areas) at (250)256-7548 for the current status.

The Fraser River Jade Reserve was set aside in 1968, and extends from the Lillooet bridge down to the Hope bridge, and on either side of the river up to the high water mark. Signed by W.A.C. Bennett himself, it was decreed as an area where the public could hunt for jade without the need for permits or licenses.

Some of the better known bars are listed here. Where applicable, the MINFILE numbers are included, to allow searching for more information and mining history.

3.	Texas Bar		49 28 20	121 25 00
4.	Channel Bar	092HSW108	49 28 06	121 24 36

Accessible from highway.

5.	Emory Bar		49 30 40	121 24 45

Park at Emory Creek bridge. Green nickel silicate and garnets are found in Emory Creek.

6.	Hill's Bar		49 32 40	121 25 40
7.	Yale Bar			

Accessible only at very low water. Turn R just after Yale and cross the railway. Park after 400 m and walk down.

8.	Sailor's Bar		49 37 05	121 24 10
9.	Wellington Bar		49 39 40	121 24 00
10.	Spuzzum	092HNW 059	49 42 00	121 25 00
11.	Alexander Bar	092HNW 061	49 41 45	121 24 25

Take the trail down to the bar opposite Alexander Lodge.

12.	Chapman's Bar		49 43 00	121 25 00
13.	Dutchman's Bar		49 43 30	121 25 50
14.	China Bar		49 48 30	121 27 30

About 3 km N of Hell's Gate, on W side.

15.	Boston Bar	092HNW 069	49 50 45	121 26 20

Several popular sites. About 1 km S of the bridge on W side of river.

16.	North Bend Bar		49 53 00	121 27 05

Site is downstream from bridge. Grossular garnet is often taken as jade. Deep pink rhodonite has been found.

17.	Kanaka Bar	092ISW 085	50 07 00	121 34 00

Through Kanaka Village. Walk down to river.

18.	Lytton Bar	092ISW 083	50 14 03	121 35 02

Cross to the W side of the Fraser on the ferry just N of Lytton, and turn S 1 km.

Other bars N of Lytton

Van Winkle Bar	092ISW 078	50 16 00	121 36 18

Cross to the W side of the Fraser on the ferry just N of Lytton, and turn N 2 km to Spences Ranch. Turn R just past the corrals and drive 400 m to park. Walk last 100 m to bar.

Stein Bar

Cross to the W side of the Fraser on the ferry just N of Lytton, and turn N 5 km.

Foster (Mile 22) Bar	092INW 089	50 30 12	121 43 30

Take Lillooet road 38 km N of Lytton. Take dry washout down to river, then head upstream a few hundred metres. Only possible in early spring. Placer gold deposits were worked from Foster Bar to Fountain (Lillooet) during the 19th century. The gold was coarse compared to the flour found further down the Fraser River, with nuggets up to 170 gm being recovered from the gravels near Lillooet. Other placer discoveries were made on the Bridge River and its tributaries, which joins the Fraser River near Fountain, and in Cayoosh Creek just W of Lillooet.

About 26 km N of Lytton, or 36 km S of Lillooet, the Ruddock Gold Pan Ranch offers the use of their Fraser River claim as part of their day rate; phone (250)455-6622.

Lillooet	092INW 071	50 42 00	121 56 30

Access above and below the main bridge across the Fraser River.

Identifying minerals on the bars

Jade: Often has a fibrous exterior, with the texture or parallel "grain". Tough to chip. Green interior. If a file can scratch it, it's serpentine; if not, it might be jade.

Rhodonite: Usually has a black surface, but pink inside. Often has a metallic sheen, as though drawn on by a soft pencil. A penknife won't scratch it. The metallic surface makes it easy to confuse with magnetite, but a compass will swing if held next to magnetite.

Agate: Is very hard (file won't scratch it) and often has a knobbly surface with small vugs (full of mud). Breaks with a conchoidal fracture, revealing translucent material.

9.5.2 WEST OF FRASER CANYON: NAHATLATCH (SALMON) RIVER

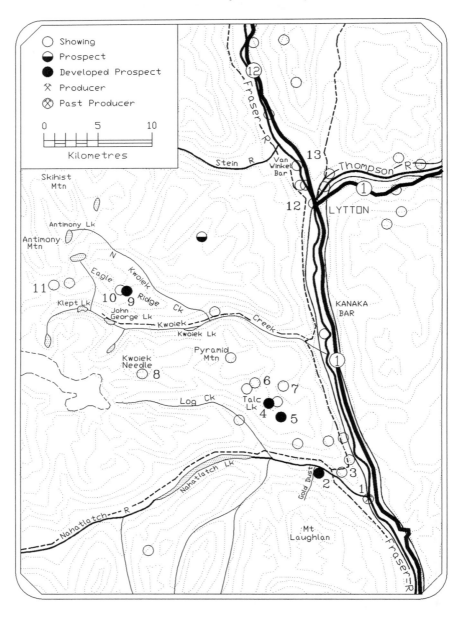

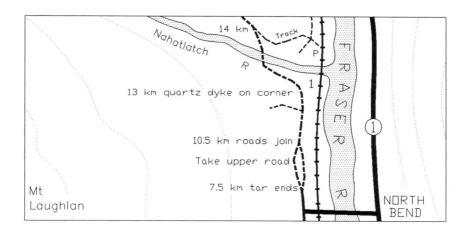

I. MINFILE NUMBER: 092HNW002
NAME(S): GISBY

Status:	Past producer, underground		
Latitude:	49 58 52	Northing:	5537367
Longitude:	121 30 55	Easting:	606448
Elevation:	200 m		
Comments:	Talc occurrence on the Nahatlatch River (sometimes known as the Salmon River). Distances refer to kilometre markers on the road. The "0" marker starts on W side of river, about 1.5 km from the centre of the North Bend bridge.		
Commodities:	Talc, silica		

MINERALS

Significant:	Talc, silica
Associated:	Quartz, calcite, magnesite, mica

Cross the Fraser River at the North Bend bridge and head N. Tar ends beyond marker 7 km. At marker 13 km, the unpaved road curves W into Nahatlatch River. The corner roadcut hosts a quartz vein and talcose schists.

The Gisby group of claims is located directly S of the Nahatlatch River, just W of the Fraser River. Access is by good logging roads, originating in North Bend, going N for about 10 km. Before 1920, the property was worked for silica, and shipments were made to Vancouver. An adit was driven on the claim, apparently in search of gold, which intersected a talc body. About 90 t of talc were extracted from the workings up to 1923. Other adits reportedly occur, but they were probably covered during road construction (which has resulted in some new exposures).

The best, and most abundant, talc is found on the Laura and Salmon River claims immediately S of the Nahatlatch River. The talc showings along the Nahatlatch River have an aggregate width of 100 m to 150 m. It is light green to pearly gray, massive to lightly laminated, with granular quartz and minor sulfide impurities. All the showings contain abundant carbonate, most of which is iron-rich magnesite.

Other showings are at the S abutment of the CPR bridge on both sides of the railway; 200 m upstream from the railway; and 50 m upstream of that, where the talc is exposed in a 5 m bank and is highly sheared. Access is from the N bank of the Nahatlatch River. Use extreme caution if approaching the railway track, as curves screen approaching trains until the last minute.

---

2. MINFILE NUMBER: 092HNW047
NAME(S): PACIFIC TALC

Status:	Developed prospect	Northing:	5539350
Latitude:	49 59 59	Easting:	602050
Longitude:	121 34 34	Elevation:	305 m
Comments:	Talc outcrop in the main pit area, 200 m S of Nahatlatch River, along the E bank of Gold Dust Creek, 5 km NW of rail bridge.		
Commodities:	Talc		

MINERALS
Significant: Talc, magnesite, chlorite

A talc body is hosted by medium to dark gray-green phyllites, ranging from 35 m to 50 m wide in the N, to 10 m wide in the S, with a strike length of 600 m. Drilling indicates the talc body extends to at least 70 m in depth. It is platy and light to dark grayish green, weathering buff to brown, and is associated with carbonates (magnesite and some dolomite), chlorite, limonite and magnetite. Up to 5% pyrite is visible, mainly along fractures, but also scattered throughout the rock.

---

3. MINFILE NUMBER: 092ISW071
NAME(S): KEEFERS

Status: Showing

The Keefers showing is located in old open cuts N of the Nahatlatch River, across the valley from PACIFIC TALC. The showings were first staked in 1954. Open cutting, surface work and diamond drilling are reported. A sample sent to Sudbury assayed 1.4% copper, 2.2% nickel, 0.2% cobalt, 3.8 gm/t platinum and 0.8 gm/t palladium.

4. MINFILE NUMBER: 092ISW063
NAME(S): NORTH ZONE, KWOIEK CREEK

Status:	Developed prospect	Northing:	5546152
Latitude:	50 03 42	Easting:	597245
Longitude:	121 38 29	Elevation:	1932 m

A talc and manganese outcrop on N side of a lake on a ridge to SE of Pyramid Mountain. A zone of talc on the N side of the lake has been exposed over a length of 200 m and a width of 100 m near the N end of the serpentinite mass. The zone continues SE across the lake for an additional 300 m, for a total strike length of up to 800 m. Inferred reserves of 4 million t grading between 30% and 45% magnesite and 50% to 65% talc have been estimated. The talc is pale green to white with a creamy buff weathered surface and contains small quantities of scattered magnetite.

5. MINFILE NUMBER: 092ISW064
NAME(S): SOUTH ZONE, KWOIEK CREEK

The H (SOUTH ZONE) talc occurrence outcrops along the same ridge and is a similar talc occurrence to H (NORTH ZONE), which lies 1.8 km to the NW. A steeply dipping lenticular zone of talc up to 110 m wide, strikes NW for 700 m in a shear zone within serpentinite. Holes drilled along the deposit indicate it continues to a depth of at least 60 m. Indicated reserves are calculated at 7.7 million t, grading 66% talc and 43% magnesite. Chlorite and minor pentlandite, pyrrhotite and magnetite are also present in the deposit.

6. MINFILE NUMBER: 092ISW102
NAME(S): NORTH TALC DEPOSIT

The NORTH TALC deposit is located 4 km SE of Pyramid Mountain, on a N tributary of Log Creek, 2.5 km NW of the TALC LAKE deposit (092ISW063), on the S rim of the Lower Stein Wilderness Area. Significant talc occurrences were first reported in the area in the early 1950s. In 1973, this site was identified by prospectors while conducting surveys for nickel, chromite and talc. Low grade (0.2%) nickel was identified over a wide area and a zone of talc-magnesite mineralization was outlined.

The area is underlain by phyllite, schist and foliated greenstone. Pods of serpentinized ultramafics occur in faults. The strata are intruded by quartz monzonite and granodiorite. Two different geological types are separated along the ridge by an intervening mass of serpentinite running

NW for 6 km, generally following the crest of the ridge, and varying up to 900 m in width. The ultramafic rock is dark green/black, and weathers buff to reddish brown. The serpentinite consists of fine-grained, massive serpentine with minor carbonate and 5% magnetite.

Since 1992, the area has been systematically surveyed and developed. The deposit consists of a lens of talc on the N side of the lake, which has been exposed over a length of 800 m and a width of 50 m to 150 m. The talc is covered by 1 m to 2 m overburden, but has been recently exposed by new logging road cuts. Serpentinite occurs on the NE side of the talc deposit, which is pale green to white with a creamy buff weathered surface. It contains small quantities of disseminated magnetite. The low brightness and high yellowness are caused by the presence of iron hydroxide minerals, the latter being indicative of surface weathering. Possible reserves based on 200 m length, 150 m width and 150 m depth are 13 million t. In 1993, a 120-t sample was shipped to Finland for tests.

---

7. MINFILE NUMBER: 092ISW103
NAME(S): JACK

Status: Showing

The JACK showing is located 6.5 km SE of Pyramid Mtn in the headwaters of 4 Barrel Creek, 2 km NE of the TALC LAKE deposit (092ISW063). The main rock type is medium to dark green/gray phyllite, striking NNW and dipping vertically. The talc mineralization is in the phyllite, and is platy and light/dark green, weathering buff to brown. Varying amounts of chlorite are also present. A talc deposit outcrops along a logging road.

---

8. MINFILE NUMBER: 092ISW052
NAME(S): KWOIEK NEEDLE

Status:	Showing	Northing:	5548550
Latitude:	50 05 06	Easting:	585400
Longitude:	121 48 23	Elevation:	1525 m
Comments:	Approximate centre of large area containing several showings.		
Commodities:	Sillimanite, kyanite, andalusite, garnet		

MINERALS

Significant:	Sillimanite, kyanite, garnet, andalusite
Associated:	Muscovite

In the Kwoiek Needle area, which lies between the Nahatlatch River and Kwoiek Creek, sillimanite, kyanite, garnet and andalusite are present in

NW-trending phyllites and schists. Garnets average 1 mm in diameter, and commonly comprise up to 15% of the rock. Aluminosilicate polymorphs commonly are 2 cm long, and comprise 6% of the rock. In some places, however, andalusite crystals up to 5 cm long are so crowded in certain layers as to form most of the rock. Locally, the aluminosilicates are completely altered to muscovite.

9. MINFILE NUMBER: 092ISW051
NAME(S): RAWHIDE, SKIHIST MOUNTAIN

Status:	Developed prospect	Northing:	5556600
Latitude:	50 09 28	Easting:	583845
Longitude:	121 49 35	Elevation:	1860 m
Comments:	Located in three recent trenches 6.3 km SE of Skihist Mtn on the S slopes above N Kwoiek Creek.		
Commodities:	Talc, asbestos		

MINERALS

Significant:	Talc, magnesite, asbestos
Associated:	Tremolite, quartz, magnetite

A lenticular, steeply dipping body of talc varying up to 75 m in width, occurs within a serpentinite belt, and strikes for a distance of 450 m. Inferred reserves are estimated at 8.7 million t grading between 40% and 60% talc, the balance magnesite. The talc is greenish white to light green and varies from being very soft and soapy, to harder and gritty in texture. Lenses of hard, massive and dark green to lighter green and talcose serpentinite are present within the talc zone.

A small trench 300 m NE of the main deposit exposes a 6 m by 2 m pod. Fibrous tremolite grades into white masses of talc and serpentine. The serpentine is a light mottled buff to brown, carbonate-rich combination of talc and serpentine. Quartz and minor magnetite occur within these talc bodies. Low grade pods up to 10 cm wide occur in fractures within dark blue serpentinite.

Asbestos occurs in tremolite-talc-carbonate pods hosted in serpentinite in a 150 m wide, fractured and sheared, serpentinite/metasediment contact zone N of the main talc body. The asbestos occurs in limited quantity, and is of questionable quality.

10. MINFILE NUMBER: 092ISW053
NAME(S): GLACIER, RAWHIDE

Status: Showing

The Glacier showing is located in an old adit close to a tributary of N Kwoiek Creek, 6.8 km SE of Skihist Mountain and 3 km NE of Klept Lake. Disseminated arsenopyrite, pyrite and minor chalcopyrite occur in massive, sugary quartz exposed at the portal of a 13 m adit in a sheared fault contact, between argillaceous phyllite and chlorite schist. There appears to be some skarning represented by actinolite, garnet, magnetite and pyrrhotite present in the zone.

The quartz vein pinches and swells along a 100 m length. Secondary quartz veins cut the major vein. Phyllites are locally fossiliferous and contain minor garnet and andalusite. The shear zone is 150 m wide and contains pods of serpentine and talc. Minor asbestos occurs.

11. MINFILE NUMBER: 092ISW029
NAME(S): GREEN GOLD

Status:	Showing	Northing:	5557100
Latitude:	50 09 47	Easting:	577050
Longitude:	121 55 17	Elevation:	2280 m

Comments: Several pits over a large area on the W slopes of Antimony Mtn, close to the saddle between Doss Pk and Antimony Mtn.

Commodities: Jade, nephrite

MINERALS
Significant: Idocrase
Associated: Grossularite, thuringite

Access is via the bridge at North Bend, crossing to the W side of the Fraser River and then N to Kwoiek Creek. The road is 2WD as far as the confluence of the North Kwoiek and Kwoiek Creeks. Thereafter, 4WD is needed to get you up Kwoiek Creek past Kwoiek and John George lakes to Klept Lake. A 1,500 m climb to Vesuvianite Lake is only for the keen. Otherwise, check the creek.

On the W ridge above Vesuvianite Lake, vesuvianite-type jade occurs within serpentinite, in thinly bedded, fine-grained, argillaceous sediments that are intruded by porphyritic hornblende-diorite sills.

There are several differing descriptions of the mineralization. A 1975 report stated that idocrase (vesuvianite) is associated with grossularite and thuringite. Where vesuvianite is the principal mineral, grossularite occurs as a reddish aggregate in veins up to 10 cm wide within the green vesuvianite.

Where grossularite is the principal mineral, it is buff-coloured, with vesuvianite occurring as green flecks or indistinct aggregates. Thuringite occurs as 1 mm to 5 mm veinlets in the buff grossularite or scattered in the vesuvianite. A 1985 report noted that, from a commercial point of view, the jade has been exhausted.

To the N of this showing, stibnite is reported on the S ridge of Antimony Mountain.

9.5.3 LYTTON AREA

12. MINFILE NUMBER: 092ISW083
NAME(S): LYTTON GEMS

Status:	Showing	Northing:	5565400
Latitude:	50 14 03	Easting:	601000
Longitude:	121 35 02	Elevation:	140 m
Comments:	Located in gravel bars of the Fraser River at Lytton.		
Commodities:	Jade, nephrite, agate, garnet		

MINERALS
Significant: Jade, agate, garnet, jasper

Nephrite (jade) boulders, agate, garnet and jasper pebbles have been found in Fraser River gravels at Lytton. See Yalakom River in the Lillooet area section for possible source rocks.

13. MINFILE NUMBER: 092ISW078
NAME(S): VAN WINKLE BAR

Status:	Showing	Northing:	5569000
Latitude:	50 16 00	Easting:	599420
Longitude:	121 36 18	Elevation:	145 m

Platinum and iridium occur in the black sands of Van Winkle Bar. Source rocks are believed to be volcanic and sedimentary rocks to the N.

9.6. THOMPSON RIVER

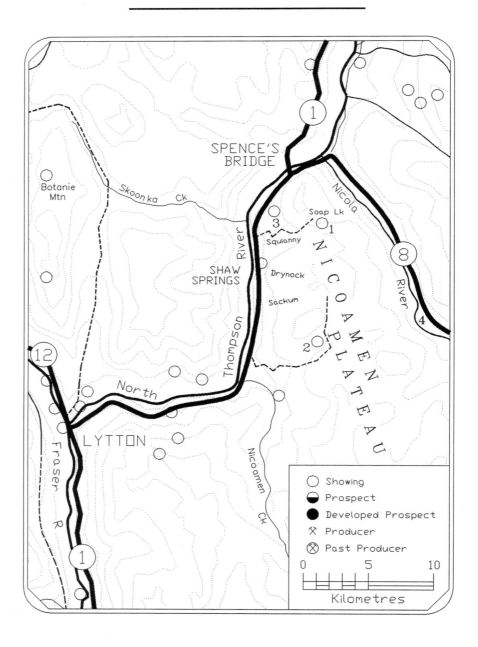

9.6.1 LYTTON – SPENCES BRIDGE

This area was first studied in 1888 by Dr. Dawson of the Geological Survey of Canada. He noted the Tertiary volcanics "of somewhat varied colour and texture, often brecciated. Chalcedony and agates, together with crystalline quartz are rather notably abundant in amygdaloidal cavities".

One of the best known agate collecting sites, the Nicoamen Plateau between Nicoamen Creek and the Nicola River is high, and access is difficult, and impossible when wet. And very steep when descending on muddy roads. 4WD is strongly advised at all times. Best hunted in the spring or fall, when the heat is off the talus slopes. Shaw Spring agates are noted for their reddish rind and smoky/gray interiors. White and pink plumes are not uncommon. Fortification, blue and black banded agates, have been discovered too. Because of the area's great popularity over the years, today you will have to work to find material, whereas before it was there for the picking.

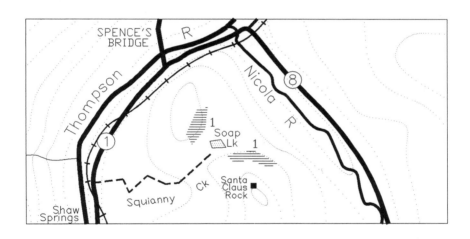

I.   **MINFILE NUMBER: 092ISW048**
     NAME(S): SOAP LAKE

Status:	Showing	Northing:	5581720
Latitude:	50 22 38	Easting:	619500
Longitude:	121 19 10	Elevation:	1000 m

Atop the ridge 5 km SE of Spences Bridge. Access via an old, steep, track about 1.5 km N of Shaw Springs (sometimes called Drynock) on Highway #1. It is often washed out; the route is 8 km long and involves a 1000 m climb. A L fork leads to the base of the bluffs that form the rim of the plateau.

In summer, take water! Caution: rattlesnakes in the dry season. The area is underlain by volcanics. Salts appear to leach from the surrounding volcanic rocks, carried into the basin by springs and concentrated there during the dry summer seasons. No outlet is visible. A sample of brine taken in 1926 yielded 81% sodium carbonate, 6% sodium sulfate and 2% sodium chloride (table salt). Salt was not produced commercially but reported as being used locally. Ecological Reserve 3 presently includes Soap Lake.

This is the home of "Shaw Springs Agate", which is known for its blue-gray colours. Plume and fortification agates are found in the small cliffs 1 km to the S of the lake, close to Santa Claus Rock, as well as on a rise NW of Soap Lake.

---

2. MINFILE NUMBER: 092ISW084
NAME(S): SHAW SPRINGS GEMS

Status:	Showing	Northing:	5572500
Latitude:	50 17 40	Easting:	619450
Longitude:	121 19 23		

Located on the W side of the Nicoamen Plateau, above the Thompson River, Highway #1 and the railway. Caution: can be rattlesnakes in summer. The occurrence consists primarily of banded agate nodules, many with plume, in various locations from Nicomen Creek in S through Sackum, Dry and Squianny creeks (the latter is 5 km S of Spences Bridge). Parking along the Highway #1 is not easy, as the pull-offs are shallow and the passing trucks many. The talus slopes above are steep and loose. Most agates have been collected between the 750 m to 1,500 m (2,000 ft to 4,000 ft) contours, in the bluffs above the railway tracks. Dry Creek, 1.5 km S of Shaw Springs, is a productive area. A large concrete culvert under the railway track identifies where to climb the loose talus slopes.

Black and gray agate nodules are also found in and below basalt bluffs on the NW side of a SW-flowing tributary of Nicoamen Creek (which can be identified by the large highway bridge 15 km E of Lytton, or 8 km S of Shaw Springs, at a sharp bend in the Thompson River). The area is underlain by volcanics. A steep unpaved track leads W from Highway #1 about 1.5 km N of the bridge, and climbs 8 km to below basalt bluffs. It is not recommended in wet weather. Agates appear as orange or brown coated nodules at the foot of the cliffs. A hammer and chisel are needed to pry material loose from the tough basalt. The trail leads finally to an abandoned ranch where several tracks lead off, one of which meets up with the Soap Lake track. Basically, all rock outcrops have potential as sources of agate.

Other agate material has been found along Highway #1 in the various dry creek beds.

3. **MINFILE NUMBER: 092ISW047**
    NAME(S): SPENCES BRIDGE

Status:	Showing	Northing:	5582550
Latitude:	50 23 08	Easting:	615950
Longitude:	121 22 09	Elevation:	700 m

The SPENCES BRIDGE coal showing is a strata-bound lignite seam, 30 m by 2 m, in a dry gully 4 km directly SW of Spences Bridge. It outcrops in a partly consolidated sandstone bed within volcanics. Two short adits were reported in 1952.

4 **NAME(S): NICOLA RIVER**

Status: Showing

Agate is reported in the Nicola River between Lower Nicola and Spences Bridge. Access is via Highway #8. A railway siding on the S side of the Nicola River, 4 km SE of the Skuhun Creek bridge, is called Agate. Be aware that much of the river is Indian Reserve, where collecting is not permitted.

9.6.2 SPENCES BRIDGE – CACHE CREEK

Driving N from Spences Bridge to Cache Creek, two lenses of limestone outcrop on the W side of the Thompson River, just N of Martel, and 23 km S of Ashcroft. The first lens consists of a triangular mass of limestone exposed over a width of 90 m in a road cut along Highway #1, 800 m N of Martel. The limestone continues NW of the highway for 120 m, and is mostly a fractured dark gray/black, veined with calcite. It becomes inter-bedded with argillite near the N edge of the lens.

Some 300 m further N, a second limestone lens is exposed in the highway roadcut, over a width of 1300 m. Extensive faulting and folding have taken place. The deposit comprises fractured, black, fine-grained lime-stone, veined with calcite, and cut by numerous dykes, which become less frequent to the NW.

Opposite the Spatsum Indian Reserve, there is an 8 m adit. Two gyp-sum outcrops, 600 m apart, occur at a locality 200 m above the Thompson River. The property was first staked in 1896. In 1913, an 8 m adit was driven on the showing, but there has been no production. It intersected a band of nearly pure white, massive gypsum, 1.5 m wide.

A lens of limestone forms a N-trending, double-crested hill, 400 m long and 200 m wide, on the N side of Cornwall Creek, just W of Highway #1 and

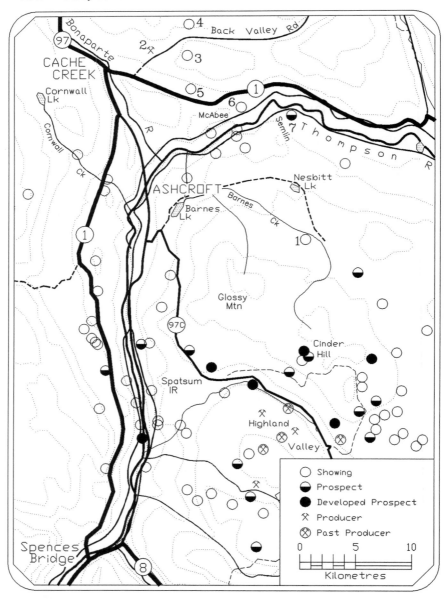

2.5 km due W of Ashcroft. The lens lies in a belt of chert, argillite, lime-stone, greenstone and ultramafic blocks. A 50 m thick bed of shale, argillite and quartzite is exposed along the central depression. The hill is com-prised of uniform light gray/mottled limestone, with a few scattered streaks of chert and irregular patches of dolomite that become more frequent on the N side of the deposit.

Ten km S of Cache Creek, a white seam on the E side of the road contains quartz crystals. One report says "Go over the hill to find petrified wood. Beware of cactus and rattlesnakes".

9.6.3 ASHCROFT AREA

The area around Ashcroft is known for its fossil deposits—ammonites, belemnites, clams, conodonts, microflora, ferns, pollen and brachiopods.

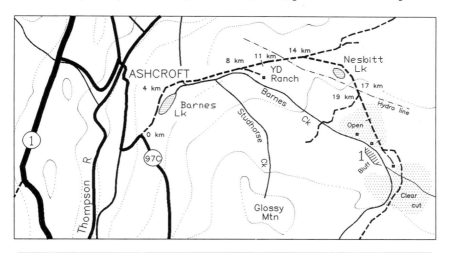

1. NAME(S): BARNES CREEK

Status:	Showing	Northing:	5616511
Latitude:	50 41 13	Easting:	634021
Longitude:	121 06 10	Elevation:	1400 m

Comments: Despite this site's considerable reputation, the author has yet to meet anyone who has actually found the spot. Reported to be on the banks of the upper Barnes Creek, beyond Nesbitt Lake.

Commodities: Fossil wood, agate

The area is underlain by Tertiary volcanics of the Kamloops Group. Opalized and agatized wood occurs along the banks of Barnes Creek, E of Ashcroft. Take the paved Highway #72C out of Ashcroft for Logan Lake, and after 6 km turn off L to Barnes Lake.

From the turnoff (0 km), the road passes Barnes Lake (4 km) and then climbs past the YD Ranch (take the L fork at 8 km). A road leads L at 14 km to Separating Lake—keep R. Near 17 km take L fork past Nesbitt Lake. At about 25 km the area opens into pasture with first views SW down to Barnes Creek. Shortly before the end of the open, the sedimentary bluff containing fossil wood may be visible down R (uncertain). Access is over private land, and it is not clear who the owner is.

Continuing on road into the forest, take L fork which loops past private property down to Barnes Creek (recently cleared). The road crosses the creek and then climbs away to SW. It may be possible to walk down to the bluff from a spot 1 km after crossing Barnes Creek. The material has been described as being "in a ravine", and that some digging is required. Bring a shovel.

9.6.4 EAST OF CACHE CREEK

The area between Cache Creek E to Battle Creek, a distance of some 15 km, is noted for its abundance of arrowheads in the creek beds. Walk upstream from Highway #1 bridges, as downstream river beds have usually been heavily disturbed during the road building process.

---

2.   MINFILE NUMBER: 092INW095
NAME(S): CACHE CREEK ZEOLITE

Status:	Producer, open pit	Northing:	5632000
Latitude:	50 49 44	Easting:	621700
Longitude:	121 16 19	Elevation:	600 m
Commodities:	Zeolite		

MINERALS
Significant: Clinoptilolite, heulandite, stilbite

The Cache Creek zeolite deposits are located about 6 km NE of Cache Creek. The area is underlain by volcanic and sedimentary rocks. The zeolitized materials in the Cache Creek area outcrop in four locations. These have been divided into two groups: A and B.

Group A is zeolitized tuffs, which are gray to light gray, and have a thickness of 6 m to 8 m. Group A1, below Group A, comprises light/dark green zeolitized tuffs. These are 5 m to 7 m thick. The contact between the two groups is sharp. The zeolite is clinoptilolite, with minor heulandite.

Group B, near McAbee, is zeolitized rhyolite, clay, shale and siltstone. Zeolites are not the main component of this sedimentary sequence. Yellow stains on fractures exposed in a bulldozer cut are probably jarosite. The stratum is light/dark brown and gray to dark green, bedded, friable and contains minor fossils. The sequence is 50 m to 70 m thick. The zeolites are heulandite, stilbite and clinoptilolite. This deposit was discovered by the BC Geological Survey Branch, and is presently being mined for use in odor-control products (Whoa and Zippity-do-dah).

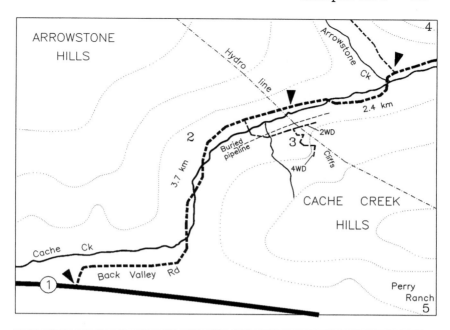

3.   NAME(S): BACK VALLEY

Status:	Showing	Northing:	5631257
Latitude:	50 49 18	Easting:	624206
Longitude:	121 14 12	Elevation:	600 m

Comments: When driving E from Cache Creek, take the Back Valley road N after 2.7 km and park at the fifth road bridge (3.7 km). Cross Cache Creek to E side and follow a service road (pipeline) for about 500 m on a sage-covered bench, crossing one shallow draw, until a larger valley opens on the right (E). Head up this side valley about 700 m to a rock outcrop in trees on S side. Agate can be found in a short rock face and a somewhat hidden rock slide.

Commodities: Agate, gemstones

MINERALS

Significant: Quartz, moss agate, tube agate

The Cache Creek Hills, which lie N of Highway #1 and S of the Back Valley road, are overlain with Tertiary volcanics, which host a variety of amygdaloidal minerals, including zeolites and agate. At the BACK VALLEY site, tube/pipe and moss agates are found in and below a rock outcrop in a draw that drains NW out from the hills. A rock hammer and chisel will be an asset.

4. NAME(S): ARROWSTONE HILL

Status:	Showing	Northing:	5633800
Latitude:	50 50 40	Easting:	624360
Longitude:	121 14 00	Elevation:	900 m
Commodities:	Opalized wood		

MINERALS
Significant: Fossils, opal

Park where the Arrowsmith Creek Road takes off from the Back Valley Road—6 km from Highway #1. The site is on the top of the hill directly N, and involves a climb of about 300 m.

5. MINFILE NUMBER: 092INW076
NAME(S): PERRY RANCH

Status:	Showing	Northing:	5628840
Latitude:	50 47 59	Easting:	625000
Longitude:	121 13 34	Elevation:	609 m
Comments:	This site is now off limits due to new ownership (1998). However, it is included here because of its reputation as a source of good cutting material, with the hope that in future years it may become available to rockhounds again. Located about 7 km E of Cache Creek, N of the Perry Ranch. Ticks in the spring; rattlesnakes in summer.		
Commodities:	Agate, gemstones		

MINERALS
Significant: Agate, quartz

Drive N to corrals to park. Material can be found from there N. A shallow valley with a creek to the NE has jasper on its W side. Some of the hills are staked. Agate is abundant in the area and may be picked up on the slopes leading up to the sedimentary beds. Quartz crystals are also reported to occur in a "white seam". Trunks of petrified trees occur in sandstone, interbedded with volcanic flows atop the hill 1 km to NE. The sedimentary beds weather to a light sandy colour, readily seen in the darker flows.

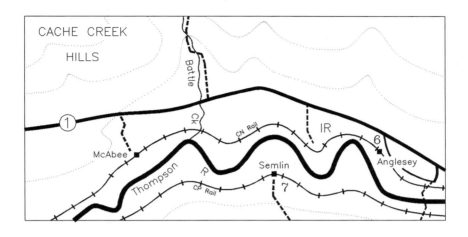

6. MINFILE NUMBER: 092INW074
NAME(S): WALHACHIN, MCABEE, ANGLESEY LOOKOUT

Status:	Showing	Northing:	5626060
Latitude:	50 46 25	Easting:	630775
Longitude:	121 08 43	Elevation:	366 m

Comments: Located 17 km E of Cache Creek, or 20 km W of the Thompson River bridge, in the cliff behind McAbee Station on the CN Railway.

Commodities: Agate, gemstones, fossils

MINERALS

Significant: Jasper, bloodstone

Park at the Anglesey Lookout on Highway #1. A track descends to below the cliffs from the E end of the parking area. Green jasper occurs in an area underlain by Eocene Kamloops Group rocks. The jasper occurs in a cliff facing the Thompson River, above McAbee Station on the Canadian National Railway. The material is often difficult to recognize, since the outer rind is the colour of the host rocks. It is very hard, and takes a good polish. Indian artifacts are also found in this area. Eocene era fossils are found — ginkgo leaves, seed pods, insects and even fish have been reported.

7. MINFILE NUMBER: 092INW087
NAME(S): RIVERSIDE PYROPHYLLITE

Status:	Prospect/Open Pit	Northing:	5626560
Latitude:	50 46 38	Easting:	634050
Longitude:	121 05 55	Elevation:	433 m
Comments:	Quarry, located S of the CP Railway tracks at Semlin Siding, 14 km NE of Ashcroft.		
Commodities:	Pyrophyllite		

MINERALS
Significant: Pyrophyllite
Associated: Quartz, calcite, pyrite, selenite

The pyrophyllite showing is in the gully of a small creek on the S side of the Thompson River. A quarry, 500 m S of the CP Railway tracks at Semlin Siding, joins two deep open cuts. A number of claims were staked in 1947 and surveyed in 1951. A rough road has been bulldozed from Semlin Siding to the quarry (ca. 1951). Other work comprised a 27 m trench S of the quarry and two smaller cuts. The host rock is a rhyolite porphyry which is schistose, greenish-gray and contains quartz, orthoclase and minor albite phenocrysts in a fine-grained ground mass. Pyrophyllite occurs with quartz, calcite and minor pyrite as wallrock alteration along a shear zone in the rhyolite porphyry. It is yellow-stained with small selenite crystals. In the quarry, the pyrophyllite is light gray-white, but very iron-stained.

9.6.5 HAT CREEK

Hat Creek is renowned for its jaspers, found among the rolling grass hills to the E of the valley. Access may be possible from the Cache Creek side, but the usual approach is via the upper level (L fork) road in Upper Hat Creek valley. Get permission from the relevant rancher. Brecciated chert and jasper are found in chalcedony, and make good cabbing material.

The valley is comprised of three different geological series. The Marble Canyon Formation is over 200 million years old, laid down in an inland sea. Much of the Cornwall Hills E of Hat Creek are composed of this material. Below the limestone, mostly on the Bonaparte River side, are the greenstones and cherts of the Cache Creek series. Next youngest materials are the sandstones, shales and coal beds of the Hat Creek valley, which were laid down 26 million to 36 million years ago. Volcanic flows from 11 million to 22 million years ago cover the valley floor and extend as far E as Tranquille and Deadman creeks. These contain chert-agate material in cavities, and were broken and brecciated due to intense folding some time after being deposited. The folding is visible on the bare hills W of the hotel in the town of Cache Creek.

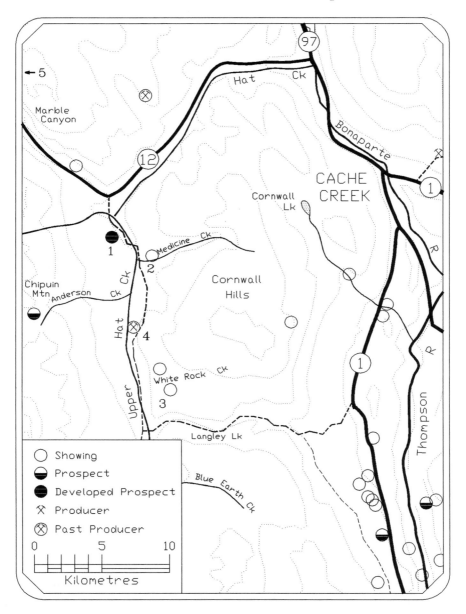

It is possible in dry weather to drive out via the S end of the valley, back E to Highway #1 near the Ashcroft turnoff. Not suitable for RVs. The road cuts across some impressive limestone bluffs that form the S end of the Marble Canyon Formation.

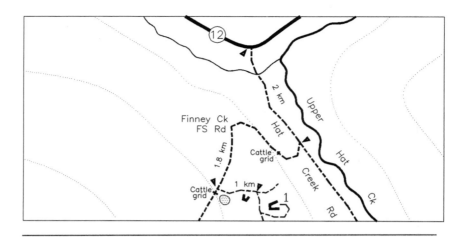

1. MINFILE NUMBER: 092INW084
NAME(S): PACIFIC BENTONITE

Status:	Developed prospect	Northing:	5625100
Latitude:	50 46 09	Easting:	597600
Longitude:	121 36 38	Elevation:	1135 m

Comments: Bentonite exposure in the W of two trenches on the property.

Commodities: Bentonite, coal

MINERALS

Significant: Montmorillonite, coal

Associated: Feldspar, cristobalite, amber, selenite, fossil wood

The prospect is located in the Hat Creek valley, 2 km S of where Highway #12 joins Hat Creek, up the Finney Creek Forest Service Road. The area is underlain by a N-trending trough containing over 1000 m of sediments, overlain by 400 m to 600 m of volcanics. The Hat Creek Formation consists of a lower unit of coal with inter-layers of siltstone, conglomerate and sandstone, overlain by an upper unit of claystone up to 600 m thick. Bentonite is common within both the coal and the claystone sequences.

A zone of bentonitic clay and sandstone, up to 100 m thick, overlain by coal, outcrops along the nose of a southward-plunging syncline, and contains zones of clean bentonite, several metres in thickness. A horizontal cut into the hill exposes (E to W) coloured claystone, coal/shale and bentonite. Near the surface, the bentonite is brown and oxidized, while the unoxidized mineral below is blue. Selenite crystals, amber and petrified wood are found in the coal strata. The wood is of poor quality.

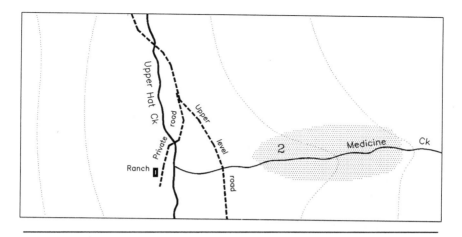

2. MINFILE NUMBER: 092INW072
NAME(S): MEDICINE CREEK

Status:	Showing	Northing:	5623750
Latitude:	50 45 32	Easting:	600640
Longitude:	121 34 23	Elevation:	1067 m

Take the Upper Hat Creek road 6 km after leaving Highway #12, and go another 2.5 km. Ask permission at the ranch. The area is underlain by volcanic and sedimentary rocks of the Eocene Kamloops Group. Jasper, agate and petrified wood occur on the ridge about 800 m E of the ranch, up Medicine Creek. One report describes petrified wood being found on the hills to the E of the road from Upper Hat Creek to Marble Canyon, a distance of almost 30 km. Jasper is found close to Medicine Creek on the N side, and is also reported on upper hillside S of the creek. Numerous large fossil wood specimens are visible from the road close to Hat Creek itself, always associated with coaly deposits.

3. NAME(S): UPPER HAT CREEK NO.2

Status:	Showing	Northing:	5611979
Latitude:	50 39 10	Easting:	601522
Longitude:	121 33 50	Elevation:	1067 m

An attractive jasper-agate is reported on the ridge NE of Upper Hat Creek, formed by the confluence of Langley and Hat creeks.

4. MINFILE NUMBER: 092INW047
NAME(S): HAT CREEK

Status:	Past producer, underground	Northing:	5618111
Latitude:	50 42 30	Easting:	599049
Longitude:	121 35 50	Elevation:	1074 m

Comments: The Hat Creek coal deposit is divided into two reserves. The No. 1 has been mined on a limited scale, while No. 2, further S, is larger but not as developed. The location coordinates indicate the centre of the entire coal field.

Commodities: Coal

MINERALS

Associated: Resin (amber), petrified wood

Three main coal seams, containing sub-bituminous rank coal, are present in approximately 425 m of strata. Physically, there is a full range of coals, from bright to dull brown, but most of it is compact, dull brown-black rock. It is flaky where sheared or weathered.

The coal is interbedded with claystone, siltstone, sandstone and minor conglomerate. Relatively continuous strata of resin beads and petrified wood fragments are common. The uppermost seam (A zone), approximately 160 m thick, consists of a relatively impure sequence. The middle seam (B zone) is 50 m thick, while the lowermost seam (D zone) is 70 m, and is separated from the former by sandy siltstone, conglomerate, sandstone, and a number of thin coal bands (C zone). Only the lower portion of the lower seam, approximately 30 m, consists of clean coal.

Proven and probable reserves are 740 million t. The volume of coal in the No. 2 reserve exceeds the No. 1 reserve, and the coal also appears to be of better quality. The potential for surface mining is greater in the No. 1 reserve, where seams are closer to the surface. A limited quantity of mining has already taken place in the No. 1 reserve.

5. NAME(S): PAVILION LAKE

Status: Showing

On the Highway #99 connector between Lillooet and Cache Creek. Fossils can be found near the foot of the rock slides of the Marble Canyon limestone, where they border Highway #99 near the W end of Pavilion Lake. The local marble takes a good polish; it is gray with reddish (iron oxide) staining at the surface.

9.7. CARIBOO COUNTRY

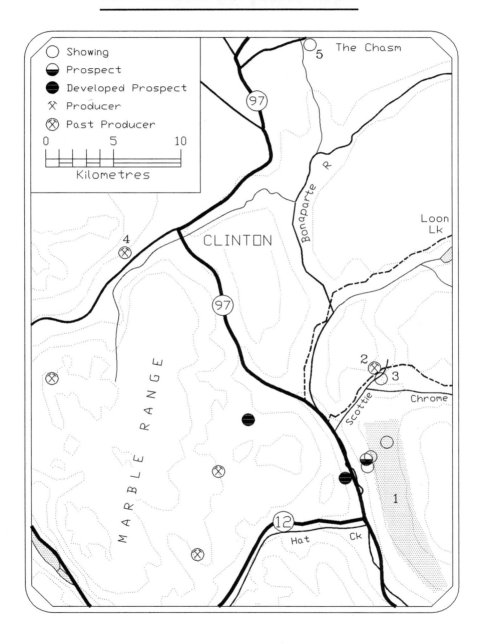

9.7.1 CACHE CREEK – CLINTON

---

1.   NAME(S): BONAPARTE RIVER HILLS

Status: Showing

The region is the centre of prehnite and chalcedony showings, covering an area stretching from S of Cache Creek to Clinton. The hills on the W and E sides of the SE-flowing Bonaparte River comprise chert, argillite, limestone, greenstone and ultramafic blocks. Chalcedony, quartz and opal occur in buff-coloured serpentine, which outcrops on both sides of the valley. When fresh, the serpentine is dark green with light green patches. Chrome garnet (uvarovite) has·also been found.

Colourless, translucent crystals of prehnite fill fissures up to 10 cm wide and 1 m long in peridotite along E side of Bonaparte Valley a short distance N of Ferguson Creek, which is 2 km S of the confluence of Scottie Creek with Bonaparte River.

Spanish topaz (citrine) has been reported along Highway #97 between Cache Creek and Clinton.

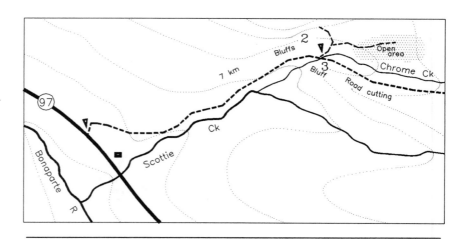

---

2.   MINFILE NUMBER: 092INW001
NAME(S): SCOTTIE CREEK

Status:	Past producer, open pit	Northing:	5650093
Latitude:	50 59 36	Easting:	612756
Longitude:	121 23 36		

Located on Scottie Creek, 5 km from its confluence with Bonaparte River and Highway #97, this chromite prospect is 20 km N of Cache Creek. The major workings are in steep soft cliffs seen from the road on the W side of the creek, just downstream from where the road turns E around the amethyst crag. The host rock is a serpentinite, and contains limestones, chert, basalt and ultramafic rocks in a matrix of chert and argillite. Locally, only serpentinite is exposed at the chromite showings. It has abundant bastite, orthopyroxene and olivine. The serpentinite is 300 m wide, with an unknown strike length. The body trends N, and is extensively fractured in many directions. The whole area is mantled by a thick cover of glacial till and alluvium.

Chromite mineralization is restricted to the dunitic parts of the serpentinite. Chromite occurs as small stringers and lenses, 2 cm to 30 cm wide and 20 cm to 40 cm long, composed of medium grained chromite. To date, exploration has failed to identify any large zones of mineralization. Approximately 450 t of ore from the adit workings were stacked and graded 22% chromite. A further 90 t of ore from a nearby open cut graded 33%. Trace amounts of platinum have been recovered from the creek. The showings were discovered in 1901 but not staked until 1915, when a small amount of trenching was done.

---

3.   MINFILE NUMBER: 092INW075
NAME(S): SCOTTIE CREEK 2

Status:	Showing	Northing:	5650093
Latitude:	50 59 36	Easting:	612756
Longitude:	121 23 36		

Amethyst occurs in a cliff on the E side above Scottie Creek, just where the road swings E (7 km from turnoff Highway #97). A large flat open space appears on the left. Caution: there may be active logging. Hill is on SE side of bend. Agate and amethyst occur in the cliff above. Specimens up to 50 kg have been found, although the crystals are small. Specimens tend to fade from purple to clear in bright sunlight. Heavy tools required to pry material loose. Mosquitoes are bad in June and July.

Placer gold and platinum have been found in Scottie Creek. The exact location is not clear. Selenite crystals up to 10 cm in length are found in carbonaceous bedding planes 200 m E of the amethyst deposit, in the bank on S side of the road.

9.7.2 CLINTON AREA

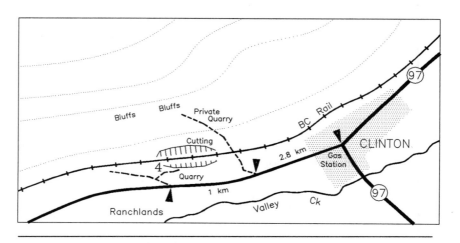

4. MINFILE NUMBER: 092P 079
NAME(S): CLINTON TUFA

Status:	Past producer, open pit	Northing:	5658801
Latitude:	51 04 29	Easting:	595609
Longitude:	121 38 07	Elevation:	969 m

Comments: Visit both the old quarry and the railway cutting above.
Commodities: Travertine, limestone

MINERALS
Significant: Calcite

A mound of tufa, up to 250 m long, 150 m wide and at least 7 m thick, is exposed in a quarry above the road and along a railway cut for 200 m, 3.8 km W of Clinton on the Pavilion Road. The deposit consists mostly of pale buff to white, roughly bedded, porous tufa that becomes dense (massive) in a few places. Twigs, branch and leaf fossils are found in the tufa. The deposit is estimated to contain 726,000 t of tufa, grading 99% calcium carbonate. A limited amount of tufa (1400 t) was produced from two small quarries near the S end of the deposit from 1948–53.

Some 300 m NW of the tufa quarries, light/dark gray, very fine-grained limestone outcrops along a series of bluffs. It is contaminated with small chert nodules. The limestone was quarried and burnt in an adjacent kiln to produce lime, some time before 1944. Travertine is found in the railway cut about 100 m up-slope of the quarry.

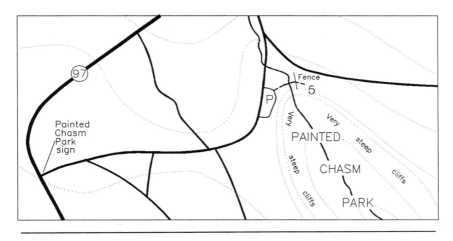

5. NAME(S): PAINTED CHASM

Status:	Showing	Northing:	5667132
Latitude:	51 12 46	Easting:	607544
Longitude:	121 28 32	Elevation:	750 m

Comments: At Chasm Park, E of Highway #97, 17 km N of Clinton. The Painted Chasm, a gorge cut in volcanics, exposes amygdaloidal flow with zeolites and opal near the top. Similar flows are found in road-cuts about 1.5 km S of the turnoff to the Chasm.

Commodities: Zeolite, opal

MINERALS

Significant: Chabazite, heulandite, analcime, opal

The area is overlain by volcanics. At the head of the gorge, amygdaloidal olivine basalts are exposed in a section 60 m thick, containing chabazite, heulandite, analcime and opal, and are most plentiful near the top of the section. The opal is mostly orange-brown in colour. Do not collect in the park. Cross the creek heading E then angle down onto steep, loose ledges (not for the nervous). A rope is recommended.

9.8. LILLOOET AREA

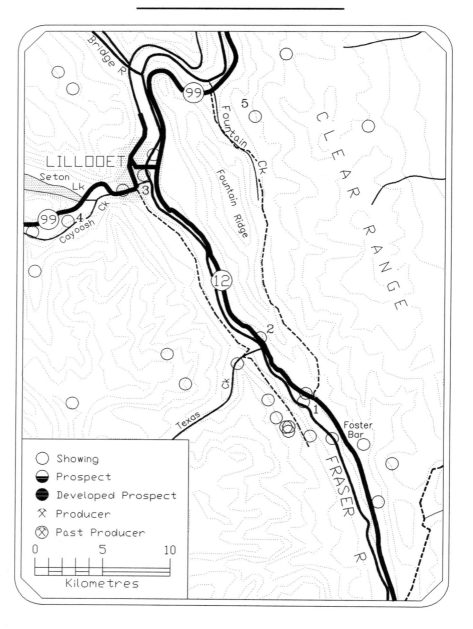

Legend:
- ○ Showing
- ◐ Prospect
- ● Developed Prospect
- ✕ Producer
- ⊗ Past Producer

0   5   10
Kilometres

9.8.1 LILLOOET

The town of Lillooet itself is worth visiting. It owes its existence to the Gold Rush of the 1860s when thousands of hopefuls streamed north to the Cariboo gold fields. The town was known locally as "Mile 0" on the Cariboo Trail. Overlanders came up Harrison and Lillooet lakes on paddlewheelers, so as to avoid the rapids of the Fraser Canyon between Hope and Lytton. Arriving in the arid backcountry of Lillooet (named, incidentally, incorrectly by Governor Douglas for the native tribes of the Pemberton area), the sourdoughs were faced with the start of the serious business of getting to the booming wealth of the Interior.

When you get to the town, take a moment to look around at the wide river below and the huge slopes that tower above this stepping stone to the Cariboo, and try to imagine what it must have felt like back then, before roads, electricity, the railway, plastic, antibiotics or even the law. There are information booths in the town, that can direct you to the Hanging Tree and other historical sites.

There is no longer a Lillooet Rockhound Club, but George and Karen Vanderwolf own the health and gift store on the main street. They have local jade and *yalakomite* (altered brecciated serpentine cut by magnesite veins) for sale, and enjoy talking rocks. Karen's grandfather came from Missouri, heading for the Cariboo, but stopped at Lillooet and stayed. Her father, Ed Osterlund, ranched a 700-acre spread on the Yalakom River. The summers were spent farming, but the fall and spring saw him hunting jade along the creeks. In 1966 he found the nephrite deposit on the upper Hell Creek, at an elevation of about 2,000 m. The family still owns the HORSESHOE BEND (092JNE117) hydraulic claim.

For rockhounds wanting an overview of this fascinating area, visit the Lillooet Museum on the main street. There are fossil and mineral displays on the ground floor (ask to see the thundereggs). In the basement, not very well displayed, is the mineral collection of Will Haylmore, who was a leading prospector in the area. Described as "an English gentleman", he arrived in 1894 and lived near Gold Bridge until shortly before his death in 1964. During that time he operated a series of placers and employed many otherwise jobless men during the Depression.

1. MINFILE NUMBER: 092INW096
NAME(S): MAGRATH PLACER

Status:	Showing	Northing:	5597915
Latitude:	50 31 43	Easting:	587740
Longitude:	121 45 44	Elevation:	183 m

Comments: Sample site on a bench of the Fraser River, just upstream from Foster Bar, about 22 km SSE of Lillooet.

Commodities: Gold

In the area of the placer lease, old workings on the bench about 30 m above the present Fraser River level may have been done by Chinese prospectors at the turn of the century. The work was apparently by hand, with a sluice box using water from the small creek in the area. The workings are in the form of trenches and cuts in the bench, with larger rocks piled up along and near the end of the box. The work is fairly extensive, with possibly as much as one-third of the bench having been worked.

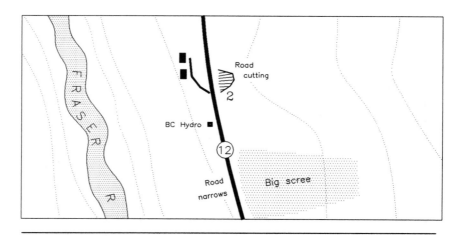

2. NAME(S): TRAVERTINE

Status:	Showing	Northing:	5603180
Latitude:	50 34 35	Easting:	584478
Longitude:	121 48 25	Elevation:	200 m

Comments: Some 44 km N of Lytton, the road narrows and curves at the Big Slide (a large scree slope). Then pass a BC Hydro box on W side. At 45 km a road cutting on E side, above the road, opposite two red-roofed houses (mailbox reads "Ford"). Or travel 17 km S of Lillooet.

Commodities: Travertine

MINERALS

Significant: Calcite

The Highways Dept has cut much of the deposit out of the hill and dumped it down-slope. A ladder, hammer and chisel would be needed to access the material above the road. Caution: the roadcut is poorly consolidated and could avalanche.

---

3. MINFILE NUMBER: 092INW071
NAME(S): LILLOOET

Status:	Showing	Northing:	5616780
Latitude:	50 42 00	Easting:	574742
Longitude:	121 56 30	Elevation:	1400 m

Comments: Placer deposits.
Commodities: Jade, nephrite, agate

MINERALS
Significant: Jasper

Agates, jade and jasper have been found on each side of the Lillooet Bridge and Bar downstream. Placer area extends about 1 km S to where the Seton River enters the Fraser at Cayoosh Park.

---

4. MINFILE NUMBER: 092JNE114
NAME(S): ST. JOHN TALC, CAYOOSH CREEK

Status:	Showing	Northing:	5611464
Latitude:	50 39 10	Easting:	570104
Longitude:	122 00 30	Elevation:	480 m

Comments: Located on both sides of the Duffy Lake Road (along Cayoosh Creek), 10 km from Lillooet. There is a small weed-filled pond about 200 m before the site (coming from the Lillooet side).
Commodities: Talc, soapstone

MINERALS
Significant: Talc
Alteration: Serpentine, talc

In the upper workings, 30 m above the road, two open cuts and strippings expose lenses 0.75 m by 2 m of serpentine and sheared soapstone. The serpentine contains small nodules of soapstone. The best and largest showing occurs 5 m to the W, where lenses of soapstone/serpentine are 0.5 m by 3 m. Light green talc is located in the hanging wall of the serpentine, in bands 0.5 m long by 5 cm thick. The soapstone is mottled gray-green and peppered by crystals of rusty ankerite.

The workings 20 m below the road are about 100 m SW across strike from the upper lenses. A large open cut contains a small amount of soapstone occurring with serpentine in lenses parallel to the enclosing schist planes.

---

5. NAME(S): LAMONT ALPINE

Status:	Showing	Northing:	5620300
Latitude:	50 43 50	Easting:	582930
Longitude:	121 49 30	Elevation:	2000 m

Comments: In Fountain Valley's upper alpine areas, SE of confluence of Fraser River and Fountain Creek.

Commodities: Thundereggs

MINERALS
Significant: Quartz, agate, calcite

Thundereggs are reported distributed widely across the flank of the mountain SE of the confluence of the Fraser River and Fountain Creek. These unusual deposits are characterized by two features: their outer surfaces are much rougher than Oregon thundereggs, and their centres are a mixture of quartz and calcite. The latter fluoresces bright green under shortwave ultraviolet light. Samples can be viewed at the Lillooet Museum. Thanks to Ailsa Lamont for this site.

9.8.2 BRIDGE–YALAKOM RIVERS

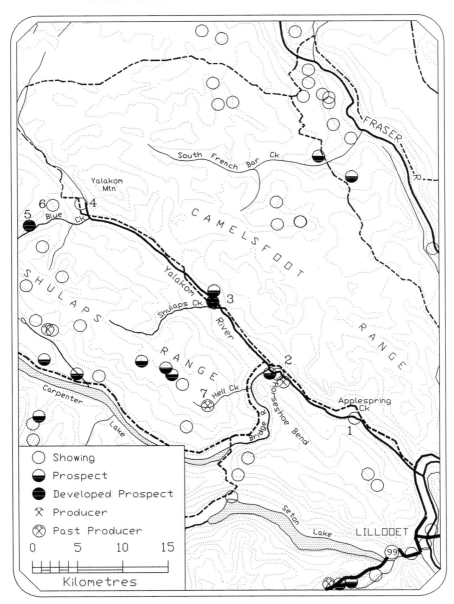

This is remote country; approach with caution. Carry plenty of gas, and don't expect outside help. There are ranches on the lower reaches of the river that remind you of what life must have been like a long time ago. A timeless aura hangs over the valley that makes you wonder how Queen Victoria is doing across the water.

1. **MINFILE NUMBER: 092JNE116**
   NAME(S):APPLESPRING CREEK

Status:	Showing	Northing:	5629194
Latitude:	50 48 45	Easting:	567615
Longitude:	122 02 25	Elevation:	360 m
Comments:	Located on W side of Bridge River, about 500 m S of the cable ferry, downstream from the mouth of Applespring Creek.		
Commodities:	Jade, nephrite		

MINERALS
Significant: Nephrite

The deposit is described as "semi-nephrite", or non-commercial type. The deposit is 45 cm to 60 cm wide, consisting of pale green to gray waxy nephrite occurring as sheared lenses, nodules and layers in sheared tremolite within a pronounced fault in serpentinite.

2. **MINFILE NUMBER: 092JNE074**
   NAME(S): HORSESHOE BEND PLACER

Status:	Past Producer	Northing:	5634342
Latitude:	50 51 35	Easting:	559043
Longitude:	122 09 40	Elevation:	410 m

The Horseshoe Bend placer deposit on the Bridge River is 1 km SE of the confluence of the Yalakom and Bridge rivers, and was probably worked as early as 1860. Between 1902 and 1945, 31 kg of placer gold were recovered. The gravels there are of four types:

1) Gravels within the river bed. These are poorly sorted with boulders up to several tonnes within finer material. These gravels have been worked in isolated patches.

2) Bank and bench gravels between low water and the river banks. Gold content of these gravels improved at depth but difficult to reach.

3) Gravel in cliffs which form the present banks of the river. These consist of unconsolidated fluvial gravels interbedded with conglomerate. Gold in these gravels is distributed throughout.

4) Gravels of the ancient river channel. Bedrock to these gravels is Shulaps serpentinite and Bridge River slate.

Horseshoe Bend is also an alluvial nephrite showing. Boulders up to several hundred kg have been found, but all originated elsewhere. There is

The productive Britannia Mine on Howe Sound, now closed, offers regular guided tours.

The Pacific Bentonite Quarry in Hat Creek exposes brilliantly coloured clays and siltstones.

Coal, amber and quartz occur throughout the Coalmont Colliery cuttings on Blakeburn Creek, south of Coalmont.

The Skagit Bluffs on Hwy #3 in Manning Park have yielded axinite, stilbite, prehnite and quartz crystals.

View from near the top of the Agate Mountain Slide to the Willis Ranch, southwest of Princeton.

The colourful strata of Vermilion Bluffs host fossil wood, agate, jasper and quartz, just west of Princeton.

Gold encrustations on quartz from the Dandy Fraction, north Texada Island.
(Ed Johanson collection)

White fossils in pink marble from Anderson Bay, at the southern tip of Texada Island.
(Ed Johanson collection)

Green epidote crystals (3 cm to 5 cm) are found around Alta Lake, near Whistler Village.
(Frank Tierney collection)

Pyrite cubes up to 2 cm/side occur at the Northair Mine on Brandywine Creek, south of Whistler. (David Singleton collection)

Quartz crystal clusters up to 10 cm across are found in the dumps at the Northair Mine, Whistler. (Frank Tierney collection)

Pyrite cubes up to 1 cm across occur in the shales of Slesse Creek, near Chilliwack.
(Frank Tierney collection)

There are extensive Jurassic-Cretaceous fossil beds on the west side of Harrison Lake. (Harley/Livia Waterson collection)

Ammonites and fossil casts occur in widespread deposits along the west side of Harrison Lake. (David Singleton collection)

Upper Jurassic "buchia" clams are found near 20 Mile Creek, west of Harrison Lake. (Adam Villazambo collection)

Almandite garnets can be panned from Ruby Creek and other rivers, north and east of Agassiz. (David Singleton collection)

Clear single quartz crystals and clusters have been found above Wahleach Power Station east of Rosedale. (Elmer/Alice Clark collection)

Typical agate and jasper pebbles collected from the Fraser River bars, from Chilliwack upstream. (Harley/Livia Waterson collection)

Tetrahedrite, freibergite and siderite are some of the rare minerals found at the Eureka Mine, high above Hope. (Frank Tierney collection)

A well-formed molybdenite specimen (12 cm) found in Texas Creek, Fraser Canyon, north of Hope. (Frank Tierney collection)

Both rough and polished green nickle silicate, found in Emory Creek below the giant BC Nickel Mine. (Cliff/Dorothy Smith collection)

River-tumbled jade boulder (20 cm) picked up on a lower Fraser River bar, and cabachons cut from it. (David Singleton collection)

Further upstream, a less tumbled jade boulder from the Yalakom River, Lillooet and a pendant made from it.

Amber nodules up to 3 cm across are found in the coal at the Pacific Bentonite Quarry, Hat Creek.

Fossil trees up to 150 cm in length lie exposed in the coal beds along the Upper Hat Creek.

Gold on quartz from the richest gold strike in BC, the Bralorne Mine, on the upper Bridge River. (Bob Bouvette collection)

The volcanics above Shaw Springs, near Lytton, are famous for banded agates with a brick-red rind. (Win Robertson collection)

The rarer plume agates can also be found above Shaw Springs near Lytton. (Yvonne Evans/John Sutherland collection)

Pyrite (or "fool's gold") is common in the Highland Valley Copper Mine area, Logan Lake. (Margaret Wright collection)

Green acicular malachite crystals up to 5 mm grow on copper ore, the Highland Valley Copper Mine. (Frank Tierney collection)

Green malachite, blue azurite, gold chalcopyrite, purple bornite from the Highland Valley Mine. (Frank Tierney collection)

Blue chrysocolla and green malachite found at Cinder Hill near Logan Lake.

Semi-transparent selenite crystals are dug from coal strata, Scottie Creek, north of Cache Creek. (David Singleton collection)

Picturesque (aplite) jewelry made from Hope Slide material, east of Hope on Hwy #3. (Cliff/Dorothy Smith collection)

Typical banded aplite boulder from the Hope Slide on Hwy #3 east of Hope.

Living room created at 1/20th scale, made from Hope Slide aplite. (Cliff/Dorothy Smith collection)

Opalized and agatized wood specimens picked up on the lower section of the Agate Mountain Slide.

Selenite crystals (up to 8 cm) resemble Christmas trees, from Highway #5A north of Princeton. (Harley/Livia Waterson collection)

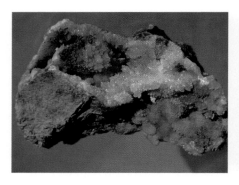

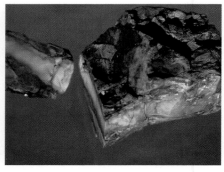

Druzy and botroidal golden travertine deposits from Bouvette Creek, Alison Lake, Highway #5A.

Bands of common opal (hyalite) up to 15 cm thick have been found on the Currie Ranch, Princeton.

"Metasequoia" and other leaf fossils are found west of Princeton along the Tulameen River.

An agatized/jasperized fossil wood specimen (30 cm long) found at Vermilion Bluffs, west of Princeton.

a contact zone in serpentinite in the W wall. Rodingite, as irregular masses, outcrops on the river bank, and is within sheared serpentinite.

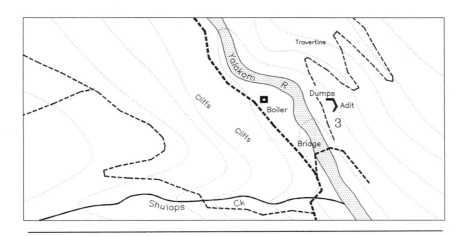

3. **MINFILE NUMBER: 092JNE062**
    NAME(S): EAGLE MERCURY

Status:	Past producer, underground		
Latitude:	50 56 25	Northing:	5643223
Longitude:	122 15 50	Easting:	551720
Elevation:	840 m		
Comments:	On the E side of Yalakom River, 13 km upstream of Bridge/ Yalakom rivers confluence, at highway marker 46 km. Both the dump and a cleared area are on the E side of the river, opposite a rusty boiler standing next to the road on the W side of the river. An overgrown adit is just S of the dump. A good (temporary) bridge 500 m S offers a way to cross with dry feet.		
Commodities:	Mercury, silver, gold		

MINERALS

Significant:	Cinnabar, pyrite
Associated:	Quartz, dolomite, travertine

The EAGLE MERCURY prospect is 500 m N of the confluence of Shulaps Creek with the Yalakom River. In 1997, a bridge allowed foot access to the E side of the river. At the mine site, greenstone and diorite-greenstone breccia are commonly altered to ankerite, which form irregular lenticular zones, laced with dolomite stringers. Cinnabar occurs as discrete grains and blebs in the dolomite veinlets or as short crosscutting hair-like stringers. A zig-zag track cuts up-slope from the site. Travertine, pudding stone and a range of other material are exposed in the dry talus slopes. In 1968, 113 t of ore were mined from which 172 kg of mercury were recovered. An earlier bulk sample collected in 1938 contained 0.44% mercury and some silver.

The RED EAGLE MERCURY prospect (092JNE078) is across the river, to the SW of GOLDEN EAGLE. The occurrence is within pillowed, green to reddish brown greenstone and greenstone breccia, with irregular bands of diabase. The rocks are considerably fractured and veined by ankerite, dolomite and quartz. Cinnabar occurs as narrow stringers, blebs, scattered grains and films on fracture planes within the breccia.

Two adits and numerous trenches explore the prospect; in 1941–42, 232 kg of mercury were produced from 23 t of ore. Reserves for the whole area are estimated to grade about 1%.

---

4. MINFILE NUMBER: 092O 014
NAME(S): SUNNY, YALAKOM RIVER

Status:	Showing	Northing:	5654800
Latitude:	51 02 44	Easting:	536750
Longitude:	122 28 33	Elevation:	1615 m
Comments:	Located 3.5 km NW of the confluence of Blue Creek and Yalakom River, on a NE-facing cliff/hillside.		
Commodities:	Magnesite		

The magnesite showing is within quartz-carbonate altered serpentinite, and is 30 m to 100 m wide and several km long. Crystalline magnesite and quartz form banded veins and comb-textured intergrowths. Enclosing rocks vary from serpentinite to quartz carbonate mariposite rock (listwanite).

---

5. MINFILE NUMBER: 092O 012
NAME(S): ELIZABETH

Status:	Developed prospect	Northing:	5653200
Latitude:	51 01 53	Easting:	531600
Longitude:	122 32 58	Elevation:	2333 m
Comments:	Located 7 km W of the confluence of Blue Creek and the Yalakom River, in the Shulaps Range.		
Commodities:	Gold, silver, lead, zinc, copper, molybdenum		

MINERALS

Significant:	Gold, arsenopyrite, pyrite, galena, sphalerite, pyrrhotite, chalcopyrite, molybdenite
Associated:	Magnetite, ankerite, calcite

The prospect is hosted within porphyritic quartz diorite, which is cut by a variety of veins. These are accessed through two portals, one on the Elizabeth 1 claim and the other on the adjacent Churn No. 1 claim. A second diorite body to the W, contains the No. 9 vein on which recent work has focused. The two diorite bodies are in serpentinized ultramafic rocks, and are adjacent to a ridge of quartz-carbonate altered rocks, or listwanite. It is 0.5 m to 1 m wide and continuous for 250 m. Vein quartz is milky white, and contains native gold (visible), arsenopyrite, pyrite, galena, sphalerite, pyrrhotite, chalcopyrite, malachite, azurite, magnetite, molybdenite, chlorite and carbonaceous material.

---

6. MINFILE NUMBER: 092O 013
NAME(S): BLUE CREEK

Status:	Showing	Northing:	5654723
Latitude:	51 02 42	Easting:	534234
Longitude:	122 30 42	Elevation:	1800 m

Comments: Adjacent to Elizabeth–Yalakom prospect access road, about 2.5 km E of the Elizabeth–Yalakom prospect.

Commodities: Jade, nephrite

MINERALS
Significant: Nephrite
Associated: Nephrite, serpentinite, amphibole, idocrase

Located in the Northern Shulaps Mountains, N of Blue Creek, and about 800 m E of the Elizabeth mine. Access is up the Yalakom road to a crossing above the confluence of the Yalakom River and Blue Creek. The showing is 8 km NW of this confluence, up an un-maintained track. It is an irregular mass of nephrite, up to 8 m wide, associated with an alteration zone within the serpentinite. The nephrite lies in a long zone of "whiterock" with small pods of botryoidal nephrite, together with minor pink amphibole and greenish vesuvianite. Contacts are not exposed, and the extent of the mineralization is not known. There has been no commercial production from this site.

---

7. MINFILE NUMBER: 092JNE063
NAME(S): HELL CREEK

Status:	Past producer, open pit	Northing:	5630399
Latitude:	50 49 30	Easting:	551358
Longitude:	122 16 15	Elevation:	2000 m

Comments: In headwaters of Hell Creek, which flows E into Bridge River, some 6 km upstream of the Bridge–Yalakom confluence. Plus some "opaque minerals" not identified. Access road takes off 38 km from Lillooet on Bridge River road.

Commodities: Jade, nephrite, talc

MINERALS

Significant:	Nephrite, talc
Associated:	Tremolite, serpentine

Jade outcrops at the head of Hell Creek, a NE-flowing tributary of Bridge River. A mass of nephrite is fault-bounded by serpentinite on the W and by slightly metamorphosed sediments on the E. The tabular-shaped mass is 2.4 m wide and trends NW for 300 m to where it is cut by a granitic intrusion. The E contact is bordered by a talc zone 30 cm wide. Cross fractures pervade the nephrite. The nephrite is described as good to fair quality, the quality being decreased by the presence of coarse tremolite patches, talc and opaque minerals.

The deposit was discovered in 1966 by Mr E. Osterlund, who used packhorses to move out material. In 1968 the property was sold to BC Gem Supply who used a helicopter until a road was built in 1969. Birkenhead Jade produced 100 t of nephrite in 1973.

9.9. UPPER BRIDGE RIVER

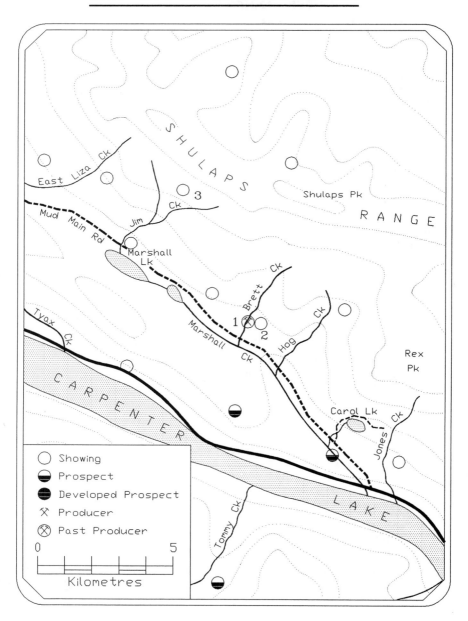

Legend:
- ○ Showing
- ◐ Prospect
- ● Developed Prospect
- ✗ Producer
- ⊗ Past Producer

0 — 5 Kilometres

9.9.1 MARSHALL CREEK

I. **MINFILE NUMBER: 092JNE065**
    NAME(S): GREENBAY, BRETT CREEK

Status:	Past producer, open pit	Northing:	5638966
Latitude:	50 54 12	Easting:	533791
Longitude:	122 31 10	Elevation:	1260 m

Comments: Follow Marshall Creek on Mud Main. Just W of Brett Creek, which flows S into Marshall Creek. Access road follows E side of Brett Creek for 800 m. A sign on Mud Main just W of turnoff reads "Brett Creek Meadows".

Commodities: Jade, nephrite

MINERALS
Significant: Nephrite
Alteration: Talc, zoisite, serpentine, garnet

Jade has been quarried on Brett Creek, 1 km up from its confluence with Marshall Creek. At the Greenbay deposit, a large tectonic inclusion of chert lies adjacent to a mass of serpentinite. Alteration along the margins of the inclusion has resulted in the development of rodingite, which is made up of hydrogarnet, clinozoisite and talc. The rodingite contains prominent small masses of thulite (pink zoisite, part of the epidote family). In places, lenses or vein-like shapes of nephrite occur either within the serpentinite body or along the rodingite-serpentinite contact. The quality of the jade is claimed to improve with depth. Approximately 800 t of nephrite have been removed and about 200 t remain. Greenbay Mining is reported to have quarried this deposit in the early 1970s.

---

2. **MINFILE NUMBER: 092JNE064**
    NAME(S): 4-TON, MARSHALL CREEK

Status: Showing
Comments: Between Brett and Hog creeks.

This nephrite showing is 500 m E east of Brett Creek, 1,200 m N of the confluence of Brett Creek with Marshall Creek. At the showing, lenses and pods of nephrite occur within serpentinite and its sheared contact with adjacent rocks. Approximately 1.5 t of extremely foliated and altered nephrite were excavated, but were not of marketable quality.

3. **MINFILE NUMBER: 092JNE111**
   NAME(S): JIM CREEK

Status:	Showing	Northing:	5643986
Latitude:	50 56 55	Easting:	531319
Longitude:	122 33 15	Elevation:	2100 m

Comments: Located at the head of Jim Creek, just W of Shulaps Peak. Turn N off Mud Main up steep bank between markers at 87 km and 88 km. Definitely 4WD, as the road claws its way up the mountain. The original operators used a tractor for access. Note the altitude—possible only in July and August.

Commodities: Jade, nephrite

MINERALS

Significant: Nephrite
Alteration: Serpentine

The showing is at the headwaters of Jim Creek, about 4 km NE of the W end of Marshall Creek. One report suggests a showing that is a cigar-shaped mass of nephrite, 1 m by 1 m by 4 m, and is within calc-silicate altered serpentinite melange (in part rodingite), and adjacent to chert. Another report suggests numerous small outcrops in the upper alpine area, overlooking the headwaters of Lisa Creek to the W.

Botryoidal nephrite occurs as thin ribbons (30 cm to 60 cm thick) within serpentinite, but is not of commercial value. The main showing is an estimated 10 t. Jim Creek, directly below the deposit, contains alluvial boulders of nephrite in such abundance as to suggest an alternate, yet undiscovered, source in the area.

9.9.2 UPPER TYAX CREEK

1. **MINFILE NUMBER: 092O 018**
   NAME(S): TUNGSTEN QUEEN

Status:	Past producer, underground		
Latitude:	51 02 10	Northing:	5653650
Longitude:	122 45 12	Easting:	517300
Elevation:	1356 m		

Comments: The deposit is adjacent to the Mud Lake road, 2.5 km SE of the Tyaughton (Tyax) and Relay creeks confluence.

Commodities: Tungsten, antimony, mercury, gold

MINERALS

Significant: Scheelite, stibnite, cinnabar, realgar
Associated: Quartz, carbonate, ankerite, chalcedony, dolomite, hematite

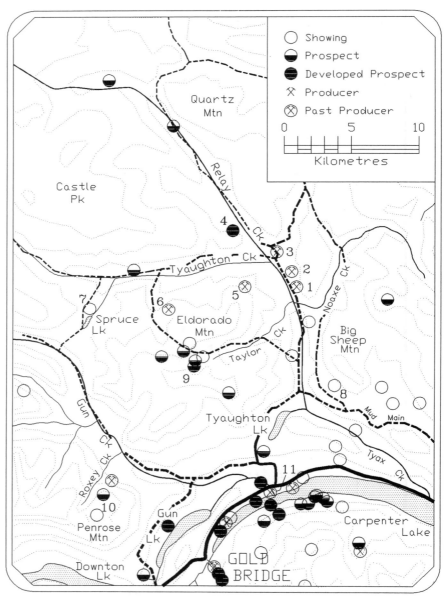

The deposit occurs near the S end of a body of altered serpentinite rock. Adjacent rocks are ribbon chert, argillite and greenstone. All are cut by dykes of feldspar porphyry (brown-weathering). The TUNGSTEN QUEEN deposit consists of eight scheelite-bearing veins of variable thickness and continuity. The principal vein (No. 6), which yielded most of the high grade ore, was up to 18 cm thick and continuous for 21 m. The other veins were much smaller. All consisted of massive, almost pure white scheelite, with stibnite, quartz and carbonate. The veins show a marked banding where comb-textured scheelite is followed inward from both walls of the vein by chalcedony, then by coarsely crystalline comb-textured quartz, and then a central band of stibnite. It is reported that between 1940 and 1953, almost 8 t of tungsten-trioxide (WO_3) were recovered from 55 t of ore. Virtually all scheelite-bearing material has been mined out.

Some 140 m SE of the TUNGSTEN QUEEN, massive/amygdaloidal greenstone contains minor cinnabar as thin sheets along shear planes, and as rims around 5 mm wide carbonate-quartz amygdules in greenstone; realgar was also identified. Feldspar porphyry close to the area contains an unexpectedly high lithium content.

---

2. MINFILE NUMBER: 092O 020
NAME(S): TUNGSTEN KING

Status:	Past producer, underground		
Latitude:	51 02 44	Northing:	5654700
Longitude:	122 45 27	Easting:	517000
Elevation:	1340 m		
Comments:	The deposit is uphill from the Mud Lakes road, 2 km SE of the confluence of Tyaughton (Tyax) and Relay creeks.		
Commodities:	Tungsten, antimony, mercury		

MINERALS

Significant:	Scheelite, stibnite, cinnabar
Associated:	Quartz, hematite

The deposit is within listwanite and dolomite, which is intensely brecciated, recrystallized and sheared. Feldspar porphyry dykes intrude the listwanite. Quartz veins with scheelite and stibnite were first discovered within a 2 m wide fracture zone in brecciated, recrystallized and sheared dolomite. Stibnite veins and disseminations occur within listwanite 75 m N. Cinnabar (for which the area was first prospected) occurs as films along shear planes. From 1942–52 about 34 t of ore were mined, grading about 5% tungsten trioxide.

---

3. MINFILE NUMBER: 092O 023
NAME(S): MANITOU, EMPIRE

Status:	Past producer, underground		
Latitude:	51 03 36	Northing:	5656300
Longitude:	122 46 05	Easting:	516250
Elevation:	1234 m		
Comments:	The mine is located on the NW side of Mud Creek, 800 m NE of the confluence of Tyaughton (Tyax) and Relay creeks.		
Commodities:	Mercury		

MINERALS

Significant: Cinnabar, pyrite, mercury
Associated: Calcite, quartz, hydrocarbon

The mercury deposit is within greenstone and along contacts between greenstone and ribboned chert. Rocks include breccia and argillite. The rocks are extremely faulted. Mercury occurs as cinnabar, chiefly with foliated green and purple volcanic rocks (greenstone) along foliations and shears. It is also found along contacts between the ribbon chert and greenstone. Cinnabar is commonly accompanied by calcite, and less commonly by quartz and native mercury, finely crystalline pyrite, and an unidentified hydrocarbon material. Recorded production, 1938–39, was 140 t of ore which yielded 540 kg of mercury.

---

4.   **MINFILE NUMBER: 092O 059**
      NAME(S): MUGWUMP, RELAY CREEK

Status:	Developed prospect	Northing:	5657250
Latitude:	51 04 07	Easting:	513700
Longitude:	122 48 16	Elevation:	1402 m
Comments:	Portal of main adit is 3 km NW of the junction of Relay and Tyaughton (Tyax) creeks.		
Commodities:	Mercury, antimony		

MINERALS

Significant: Cinnabar, stibnite
Associated: Quartz, carbonate

The MUGWUMP mercury prospect is hosted in conglomerate. Cinnabar and stibnite occur as disseminated grains, smears on fractures, blebs, streaks and partly massive seams associated with quartz veinlets, calcite and hematite along fractures and joints within pebble conglomerate. Cinnabar is relatively abundant as disseminations within listwanite. Stibnite, as acicular needles, forms drusy clusters that occupy vugs, and also semi-massive seams along quartz veinlets in the conglomerate. The main mineralized shear has been traced for 450 m.

---

5.   **MINFILE NUMBER: 092O 017**
      NAME(S): SILVERQUICK MINE

Status:	Past producer, underground		
Latitude:	51 02 26	Northing:	5654125
Longitude:	122 49 00	Easting:	512850
Elevation:	1669 m		

Comments: Approximately 3 km SW of the confluence of Relay and
              Tyaughton creeks.
Commodities: Mercury

MINERALS
Significant: Cinnabar
Associated: Quartz, calcite, limonite, clay, dickite

The Silverquick mercury deposit, approximately 4 km NE of Eldorado
Mountain, is within chert pebble conglomerate and interbedded
sandstone-shale. Cinnabar is present as disseminated grains, streaks and
small lenses within brecciated conglomerate, as smears on faults, and in the
mud of gouge seams. The area around the mine has undergone large scale
folding and thrust faulting. The mine produced most of its ore in the 1960s,
yielding over 3 t of mercury.

---

6. **MINFILE NUMBER: 092O 026**
    NAME(S): ROBSON, BONANZA, PEARSON

Status: Past producer, underground
Latitude: 51 01 23   Northing: 5652180
Longitude: 122 53 15   Easting: 507900
Elevation: 1737 m
Comments: The Robson adit is 6 km E of Spruce Lake, S of Tyaughton
             (Tyax) Creek, and 3.5 km NW of Eldorado Mtn.
Commodities: Gold, silver, lead, zinc, copper

MINERALS
Significant: Arsenopyrite, pyrite, jamesonite, sphalerite, chalcopyrite,
              stibnite, boulangerite, pyrargyrite, pyrrhotite
Associated: Quartz

This polymetallic vein is within hornfelsed and altered sedimentary rocks,
and consists of seams and veins of arsenopyrite along a SW-trending zone
that seems to be part of a set of fractures that radiate from a pluton. The
vein seems to partly grade into altered granodiorite. Other metallic minerals present include pyrite, jamesonite, sphalerite, chalcopyrite, stibnite,
boulangerite, pyrrhotite and pyrargyrite. The deposit was mined 1939–
40, producing a total of 34 t of ore, which yielded 18 kg of silver, 2.2 kg of
gold, 193 kg of copper and 2.6 t of lead.

7. NAME(S): SPRUCE LAKE

Status:	Showing	Northing:	5539061
Latitude:	50 00 21	Easting:	502090
Longitude:	122 58 15	Elevation:	1500 m
Comments:	Fossils		

There are two BC Forest campsites, on the E and N sides of Spruce Lake. The peak on the N side of the lake (good fishing), located some 15 km NW of Gun Lake up the Gun Creek, is reported to have extensive fossil beds.

9.9.3 TYAUGHTON (TYAX) LAKE AREA

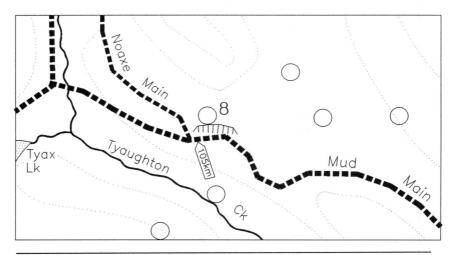

8. MINFILE NUMBER: 092JNE149
NAME(S): MUDMAIN

Status:	Showing	Northing:	5646400
Latitude:	50 58 15	Easting:	520020
Longitude:	122 42 54	Elevation:	1265 m
Commodities:	Magnesite, antimony		

MINERALS
Significant:	Magnesite, dolomite
Associated:	Druzy quartz

The MUDMAIN magnesite showing is exposed in a brown talus slope on the N side, at the junction of the Noaxe and Mudmain Forest Service roads. The exposure is at least 50 m by 30 m of quartz-carbonate-fuchsite altered serpentinite. Magnesite, which occurs as bright green crystalline masses in the outcrop, contains anomalous mercury and antimony.

9. MINFILE NUMBER: 092JNE045
NAME(S): LUCKY STRIKE

Status:	Prospect	Northing:	5647762
Latitude:	50 59 00	Easting:	509711
Longitude:	122 51 42	Elevation:	1950 m
Commodities:	Gold, silver, zinc, lead, copper		

MINERALS

Significant:	Arsenopyrite, sphalerite, jamesonite, pyrite, chalcopyrite, galena, stibnite
Associated:	Quartz

Access via Tyaughton (Tyax) Lake and Taylor Creek, which can be 4WD at times. Arsenopyrite is massively crystalline, and found on the dump. The Lucky Strike prospect is 4 km SSW of Eldorado Mountain, at the headwaters of Taylor Creek. The occurrence is hosted in a band of serpentinite which contains greenstone, sandstone and phyllite. The claim has widespread mineralization occurring in veins and fractures in both dykes and sedimentary hosts. The veins are mostly narrow and faulted or feathered and pinched. The veins occur on either side of a felsic dyke contacting cherts to the E, and ultramafics to the W. The mineralized contact zone strikes N–S and dips almost vertically.

There are 2 adits on the property. The No. 1 adit, in the NW corner of the claim, explores a zone 3 m to 10 m wide, showing a coarse porphyry dyke, altered serpentines and iron-rich carbonates. The shear zone continues for nearly 80 m and contains irregular pods, lenses and streaks of sphalerite, jamesonite, pyrite, chalcopyrite, galena, massively crystalline arsenopyrite and minimal quartz gangue.

The No. 2 adit is 200 m SW of No. 1 adit, and runs S along a mineralized zone between a hornblende andesite dyke and surrounding serpentines. A 10 cm vein shows arsenopyrite, jamesonite, sphalerite, pyrite and minor chalcopyrite.

10. MINFILE NUMBER: 092JNE068
NAME(S): LITTLE GEM

Status:	Prospect	Northing:	5638023
Latitude:	50 53 45	Easting:	503125
Longitude:	122 57 20	Elevation:	1820 m

Comments: Access is up the Gun Creek Rd (4WD). Located on SE slope, approximately 200 m above Roxey Creek, a tributary off Gun Creek, N of Mt Penrose and W of Gun Lake.

Commodities: Cobalt, gold, uranium, molybdenum

MINERALS

Significant: Danaite, lollingite, safflorite, arsenopyrite, molybdenite, gold, skutterudite, uraninite, cobaltite, scheelite

The LITTLE GEM prospect is a hypothermal, cobalt-sulfarsenide uranium and gold vein, 2 km ENE of Dickson Peak. Shears in the zone contain two parallel ore shoots, ranging in width from a few centimetres to a few metres. Irregular lenses of almost solid sulfides contain cobalt and gold values in association with danaite, loellingite, safflorite, arsenopyrite, scheelite and minor molybdenum. Uranium, in the form of uraninite, occurs in the gangue along with coarse-grained allanite, apatite, feldspar, quartz, chlorite, sericite, calcite, erythrite and limonite. Gold occurs mainly as microscopic veinlets of native metal within and adjacent to the sulfarsenide minerals. Surrounding the ore, strongly bleached granodiorite containing sulfides, residual quartz, feldspar and kaolin grades into unaltered granodiorite.

Two adits follow the ore shoots. The upper adit, sampled over 36 m, graded 26 gm/t gold, 0.4% uranium and 3.1% cobalt. The lower adit, sampled over 2 m, graded 55 gm/t gold, 0.3% uranium and 3.2% cobalt.

9.9.4 CARPENTER LAKE

In 1925, BC Hydro's predecessor, the BC Electric Co., sent E. Carpenter to survey the Bridge River and Seton Lake watersheds. Carpenter quickly realized that the 400 m drop between the river to the N and Seton Lake to the S was the key to future hydro power in the province. In 1927 a contract was awarded for the first of two 4 km long, 4.3 m diameter tunnels that would bring water from the Bridge River to new generating stations on Seton Lake. Starting at both ends, the tunnel was completed in June 1930, meeting in the middle with an offset of less than 3 cm! Carpenter Lake is the man-made reservoir that now diverts the Bridge River catchment S through the tunnels.

It's interesting to note that during the Depression, many would-be miners used the as-yet unflooded tunnel to walk from Lillooet to Bridge River, in search of work.

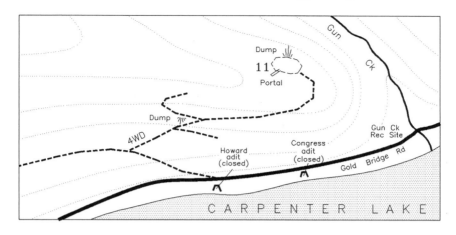

11. MINFILE NUMBER: 092JNE029
NAME(S): CONGRESS MINE

Status:	Past producer, underground		
Latitude:	50 53 38	Northing:	5637829
Longitude:	122 46 53	Easting:	515375
Elevation:	749 m		
Comments:	On the N side of Carpenter Lake, just W of Gun Creek. The Howard, Congress and Contact adits (all close to lake level) are now closed, and their dumps not obvious, but 4WD access to an upper portal offers great views of the lake and several dumps.		
Commodities:	Gold, silver, copper, antimony, mercury, zinc		

MINERALS

Significant:	Stibnite, pyrite, marcasite, kermesite, cinnabar, sphalerite
Associated:	Crystalline quartz

The CONGRESS MINE is underlain by volcanics, cherts and argillites. Mineralization was in the form of three steeply plunging ore shoots in a NE trending shear zone, traced for 550 m.

Veins several centimetres wide contain massive stibnite and fine-grained pyrite, and marcasite on the borders with kermesite. Cinnabar is found in fractures and as impregnations between fractures. Wallrock is altered up to 5 m on either side of the shear, with ankerite, carbonate and dense to finely crystalline quartz.

9.9.5 **GOLD BRIDGE**

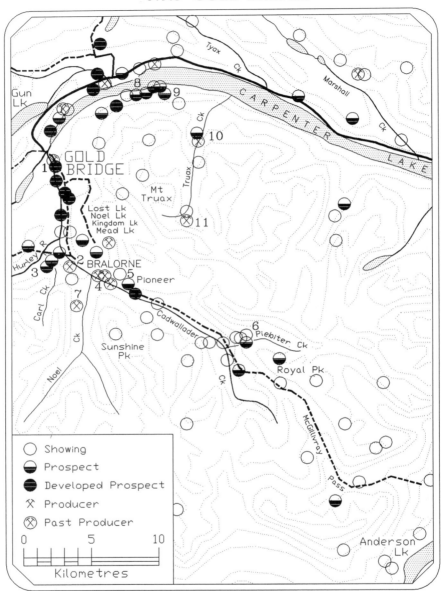

The geology of the area includes a number of Paleozoic and Mesazoic terranes, intruded by plutonic rocks of the Coast Crystalline Complex, and NW-striking faults. The area is noted for its very varied terranes and their mineralization.

The area is also famous for its historical gold production. The Bridge River camp, as it is known, has produced more than twice the gold of the next two largest producers in BC. More than 87 t have come from BRALORNE,

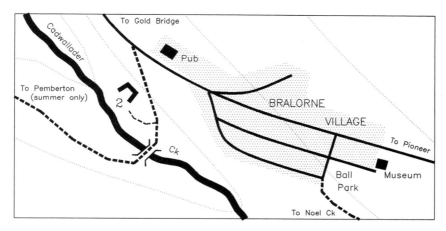

while the neighbouring PIONEER mine has produced over 41 t.

The area is well worth visiting. Great forested slopes and alpine meadows are capped by snow-clad peaks. Long lakes reflect the brilliant colours of the sky. This is BIG country. There is a wildness and emptiness that belies how close the visitor is to the city of Vancouver.

Because of the extreme remoteness of the two towns of Gold Bridge and Bralorne, there is a close sense of community. Bralorne was a "mine town", built with pleasing architecture, so there is a harmony of style not often seen in a small neighborhood. In the late '90s, however, low employment means many of the homes are now abandoned. The only new building is the Mines Motel at (250)238-2355, run by Linda and Nick Skutnik.

Access to the area is either from Lillooet in the E, via the Bridge and Yalakom rivers and the very dramatic Bridge River Canyon, or from Pemberton in the SW (summer road only). Gas is available in Gold Bridge.

I.   MINFILE NUMBER: 092JNE026
NAME(S): HAYLMORE PLACER

Status:	Past producer, open pit	Northing:	5632629
Latitude:	50 50 50	Easting:	511244
Longitude:	122 50 25	Elevation:	670 m

Comments: At the mouth of the Hurley River. Principal production from E rim. Will Haylmore was a noted "English gentleman" who prospected the area from 1894 onwards and owned several mines. A small part of his mineral collection is on show (unlabeled) at the Lillooet Museum.

Commodities: Gold

At the mouth of the Hurley River, from the E rim, "over 1000 ounces" of coarse gold are reported to have been recovered from serpentine bedrock or gravels. The largest nugget weighed 368 gm, but more common were 30 gm to 140 gm nuggets.

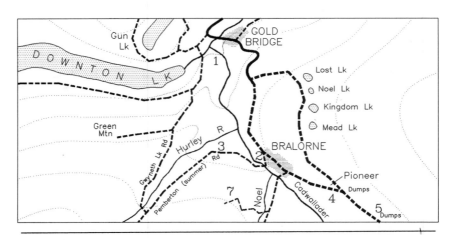

2. MINFILE NUMBER: 092JNE001
NAME(S): BRALORNE MINE

Status:	Past producer, underground		
Latitude:	50 46 40	Northing:	5624910
Longitude:	122 49 15	Easting:	512632
Elevation:	960 m		
Comments:	The major mine in the area. Located in Cadwallader Creek below the town of Bralorne. Shafts over 1.5 km deep. Still serviced by a maintenance crew, but not operational.		
Commodities:	Gold, silver, lead, zinc, copper, tungsten		

MINERALS

Significant:	Gold, pyrite, arsenopyrite, sphalerite, galena, chalcopyrite, pyrrhotite, tetrahedrite
Associated:	Quartz, calcite, mariposite, talc, scheelite

A 60 m wide belt of serpentinite borders the diorite on the SE. The principal host rock is diorite, and an abnormal richness in gold was noted when veins neared the serpentinite. The lens hosting quartz veins is 5 km long by 2 km wide, and has a complex interlacing fault system. The faults grow wider with depth. The veins are persistent, having been mined to nearly a 2 km depth. The mine was accessible by four main shafts and worked on 44 levels, with over 150 km of tunnels. Indicated reserves are 965,000 t grading 9.4 gm/t gold.

A small mine museum at the top of Bralorne village is worth a visit (open Fri–Sun); follow the signs from Bridge River.

3. MINFILE NUMBER: 092JNE016
NAME(S): SHORT O'BACON

Status:	Prospect	Northing:	5624906
Latitude:	50 46 40	Easting:	511261
Longitude:	122 50 25	Elevation:	1130 m

Comments: The main vein is just S of Carl Creek, 1 km SE of its junction with the Hurley River.

Commodities: Gold, silver

MINERALS
Significant: Cubic, pyrite, gold
Associated: Quartz

The main SHORT O'BACON showing is hosted in greenstone near its contact with serpentinite. Cherts and argillites are exposed to the E and S. The vein is in a shear zone striking NW and dipping steeply, containing quartz and sheared greenstone with quartz stringers. It has been followed for 150 m.

Directly E of the Short O'Bacon adit is another vein on the E bank of Carl Creek, in a wide shear zone, also in greenstone near the serpentinite contact. The rock is talcose, highly sheared and contains abundant mariposite and cubic pyrite. A 30 cm quartz vein is sparingly mineralized with pyrite and a little gold. About 200 m W of the Short O'Bacon vein is another greenstone-hosted vein-shear striking SE and dipping steeply W. Sericite, chlorite and iron sulfides occur in approximately 1 m of quartz.

4. MINFILE NUMBER: 092JNE004
NAME(S): PIONEER

Status:	Past producer, underground		
Latitude:	50 45 40	Northing:	5623064
Longitude:	122 46 45	Easting:	515575
Elevation:	1215 m		

Comments: This was the second major mine (with regard to gold production) in the area (after Bralorne), although it started years earlier. Access on the lower road through the village of Bralorne.

Commodities: Gold, silver, lead, zinc, copper, antimony, tungsten

MINERALS
Significant: Arsenopyrite, pyrite, gold, sphalerite, galena, chalcopyrite, pyrrhotite, marcasite, stibnite, scheelite

Pioneer was first staked in 1897, but the first shaft was only sunk in 1916. In the mid-1920s the miners really began to hit paydirt. By the time it closed in 1962, the mine was worked on 27 levels to a depth of 1 km from

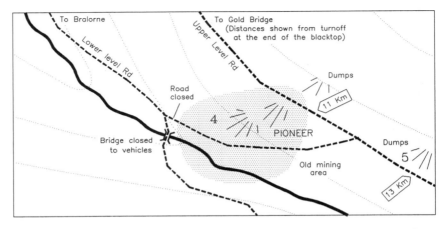

five shafts. The veins are hosted mainly in greenstone and granite. The mineralized veins were composed mainly of quartz gangue, with fractures filled with calcite and ankerite. Small shoots of scheelite occur in the main vein and tourmaline is said to occur in cavities in one vein. The quartz ribbons contained chlorite, sericite, mariposite, gouge sulfides and gold. The principal sulfides, arsenopyrite and pyrite, occur as disseminations in massive quartz or in the ribbon partings. Massive arsenopyrite is often associated with free gold. Other sulfides include sphalerite, galena, chalcopyrite, pyrrhotite, marcasite and stibnite.

The PIONEER property was consolidated with Bralorne Mines in 1959. In 1997 the buildings were demolished. The Upper Level Road (see CADWALLADER CREEK) provides access to the PIONEER dumps, which are above that road, 11 km from the turnoff from the Gold Bridge–Bralorne road. At PIONEER EXTENSION (092JNE 009) small dumps are found above the road at 13 km.

Access to upper Cadwallader Creek beyond Pioneer has been closed off at the PIONEER mine bridge. The result is that the only route to the valley to the S is now via the Upper Level Road. To reach this from Gold Bridge, drive a few km S toward Bralorne, and take the unpaved road left (E) where the main road paving ends, at the top of the zig-zags. A road sign indicates Lost, Noel, Kingdom and Mead lakes.

---

5. MINFILE NUMBER: 092JNE113
NAME(S): CADWALLADER CREEK

Status:	Showing	Northing:	5623869
Latitude:	50 46 06	Easting:	516258
Longitude:	122 46 10	Elevation:	1280 m
Comments:	Located beyond the Pioneer mine. Incidentally, E.		
	Cadwallader (there seems to be no record of what "E"		

stood for) was an experienced Scottish prospector who led a team of Italian miners into the area in 1863 (the time of the great gold rush up the Fraser River). He appears to have been an influential character, because he was grubstaked by a public subscription from Lillooet, plus £50 from Governor Douglas.

Commodities: Talc, chromium

MINERALS

Significant: Talc, chromite, magnetite

The CADWALLADER CREEK talc showing occurs in sediments consisting of chert and argillite. Serpentinite also occurs. Generally, the talc is associated with approximately equal amounts of ankerite and contains serpentine, disseminated sulfides (mostly pyrite), magnetite and chromite. The colour varies from creamy white to dark reddish purple.

In the PIONEER EXTENSION workings, a shaft cuts through 30 m of highly talcose rock lying beneath an albitic dyke. Nodules of chert and argillite are found within the talc bed. A 30 m wide zone of talc rock is also found on the N border of a serpentinite belt separating the altered ultramafics from soda-granite. Albite dykes intrude the talcose zones.

---

6.   MINFILE NUMBER: 092JNE044
       NAME(S): CHALCO 12

Status:	Showing	Northing:	5619027
Latitude:	50 43 28	Easting:	525549
Longitude:	122 38 17	Elevation:	1783 m

150 m up-slope of CHALCO 5. Limestone lenses in the schist are altered to skarn; they contain massive chalcopyrite and smaller masses of pyrite and pyrrhotite with associated blebs of quartz and green diopside. Well crystallized garnet and epidote occur with scattered grains of scheelite throughout the veins.

The CHALCO 5 site is located along Piebiter Creek, E of its confluence with Cadwallader Creek, at the 19 km marker on the Cadwallader ML. A 4WD track leaves the Cadwallader Creek road just N of Piebiter Creek. The upper workings (CHALCO 12: 092JNE044) can be seen on the N side of Piebiter Creek, from the open cut 500 m further S along Cadwallader Creek Road.

The area is underlain mainly by hornblendite and limestone, in contact with the Bendor pluton to the NW. A NW-trending belt of serpentinite separates hornblendite from Bridge River metasediments to the W. At least five skarn zones occur in laminated hornblendite and crystalline limestone, within 300 m of the Bendor pluton contact. Mineralization consists of

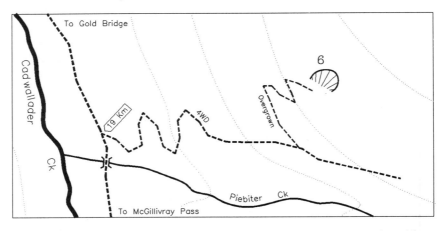

chalcopyrite and scheelite with minor molybdenite in quartz-diopside-garnet-epidote skarn. Exploration in 1969 defined a zone up to 50 m long and 3 m by 4 m wide, with grades of over 6% copper, 2% tungsten trioxide and 85 gm/t silver.

McGillivray Pass is often closed by a gate beyond Piebiter Creek. There are reports of significant magnesite, silver, galena, pitchblende and garnet deposits in the upper alpine areas.

---

7. MINFILE NUMBER: 092JNE118
NAME(S): NOEL CREEK, ROYAL JADE MINE

Status:	Past producer, open pit	Northing:	5621358
Latitude:	50 44 45	Easting:	513091
Longitude:	122 48 52	Elevation:	1530 m

Comments: Located on W side of Noel Creek, 3.5 km S of Bralorne. Follow signs to museum (in Bralorne village). Follow Lorne Street down past ballpark and bear left onto Noel ML. Road has serious tension cracks at 4 km mark. 4WD recommended. Road crosses creek on OK bridge and climbs onto W side of valley. Old cabins indicate where track climbs into alpine.

Commodities: Jade, nephrite, gold

MINERALS
Significant: Nephrite, gold
Associated: Tremolite, titanite, talc, magnesite, calcite, quartz

Jade has been quarried on the W side of Noel Creek. Two deposits have been reported. One is a "semi-nephrite" with shredded tremolite, clinozoisite and titanite, and is associated with listwanites (quartz-calcite-magnesite). The other deposit, about 300 m to the N, is a S-dipping band of semi-nephrite,

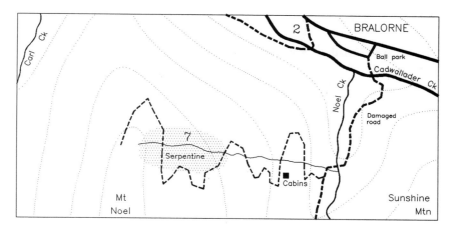

and occurs between the hanging wall and a contact zone on the footwall.

Reports on the old workings describe similar carbonate-altered serpentinite and listwanites. Possible reserves are 480 t and probable reserves are 45 t in rejected 13.5 t block-cuttings and boulders. Visible gold was said to have been found in quartz stringers in low grade jade or silicified greenstone, although recent attempts (1981) to locate such an occurrence were unsuccessful.

In 1969, several t of low grade nephrite were cut and sold from the west side of Noel Creek. During the early 1970s, Harry Street (owner) was reported to be producing jade from a contact zone between diorite and ultramafic rocks.

9.9.6 SOUTH OF CARPENTER LAKE

To reach the road on S side of Carpenter Lake, take any one of the three streets in Gold Bridge, which converge on the E side of town. The lake road is an active (and good) logging road, although narrow.

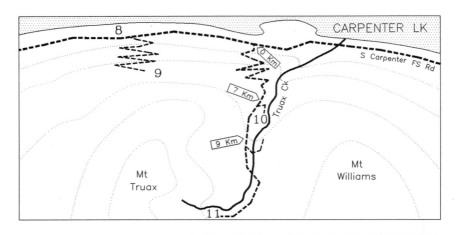

8. **MINFILE NUMBER: 092JNE152**
    NAME(S): ENIGMA

Status:	Prospect	Northing:	5637960
Latitude:	50 53 42	Easting:	518620
Longitude:	122 44 07	Elevation:	945 m

Comments: Vein exposed in trench on shore of Carpenter Lake.
Commodities: Gold, antimony

MINERALS
Significant: Stibnite, pyrite, arsenopyrite
Associated: Calcite

A stibnite vein is exposed in a trench on the S shore of Carpenter Lake, about 8.5 km E of Gold Bridge. The vein is within brecciated ribbon chert, and is composed of quartz and orange-brown calcite, with up to 70% of the vein occupied by bladed to massive stibnite, with small amounts of interstitial arsenopyrite. Minor fine-grained pyrite is present along vein margins. Both quartz and calcite are vuggy. Vein margins are sharp but not foliated. Red staining on vein material is probably kermesite (after stibnite).

9. **MINFILE NUMBER: 092JNE130**
   NAME(S): OLYMPIC, HILLSIDE

Status:	Prospect	Northing:	5637596
Latitude:	50 53 30	Easting:	519537
Longitude:	122 43 20	Elevation:	990 m

Comments: Location on S side of Carpenter Lake, about 8.5 km NE of Gold Bridge. First few hundred metres of the track are the worst. Thereafter the quality improves up a long line of switchbacks. Fantastic views of Carpenter Lake. At the mine, numerous dilapidated buildings are scattered around in the forest.

Commodities: Antimony, gold

MINERALS
Significant: Stibnite, arsenopyrite, pyrrhotite
Associated: Quartz, carbonate

The No. 1 adit zone follows a steeply dipping, SE-trending, brecciated shear zone at the faulted contact between andesitic and silicic tuffs, crystalline carbonates and diorite. Two parallel, narrow, quartz-carbonate veins follow the shear and are heavily mineralized with large stibnite crystals and finely scattered arsenopyrite and pyrrhotite.

10. **MINFILE NUMBER: 092JNE067**
    NAME(S): MARY MAC (MAIN/NORTH)

Status:	Past producer, underground	Northing:	5633899
Latitude:	50 51 30	Easting:	521995
Longitude:	122 41 15	Elevation:	1372 m

Comments: From the end of the blacktop in Gold Bridge, go 11.5 km along S side of Carpenter Lake before turning S up Truax Creek. Good 2WD road climbs via many switchbacks up steep slopes to upper Truax valley, which is flat. Pass claim posts at 18.6 km. The Truax road is km-posted from turnoff at Carpenter Lake. A steeply dropping track (4WD) between 7 km and 8 km posts takes you down to the creek (400 m) and the crumbling mine buildings.

Commodities: Gold, antimony, molybdenum, silver, copper

MINERALS
Significant: Stibnite, molybdenite, arsenopyrite, pyrrhotite, chalcopyrite, silver
Associated: Quartz, carbonate

There are two distinct types of occurrences: earlier molybdenum mineralization, followed by later stibnite-gold mineralization. The molybdenum is concentrated along the margins of quartz stringers, forming a reticulate pattern in the hornblende feldspar porphyry. The mineralization extends into the host rock, where molybdenum is fine-grained and appears as a purplish gray sheen.

The gold-bearing quartz-carbonate-stibnite veins transect all the rock types; they are well defined in the volcanics, and become more diffuse as they crosscut the porphyry stockwork. The veins range from 0.5 m to 2 m in width and trend WNW, with the dykes, fractures and shears all following. Mineralization consists of massive, coarsely crystalline stibnite with associated gold, arsenopyrite, pyrrhotite, chalcopyrite, limonite and traces of tetrahedrite and/or jamesonite. High but spotty values of silver are reported.

Chloritic alteration is widespread with local sericite and abundant pyrite. The main zone is about 100 m wide. The N zone was the source of ore used in an antimony mill, which operated in 1974, producing about 4 t of rough stibnite concentrate per day. The grade was reported at 20%. Other workings on the property include several adits.

II. MINFILE NUMBER: 092JNE066
NAME(S): GRAY ROCK

Status:	Past producer, underground		
Latitude:	50 48 15	Northing:	5627872
Longitude:	122 41 55	Easting:	521237
Elevation:	2130 m		
Comments:	At headwaters of Truax Creek. Road becomes 4WD for last few km.		
Commodities:	Silver, antimony, lead, zinc, gold, copper		

MINERALS

Significant:	Stibnite, galena, pyrite, copper, sphalerite, arsenopyrite, realgar, tetrahedrite
Associated:	Quartz

Metasediments of graywacke, hornfels, minor conglomerates, recrystallized chert breccia and silicified limestone and volcanics are intruded by dykes of granodiorite, aplite, granite, quartz diorite and quartz latite. Quartz-filled parallel fissures cut both metasediments and dykes. The mineralized veins are found mainly in the meta-graywacke.

There are three main veins that strike NE, varying in width from several centimetres to 2 m, with numerous minor offshoots. The main (No. 1) vein is continuous for at least 120 m, averaging 1 m in width. The mineralization occurs in lenticular masses and is constant throughout the length of the vein. Stibnite occurs as disseminations and streaks in the quartz gangue and as massive layers on the vein walls. Smaller amounts of pyrite, grey copper with associated silver, sphalerite, galena, arsenopyrite, tetrahedrite and fuchsite are found in the No. 1 vein. Nos. 2 and 3 veins contain only discontinuous lenses of high grade stibnite.

Ore reserves proved 4% antimony, 2% lead and 340g/t silver. In 1951, over 3 t of antimony were recovered from 7 t of sorted ore. There are two adits (at 1,950 m and 2,050 m) with "several hundred feet" of drifting on the No. 1 vein. There are numerous nearby prospects; all are located near the head (S end) of Truax and Fergusson creeks. Some well-formed quartz crystals up to 15 cm in length have reportedly been found in the area.

The showing TRUAX (092JNE059) is directly SE of Mount Truax, W of Truax Creek and N of GRAY ROCK. Three parallel quartz veins in a shear zone contain stibnite and arsenopyrite, with associated gold values.

9.10. HOPE – MERRITT

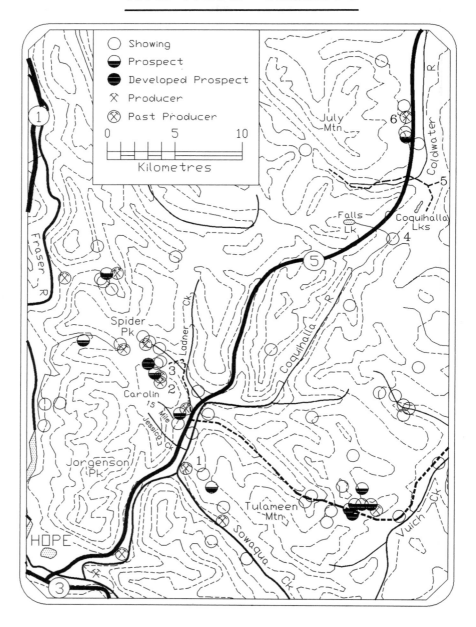

9.10.1 COQUIHALLA HIGHWAY

Ultramafic rocks are rich in magnesium and iron, so olivine and pyroxene are common. When altered, they form serpentine, and are associated with deposits of asbestos, nickel, chrome and jade. In the case of jade, the weathered exterior rarely resembles the glossy material seen in art galleries. In the field, jade is recognized by a platy or fibrous surface. The mineral is translucent when viewed through a thin section. BC jade is formed from fibres of nephrite, and it is these that give jade its great toughness (resistance to breaking). Toughness is not the same as hardness (which is resistance to scratching). Jade boulders have been found in both the Fraser and Coquihalla rivers, derived no doubt from the serpentine belt that runs NW–SE, cutting the rivers at Nahatlatch and Sowaqua creeks respectively.

The Sowaqua Valley formed part of the Hudson Bay Company's Hope–Brigade Trail, with the turnoff to the Ghost Pass Trail leading to the Sumallo River and S, coming out at Manning Park. Placer claims (092HSW148, Lat 49 24 30, Long 121 13 16) were located along Sowaqua Creek, beginning about 4 km above the junction of the creek with the Coquihalla River, and extending back about 4.5 km. The road on the N side of the creek is narrow, steep, exposed, and in 1997, was an active logging area. Further, it traverses the slope 500 m above the creek, and does not offer easy access to the river below.

The creek flows through the Coquihalla Serpentine Belt, which is comprised chiefly of serpentine intersected by a number of both large and small dykes, or less regular masses of diorite and a few dykes of quartz-porphyry. In the 1920s, considerable surface sluicing was done with several open cuts and trenching along the low benches along the creek.

---

1. **MINFILE NUMBER: 092HSW097**
   NAME(S): STEVEN, JADE KING 2

Status:	Past producer, open pit	Northing:	5478224
Latitude:	49 26 44	Easting:	626130
Longitude:	121 15 36	Elevation:	380 m

Comments: The original deposit was discovered by a bulldozer operator when a pipeline was laid down the valley. The jade quarry was just E of Highway #5, where Sowaqua Creek joins the Coquihalla River. A new development at the junction of Sowaqua Creek and Coquihalla River (15 cottages) may make access better or worse.

Commodities: Jade, nephrite

MINERALS

Significant: Nephrite

Associated: Talc, serpentine, quartz, pyrite

A small amount of nephrite was mined from a rock quarry 100 m SE of the Coquihalla Highway. Jade occurs in serpentinite-filled fault zones cutting ribbon cherts and basaltic volcanics. One such zone exposed in the old rock quarry, the West Zone, trends N, and pinches and swells over short distances. Widths vary from 0.5 m to 1.5 m. The zone can be subdivided as follows from west to east:

1) Highly altered chert and quartz lenses and veins, minor pyrite
2) Talc and serpentinite
3) Nephrite jade seams and lenses
4) Serpentinite
5) Altered basaltic volcanics and chert.

The serpentinite is comprised of black to dark green, highly sheared and abundantly slickensided, massive to foliated serpentine. Near the surface, jade is recovered as plates 2 cm to 5 cm thick. The jade consists of apple-green, translucent, fracture-free, mottled nephrite of jewelry grade with very few impurities. R. Fulbrook of Vernon periodically quarried jade from this deposit between the late 1970s and 1987, but no production figures are available.

---

2. MINFILE NUMBER: 092HNW003
NAME(S): AURUM MINE

Status:	Past producer, underground		
Latitude:	49 30 17	Northing:	5484769
Longitude:	121 16 47	Easting:	624550
Elevation:	1000 m		
Comments:	Mine, located on the SW fork of Ladner Creek.		
Commodities:	Gold, silver, talc, copper, soapstone		

MINERALS

Significant:	Arsenopyrite, gold, talc, chalcopyrite, pyrrhotite, pyrite, millerite
Associated:	Quartz, calcite

The mine operated intermittently from 1928–42. Some 500 m S of the CAROLIN MINE (092HNW007), which mined the Idaho deposit until 1984, the AURUM MINE is hosted in a NW, trending belt of serpentinite that is badly sheared and altered to talc over an average width of a few metres. The talc seam, which hosts other gold ore bodies, has been followed by many metres of workings. High grade mineralization occurs in ore shoots hosted by a "talc seam" or talc schist on the serpentinite contact.

The talc is mottled, mostly impure, foliated, light gray to dark green and free of grit. It has a smooth greasy slip in powdered form. Impurities with the talc include sulfides, imperfectly altered serpentine and minor amounts of quartz and calcite.

Gold occurs primarily as free gold and is coarse-grained. It also occurs associated with one or more of pyrrhotite, pyrite, chalcopyrite, arsenopyrite and possibly millerite. The gold and associated sulfides commonly occur as very thin, polished films over slickensided surfaces of serpentinite and talcose rock. Gold also occurs as plates, thin wedges or irregular prongs, and as small, roughly corrugated beads distributed sporadically in the more massive bodies of the talcose rock. The arsenopyrite forms well-defined bands, up to 1 cm in width, separated by partings of calcite, quartz and foliated talc. Native gold favours some of these bands and occurs either scattered or as thin, vein-like segregations of particles varying from dust-like points to grains, short wire or leaves of more substantial size. Apparently, soapstone production from this location was attempted in 1932.

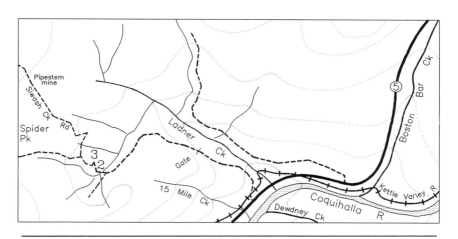

3.   MINFILE NUMBER: 092HNW007
NAME(S): CAROLIN MINE

Status:	Past producer, underground		
Latitude:	49 30 32	Northing:	5485225
Longitude:	121 17 15	Easting:	623975
Elevation:	1036 m		
Comments:	Portal is 4 km SSE of the summit of Spider Peak. Road is posted on Highway #5—steep and 4WD only. A gate at 3 km may be locked, as the area is currently under claim.		
Commodities:	Gold, silver, copper, zinc		

MINERALS

Significant: Pyrrhotite, arsenopyrite, pyrite, chalcopyrite, bornite, gold, sphalerite

Mineralization at CAROLIN MINE is characterized by sulfide disseminations and veinlets, deformed, multi-phase quartz veins, and intense albitic alteration; however, not all areas containing these features are enriched in gold. Opaque minerals make up to 15% of the ore; these are, in decreasing order of abundance, pyrrhotite, arsenopyrite, pyrite, magnetite, chalcopyrite, bornite and gold. Traces of sphalerite occur sporadically. Visible gold occurs as inclusions in the pyrite and arsenopyrite crystals, or as rims on the pyrite and chalcopyrite. Gold is also found independent of the sulfides as minute grains within some quartz, calcite and feldspar crystals.

Milling of ore began in 1981 and closed in 1984, due to poor gold recoveries, environmental concerns and low gold prices.

4. MINFILE NUMBER: 092HNW067
NAME(S): COQUIHALLA

Status:	Showing	Northing:	5499471
Latitude:	49 38 00	Easting:	640811
Longitude:	121 03 00	Elevation:	1500 m

Comments: Exposed along abandoned Kettle Valley Railway cutting.
Commodities: Mica, feldspar, silica

MINERALS
Significant: Orthoclase, quartz, muscovite

Pegmatites are a common occurrence in the Eagle granodiorite. These are exposed along the railway cuttings between Coquihalla and Romeo and have been observed on both sides of the Coquihalla River at various points. The pegmatites are up to several metres wide, and consist of pink orthoclase, milky quartz and muscovite. The coarser varieties contain crystals up to 4 cm long.

5. MINFILE NUMBER: 092HNE006
NAME(S): INDEPENDENCE

Status:	Prospect	Northing:	5500160
Latitude:	49 38 17	Easting:	646880
Longitude:	120 57 57	Elevation:	1649 m

Comments: Portal of the main adit is 1 km SW of the summit of Mt Henning, 2.3 km E of Coquihalla Lakes. Turn off Highway #5 at Exit 228.
Commodities: Copper, molybdenum, zinc, gold, silver

MINERALS
Significant: Pyrite, chalcopyrite, molybdenite, sphalerite, chalcocite, tetrahedrite, cuprite
Associated: Quartz, pyrrhotite

The area at the headwaters of Henning Creek is underlain to the W by foliated granodiorite and to the E by metavolcanics (foliated greenstone), which are intruded along the contact by a dyke-like body of quartz-feldspar-biotite porphyry. The body trends NNW for 4 km and is up to 400 m wide. This is in turn cut by feldspar porphyry dykes. The porphyries are mineralized with disseminations of pyrite, chalcopyrite and minor molybdenite.

The deposit has been periodically assessed by various operators since first being staked in 1901. It was explored underground between 1906 and 1908, when more than 300 m of tunnelling was completed.

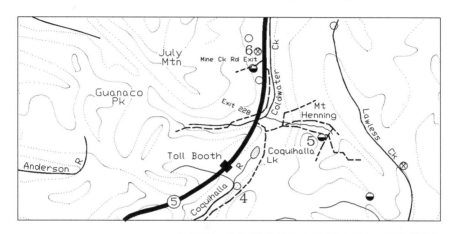

6.   MINFILE NUMBER: 092HNW024
NAME(S): KEYSTONE

Status:	Past producer, underground	Northing:	5506175
Latitude:	49 41 35	Easting:	642550
Longitude:	121 01 25	Elevation:	1300 m

Comments: Location right off Highway #5, 4.5 km N of the toll booth. Take Mine Creek Road exit. Widespread manganese staining is reported within the shear zone.

Commodities: Silver, gold, zinc, lead

MINERALS

Significant: Pyrite, sphalerite, galena, hematite, tetrahedrite, chalcopyrite, magnetite

Associated: Quartz, carbonate, rhodochrosite, calcite

The mine is located on the W side of the Coldwater River, approximately 6 km N of the Coquihalla Lakes. Base and precious metal mineralization were originally discovered in the early 1900s, and underground development had taken place by 1936. The only production from the mine occurred in 1955, when 81 t of ore were shipped.

The KEYSTONE mine is situated near the centre of a quartz diorite stock, which has been estimated to be approximately 1300 m by 2200 m. The S half of the stock is brecciated, as is the older granodiorite adjacent to it. In the area of the mine, rhodochrosite, sphalerite and hematite with galena and minor chalcopyrite and magnetite occur with or without quartz(-carbonate) as veins, veinlets and stringers in shears and brecciated zones. Erratically distributed gold and silver values reportedly occur with the quartz.

The dominant structure shows conspicuous rock alteration and manganese (black) staining. This extends from an adit (092HNW034 and 092HNW023) on Mine Creek NE past the KEYSTONE mine, attaining widths in excess of 150 m.

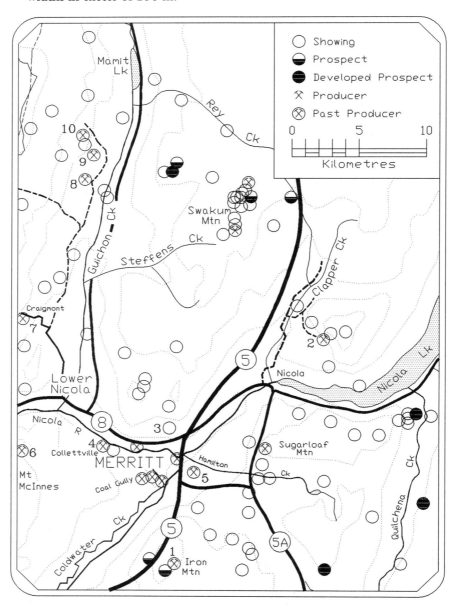

9.10.2 MERRITT AREA

The Promontory Hills are underlain by steeply dipping volcanics. They are bounded to the N by the Guichon Creek batholith (which hosts the Highland Valley and Bethlehem mines) and covered by extensive gravel overburden.

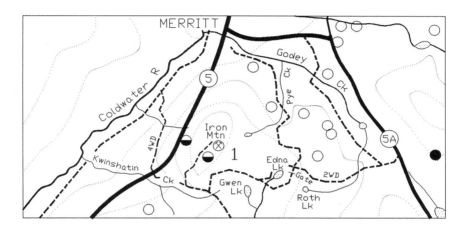

1. **MINFILE NUMBER: 092ISE052**
   NAME(S): LEADVILLE, IRON MOUNTAIN

Status:	Past Producer	Northing:	5545000
Latitude:	50 02 16	Easting:	660172
Longitude:	120 45 48	Elevation:	1633 m

   Comments: Iron Mountain lies within the W belt of the Nicola Group, consisting mainly of an E-facing sequence of calc-alkaline flows which grade upward into pyroclastic rocks, epiclastic sediments and limestone.

   Commodities: Lead, zinc, silver, copper

   MINERALS

   Significant: Galena, sphalerite, barite, specularite, chalcopyrite, malachite, azurite

   Associated: Barite, quartz specularite

In the vicinity of the Leadville deposit are brown/pink feldspar-rich dacite and rhyolite flows, flow breccias, and white to green rhyolite. These units are interbedded with amygdaloidal andesite agglomerate, tuff and breccia. Mineralization consists of specularite and chalcopyrite in irregular fractures, scattered randomly in a 600 m diameter zone. Malachite and azurite staining are present. The average copper grade was less than 0.1%. Felsic units host galena and sphalerite mineralization in barite veins.

The LEADVILLE shaft was sunk on a zone of banded veins and bedded lead-zinc-barite in sheared, flow-banded rhyolite. The mineralized zone was over 50 m long and less than 1 m wide.

---

2. MINFILE NUMBER: 092ISE055
NAME(S):TURLIGHT

Status:	Past producer, underground		
Latitude:	50 11 35	Northing:	5562614
Longitude:	120 36 30	Easting:	670713
Elevation:	1214 m		
Comments:	Turn N through Nicola onto the Clapperton Ck Rd.		
Commodities:	Copper, silver, gold		

MINERALS
Significant: Bornite, chalcopyrite, chalcocite, malachite
Associated: Quartz

The property is located near the SW perimeter of the Nicola batholith, which locally consists of gneissic granodiorite to quartz monzonite. To the SW the batholith intrudes intermediate rocks and sediments belonging to the Nicola Group. Shear zones contain lenses of mineralized vein matter.

It consists of an inclined shaft 140 m deep, underground workings on six levels and several trenches. At the shaft, copper mineralization occurs in a quartz vein up to 1.5 m wide with well-defined walls. The quartz hosts irregular masses, veinlets and disseminated grains of bornite, chalcopyrite, minor chalcocite and some malachite.

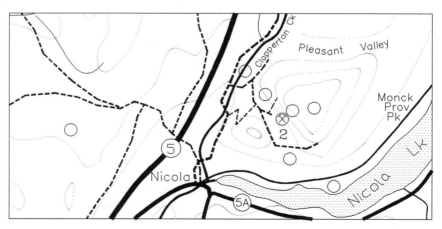

3. **MINFILE NUMBER: 092ISE140**
    NAME(S): MERRITT GYPSUM

Status:	Past producer, open pit	Northing:	5553882
Latitude:	50 07 06	Easting:	657159
Longitude:	120 48 06	Elevation:	670 m
Commodities:	Gypsum		

MINERALS

Significant:	Gypsum, coal
Associated:	Calcite

Immediately to the N of Merritt, sedimentary beds overlie the Nicola Group volcanics. The sediments consist of sandstone, conglomerate, shale and local coal seams. On the benches of the hills, gypsum occurs as irregular patches exposed by erosion. Pockets vary in thickness up to 3 m. Calcite, sand and vegetable matter vary the purity of the gypsum. Shipments of 450 t were reported in 1911. Since then the trenches and pits have filled with debris.

4. **MINFILE NUMBER: 092ISE121**
    NAME(S): COPPER BELLE

Status:	Past producer, underground		
Latitude:	50 07 18	Northing:	5554183
Longitude:	120 50 06	Easting:	654765
Elevation:	671 m		
Comments:	S side of Nicola River, about 4 km W of Merritt through Collettville on the Linley Ck Rd.		
Commodities:	Copper, silver		

MINERALS

Significant:	Chalcopyrite, specularite, rutile
Associated:	Quartz, calcite

The COPPER BELLE mine lies in rocks which consist of andesitic and basaltic flows, minor volcanics, sediments and granite/gabbro intrusives. The orebody runs E and consists of quartz and calcite with specular hematite, chalcopyrite and copper carbonates. Mineralized outcrops occur as discontinuous lenses 5 cm to 60 cm wide and 1 m to 9 m long. The deposit has been developed by four adits, shallow inclined shafts, and open cuts which expose fracture zones up to 1.5 m wide. One such cut contains rutile-bearing quartz with chalcopyrite, hematite and calcite, is 45 cm wide and is exposed for a length of 3 m.

5. MINFILE NUMBER: 092ISE058
NAME(S): MERRITT COAL

Status:	Past producer, underground		
Latitude:	50 06 03	Northing:	5552063
Longitude:	120 44 34	Easting:	661427
Commodities:	Coal	Elevation:	663 m

Up to ten coal seams containing high volatile bituminous coal occur in the Coldwater Formation interbedded with sandstone, shale and conglomerate. The seam numbers and thicknesses vary across the Merritt coal field, with seams lensing out into shale laterally, and commonly containing seam splits. The best outcrop of the coal measures occurs in the COAL GULLY area (092ISE066), where four seams are present in a 230 m section. In the adjacent MIDDLESBORO mines (092ISE081), up to eight seams 0.5 m to 8 m thick were recognized in 235 m of section. In the NORMANDALE area (092ISE061), two holes drilled in 1982 intersected six and eight coal seams, ranging in thickness from 0.2 m to 2 m. A small tonnage was mined from this area in the early 1900s.

South of Merritt, three coal seams outcrop in the Coldwater Hill area. In addition, several shaly coal units are present. The No. 2 mine (092ISE081) was located here. E of the town and S of the Nicola River, are the DIAMOND VALE No. 3 and 4 mines (092ISE142). Six coal seams occurred in 100 m of strata, of which two were mined by the above mentioned mines. In total, nearly 2.7 million t of thermal coal were mined (underground) from the coalfields from 1906 until the late 1950s.

Both the W and E margins of the basin appear to be structurally most complex. The basin overlies a volcanic surface and is partially overlain by younger basalts. Measured geological reserves for the Merritt coalfield are 10 million t, and inferred reserves are 40 million t.

---

6. MINFILE NUMBER: 092ISE148
NAME(S): LAW

Status:	Past producer, open pit	Northing:	5553259
Latitude:	50 06 54	Easting:	648353
Longitude:	120 55 30	Elevation:	1250 m
Commodities:	Copper, lead, zinc, gold, silver		

MINERALS

Significant::	Chalcopyrite, pyrite, bornite, specularite, sphalerite, magnetite

The NE slopes of Mount McInnes are underlain primarily by a succession of andesitic and basaltic flows with interbedded volcanic breccia, tuff and sandstone. Volcanics and sedimentary rocks and dioritic intrusions are exposed N of the Nicola River and in the valley of an unnamed creek W of Logan Creek. The rocks are intensely altered. Lenses of crystalline limestone host skarn. A dark gray, 3 m wide, diabase dyke strikes NE, and contains minor magnetite, chalcopyrite and specular hematite along widely spaced fine fractures. Small sphalerite veinlets and weak disseminations of pyrite, chalcopyrite and bornite are exposed at widely separated locations in Nicola Group rocks and their skarn equivalents.

---

7. MINFILE NUMBER: 092ISE035
NAME(S): CRAIGMONT MINE

Status:	Producer, open pit/Underground		
Latitude:	50 12 27	Northing:	5563533
Longitude:	120 55 29	Easting:	648090
Elevation:	1220 m		
Comments:	Centre of open pit.		
Commodities:	Copper, iron, silver, gold		

MINERALS
Significant: Magnetite, chalcopyrite, specularite, copper, chalcocite, bornite, calcite, hematite
Associated: Pyrite

In the vicinity of the mine, the Guichon Creek batholith varies in composition from quartz diorite to granodiorite. These rocks intrude a thick volcanic and sedimentary series of agglomerate, breccia, andesitic flows, limestone, argillite and graywacke. The mine lies next to the S margin of the batholith. Five main orebodies are confined to a limy horizon between walls of graywacke and andesite. Mineralization consists of magnetite, hematite and chalcopyrite, occurring as massive pods and lenses extending through that horizon. Chalcopyrite commonly encloses the magnetite, and is the principal ore mineral, occurring as veins and streaks. Bornite is present in small amounts. Pyrite is confined to areas of heavy garnet alteration. Approximately 20% of the ore (by weight) comprised magnetite and hematite, and occurred in the skarn.

The original Craigmont copper mine went into production in 1962, with underground mining ceasing in February 1982, as a result of the falling price of copper. The concentrator remained in operation processing the iron ore stockpiles until November 1982, when it was also shut down.

From 1962–1970, the operators did not recover the magnetite in the milling process; there was thus an estimated 5 million t of magnetite in the tailings deposit. Since ceasing production in 1982, magnetite has been shipped from the stockpiles to western coal producers, to be used in their heavy media separation process.

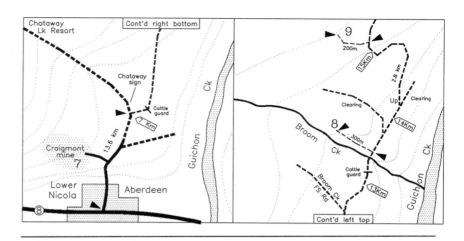

8. MINFILE NUMBER: 092ISE024
NAME(S): ABERDEEN

Status:	Past producer, underground		
Latitude:	50 18 13	Northing:	5574375
Longitude:	120 51 26	Easting:	652592
Elevation:	1036 m		

Comments: Access is not possible off Highway #97C on the E side of Guichon Creek. Approach on the W side of the creek from the S via Lower Nicola past the Craigmont Mine. Leave the Chataway Lake Resort road at marker 7 km (there is a Chataway sign) by bearing R onto smaller unpaved 2WD road. This is 13.6 km after leaving Highway #8. Shortly after crossing a cattle guard (19 km from Highway #8) cross Broom Creek and turn L 300 m upstream.

Commodities: Copper, silver, gold

MINERALS
Significant: Chalcocite, specularite, copper, chalcopyrite, pyrite, bornite, malachite

Associated: Tourmaline, quartz, hematite

The ABERDEEN deposit lies along a mass of greenstone between two coarse joint planes in the plutonic rocks. A series of high-grade lenses occur in a fracture zone to a depth of 30 m. The mine was developed by a vertical shaft from which levels were run at depths of 15 m, 30 m, 45 m and 60 m. Several of these drifts are reported to be 125 m long.

9. MINFILE NUMBER: 092ISE023
NAME(S): VIMY MINE

Status:	Past producer, underground	Northing:	5576406
Latitude:	50 19 18	Easting:	653181
Longitude:	120 50 53	Elevation:	1071 m
Comments:	Access is from the S through Lower Nicola off Highway #8.		
Commodities:	Copper, gold, silver, molybdenum		

MINERALS

Significant: Bornite, copper, chalcocite, chalcopyrite, covellite, cuprite, specularite

The VIMY MINE is located on the E side of an unnamed stream which flows S into Broom Creek. The area is underlain by the Guichon Creek batholith which intrudes volcanic rocks in the E. Mineralization is found as sprinklings and veinlets of bornite, native copper, chalcocite and chalcopyrite, with minor covellite and cuprite concentrated in a zone of intense brecciation and alteration at the intersection of N and NW trending faults.

10. MINFILE NUMBER: 092ISE063
NAME(S): WIZ, CHATAWAY

Status:	Past producer, underground	Northing:	5577849
Latitude:	50 20 06	Easting:	652297
Longitude:	120 51 36	Elevation:	1377 m
Commodities:	Copper, molybdenum, silver, gold		

MINERALS

Significant: Chalcocite, chalcopyrite, bornite, copper, malachite, azurite, pyrite, molybdenite

Associated: Quartz, carbonate

The property is located S of Gypsum Lake, near the SE border of the Guichon Creek batholith. The area is underlain by granodiorite, which represents the oldest rocks in the batholith. The bedrock varies from fine-grained quartz monzodiorite to coarse-grained granodiorite. Copper mineralization occurs in a strong shear zone which strikes N. The length of the zone is greater than a km, though drill results indicate significant mineralization is confined to about half this distance. The shear zone comprises a number of near-parallel, steeply dipping faults, quartz and carbonate pods, gouge and breccia. High grade mineralization consists of massive chalcocite, blebs and stringers of chalcopyrite, bornite, native copper, malachite and azurite, and numerous secondary copper minerals in clay gouge and quartz-filled tension fractures. Mineralization is cut off to the N by the Gypsum Lake fault, and the grade also decreases to the S.

9.11. EAST OF MERRITT

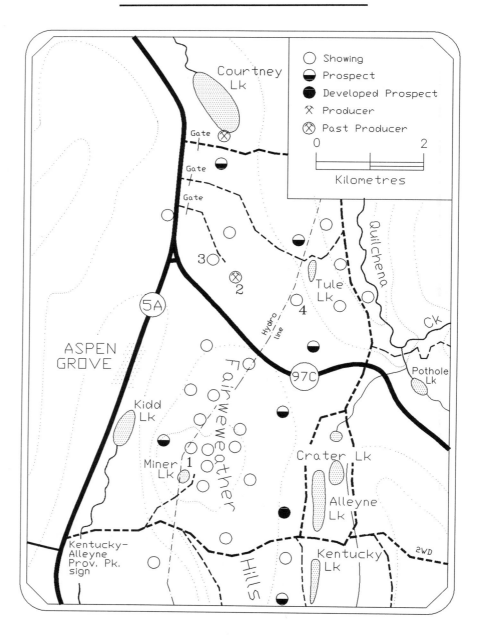

9.11.1 ASPEN GROVE

Aspen Grove lies in the Central belt, which mainly consists of red or purple/green porphyritic, andesitic and basaltic flows, volcanic breccia and tuff, and minor argillite and limestone. The volcanics are locally intruded by bodies of diorite. The region is characterized by mostly N-striking faults and fracturing. Two important fault systems in the area, the Kentucky–Alleyne fault and the Allison fault, converge just S of Courtenay Lake, which is N of the Okanagon Connector (Highway #8).

Aspen Grove is a collection of houses, with no services. The best place to stay, which also offers good access to the mineral area along the Fairweather Hills, is the Kentucky–Alleyne Provincial Park. From there, drive or walk to Miner Lake, where there are numerous old adits, cuttings and trenches along the crest of the hill.

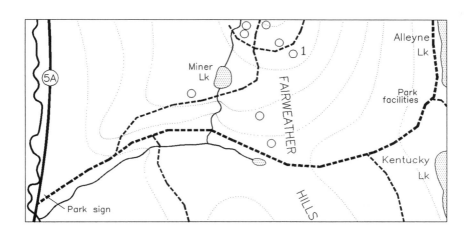

I. **MINFILE NUMBER: 092HNE084**
   NAME(S): CINCINNATI

Status:	Developed prospect	Northing:	5531610
Latitude:	49 54 49	Easting:	673710
Longitude:	120 34 50	Elevation:	1204 m

Comments: Centre of an area of trenching and tunnelling, 1 km NW of the S end of Alleyne Lake, and 3 km NNW of the S end of Kentucky Lake. Access road leads off park road 1 km in from Highway #5A.

Commodities: Copper, silver

MINERALS

Significant: Chalcocite, copper, chalcopyrite, bornite, cuprite
Alteration: Malachite, azurite, pyrite

The area is underlain by volcanics and associated diorite to monzonite intrusions. Locally, the area is underlain by red and green breccias, andesite porphyry and minor sediments. Mineralization consists primarily of chalcocite and native copper, accompanied by lesser malachite and azurite. Mineralization is exposed along the crest and E flank of a small N-trending ridge, over a N–S distance of 400 m. The Cincinnati deposit was first explored in the early 1900s. A number of trenches, and one adit 120 m long, were excavated between 1899 and 1913.

---

2. MINFILE NUMBER: 092HNE073
NAME(S): BIG SIOUX

Status:	Past producer, open pit, underground		
Latitude:	49 57 08	Northing:	5535860
Longitude:	120 36 03	Easting:	672100
Elevation:	1134 m		
Comments:	Cribbed shaft N of Highway #8 just E of the Aspen Grove interchange. Follow the hydro cables.		
Commodities:	Copper, gold, silver		

MINERALS

Significant:	Pyrite, chalcopyrite, chalcocite, bornite
Associated:	Calcite, epidote

The deposit is located at the N end of an area of hilly upland known as the Fairweather Hills. These are underlain by porphyritic pyroclastics and flows, and associated diorite intrusions. Locally, the area is underlain by red and green breccias, andesite porphyry and minor sediments. Copper mineralization is exposed in a 300 m long roadcut and in various old workings N of the roadcut, in an area 500 m by 300 m. Mineralization consists primarily of pyrite and chalcopyrite. Pyrite also forms thin bands, comprising up to 25% of the host rock. Malachite occurs along fractures in many surface exposures. Chalcocite forms fracture fillings in one prominent 2 m wide shear zone.

This deposit was one of the first showings to be explored in the Aspen Grove copper camp, and was staked in 1899. A shaft 10 m deep, an adit 45 m long, and numerous pits and trenches were excavated from 1900–14. Over 40 t of ore were shipped in 1918, grading almost 10% copper. The occurrence was re-staked in 1989, after copper mineralization was exposed in a roadcut along the N side of the recently completed Okanagan Connector (Highway #8).

3. **MINFILE NUMBER: 092HNE075**
    NAME(S): MAGGIE

Status:	Showing	Northing:	5535940
Latitude:	49 57 11	Easting:	671700
Longitude:	120 36 23	Elevation:	1103 m

Situated W of BIG SIOUX. Pyrite and chalcopyrite occur disseminated in green/gray fractured and sheared andesite. The fractures are occasionally filled with yellowish white serpentine or white chalcedony. A shaft, 15 m deep, was excavated in the mineralized shear zone 1901–05.

4. **MINFILE NUMBER: 092HNE181**
    NAME(S): ASPEN GROVE AGATE

Status:	Showing	Northing:	5535230
Latitude:	49 56 47	Easting:	672650
Longitude:	120 35 37	Elevation:	1158 m

Agate is reported to outcrop along a logging road, E of Big Sioux and 1.7 km SSW of the S end of Tule Lake. Access is via closed ranching property. Ask for information in Aspen Grove. The site is described as "Drive 3 km N of Aspen Grove [past the modern junction of Hwy #97C, we assume]. Turn R up logging road about 2.2 km to a massive agate site."

9.11.2 STUMP LAKE

This historic mining camp was located on Mineral Hill, on the SE side of Stump Lake, within a belt of volcanics and sediments. Access is via Highway #5A, which is reached by turning off the Coquihalla Highway #5 at Merritt, and following, around Nicola Lake for 44 km. The greenstones consist of andesite and basalt, augite porphyry, andesitic flow breccia and tuff, and minor interbedded argillite, conglomerate and limestone.

The tuff and sedimentary beddings suggest that a syncline passes through Mineral Hill. Both W and NE of Stump Lake, the volcanics are intruded by granitic batholiths. Andesitic rocks are bleached, heavily silicified, pyritic and brecciated. Mineralization occurs in numerous quartz (and less commonly calcite) veins, which strike generally N and dip steeply E.

Access to the mineral area is via Planet Mine Road (paved) off Highway #5A. Coming from Merritt, it takes off R about 1 km after Peter Hope Road, and is through a private grazing area. From the turnoff, an old adit is visible R after 1 km. At 2 km there are two tailings dumps on R. At 3.1 km, ENTERPRISE dump is on R. Lake cottages are at 4 km.

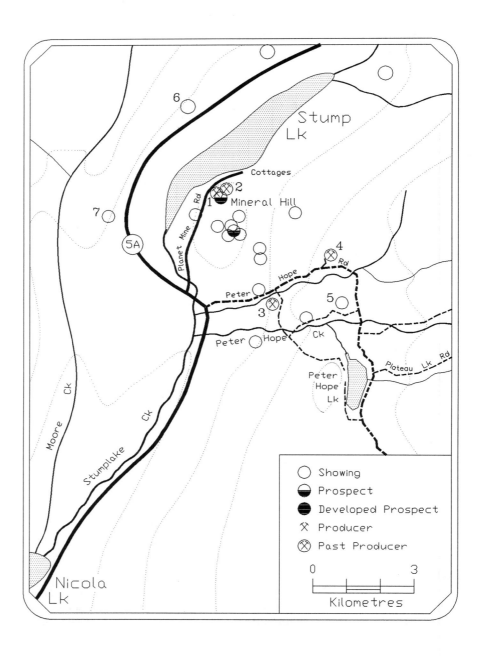

I. **MINFILE NUMBER: 092ISE028**
    NAME(S): ENTERPRISE, KING WILLIAM

Status: Past producer, underground
Latitude: 50 20 52   Northing: 5580345
Longitude: 120 23 18   Easting: 685810
Elevation: 846 m
Commodities: Silver, gold lead, zinc, copper

MINERALS
Significant: Pyrite, galena, sphalerite
Associated: Quartz, calcite

The ENTERPRISE mine consists of a 100 m deep shaft, a 230 m adit and approximately 2 km of underground development on six levels. The bottom level was extended over 400 m to the NW to intersect the TUBAL CAIN (092ISE108) and JOSHUA (092ISE109) veins. The Enterprise vein's width was generally less than 60 cm, but swelled up to 2 m. Mineralization consisted of galena, sphalerite and pyrite, with associated gold and silver values.

2. **MINFILE NUMBER: 092ISE109**
    NAME(S): JOSHUA

Status: Past producer, underground
Latitude: 50 20 57   Northing: 5580512
Longitude: 120 22 52   Easting: 686312
Elevation: 866 m
Commodities: Silver, gold lead, zinc, copper, tungsten

MINERALS
Significant: Pyrite, galena, sphalerite, chalcopyrite, tetrahedrite, scheelite
Associated: Quartz

The JOSHUA mine originally consisted of a 230 m deep shaft with workings on six levels. The Joshua vein varied in width from 5 cm to 75 cm, with numerous smaller veins and stringers feathering out. Mineralization consisted of pyrite, galena, sphalerite, chalcopyrite and tetrahedrite in variable amounts. Surface trenching has exposed similar mineralization within the altered andesites NW and SE of the Joshua shaft. Scheelite masses up to 10 cm in diameter have been found in dump material.

3. MINFILE NUMBER: 092ISE031
NAME(S): JENNY LONG

Status: Past producer, underground
Latitude: 50 18 59   Northing: 5576912
Longitude: 120 21 49   Easting: 687700
Elevation: 827 m
Comments: Peter Hope Rd is 43 km from Merritt–Highway #5 turnoff.
Commodities: Silver, lead, zinc, gold, copper, tungsten

MINERALS
Significant: Galena, sphalerite, pyrite, chalcopyrite, scheelite
Associated: Quartz

The site is located SE of Mineral Hill, off the Peter Hope Road, within a belt of intermediate volcanics and sediments. It originally consisted of an 85 m deep shaft with underground workings on three levels and several surface trenches and pits. A quartz vein system within andesitic rocks pinches and swells up to 2 m in width, but is generally less than 75 cm wide. Mineralization consists of variable amounts of galena, sphalerite, pyrite and chalcopyrite. Narrow bands of scheelite were found in quartz samples from the dump.

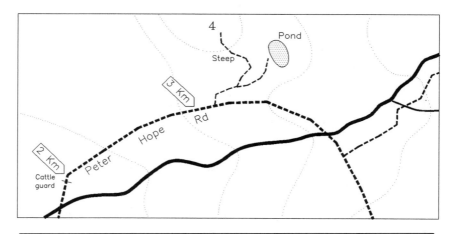

4. MINFILE NUMBER: 092ISE115
NAME(S): MARY REYNOLDS

Status: Past producer, underground
Latitude: 50 19 47   Northing: 5578470
Longitude: 120 20 22   Easting: 689360
Elevation: 1061 m
Comments: Take Peter Hope Rd 3.3 km and turn L up steep track
                (4WD) 400 m to site. Lots of old mining gear in the bush.
Commodities: Silver, lead, zinc, gold, copper

MINERALS

Significant: Pyrite, galena, sphalerite, tetrahedrite, chalcopyrite
Associated: Quartz, calcite

The property hosts a major NNE-trending, gold-silver bearing shear zone that has an overall length of 1 km and widths of 40 m to 300 m. Mineralization occurs sporadically within quartz-carbonate veining, and comprises very fine-grained pyrite, galena and sphalerite with minor tetrahedrite and chalcopyrite.

Approximately 750 m to 900 m S, old trenches and an inclined shaft have exposed a broad zone of carbonate-altered andesite hosting one or more quartz veins. Grab rock samples of quartz vein dump material mineralized with pyrite and galena assayed up to 166 gm/t silver and 2.3 gm/t gold.

Another zone is located 300 m WNW and parallel to the main zone. It covers an area of discontinuous N-trending shears, ranging from 1 m to 3 m in width, and comprises very fine-grained pyrite and minor galena.

---

5.   MINFILE NUMBER: 092ISE158
NAME(S): CIG 100

Status:	Showing	Northing:	5577000
Latitude:	50 18 59	Easting:	689750
Longitude:	120 20 05	Elevation:	1061 m
Commodities:	Copper, gold, silver, zinc		

MINERALS

Significant: Pyrite, chalcopyrite, argentite, sphalerite
Associated: Quartz vugs, carbonate, calcite

Various old workings are located in the NW corner of the property. Trenches and outcrops reveal two types of mineralization within the andesite. The first comprises occasional blebs of chalcopyrite in quartz-calcite veins, with vugs lined with quartz crystals. The second type comprises narrow quartz-calcite veins with an alteration zone where hornblende is replaced by feldspar and pyrite is evident.

6. MINFILE NUMBER: 092ISE107
NAME(S): BAG

Status:	Showing	Northing:	5582500
Latitude:	50 22 02	Easting:	685335
Longitude:	120 23 38	Elevation:	915 m

Comments: On W side of Stump Lake, about 150 m above Hwy #5A.
Commodities: Gold, silver

MINERALS
Significant: Pyrite
Associated: Quartz, chalcedony, calcite

The area is underlain by interbedded volcanics and sediments. In the SW corner of the property, rhyolites and tuffs have undergone alteration. Kaolinite clay minerals occur on either side of a quartz-chalcedony sheeted vein up to 5 m wide, which has been exposed intermittently for over 300 m. It has been suggested that this vein is the extension of the ENTER-PRISE MINE (092ISE028), 2 km SE.

At the N end of the property, numerous narrow quartz-chalcedony veins can be traced for distances up to 1200 m.

7. MINFILE NUMBER: 092ISE187
NAME(S): TIC-TAC-TOE

Status:	Showing	Northing:	5579434
Latitude:	50 20 26	Easting:	682700
Longitude:	120 25 57	Elevation:	1010 m

Commodities: Copper, silver

MINERALS
Significant: Tetrahedrite, chalcopyrite, bornite
Associated: Quartz, calcite, chalcedony, pyrite, magnetite

On the TIC-TAC-TOE occurrence, an E-trending alteration envelope, 1000 m long and up to 200 m wide, occurs along the N edge of the main ultramafic mass. This highly calcitic zone consists of rusty siderite-quartz-fuchsite rock, cut by abundant quartz-calcite stringers. Hematinic and kaolinitized sections are irregularly distributed. Stringers contain scattered tetrahedrite, chalcopyrite and pyrite, and locally give the rock a crackle breccia appearance. Banded veins up to 6 cm wide consist of alternating yellow calcite and white chalcedonic quartz bands, and contain fine specks of pyrite, chalcopyrite and tetrahedrite. Bornite was also reported in a shear 500 metres NE.

9.12. NORTH OF MERRITT

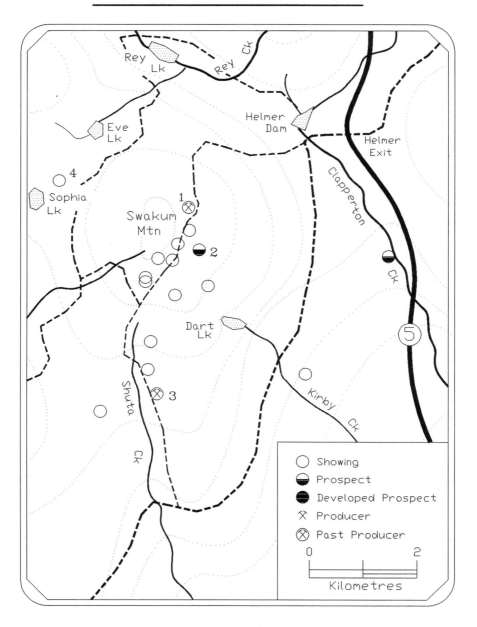

9.12.1 SWAKUM MOUNTAIN

The area around Swakum Mountain, due N of Merritt, consists of folded volcanic rocks with interbedded sedimentary strata. These rocks are intruded by large felsic intrusions (batholiths) E and W of the mountain. The volcanics on the mountain strike N to NE and dip steeply. For a large part they consist of andesitic flows and tuffs, agglomerates, and occasional basalts and rhyolites. Most of the old workings on the mountain occur in close proximity to or within this volcanic-sedimentary unit. The local deposits consist of polymetallic skarn-type mineralization, lead-zinc-silver bearing quartz veins and replacements, and polymetallic quartz veins.

Access is from the N up a 4WD track from the Helmer Lakes exit on Highway #5. Closed in winter. There may be active logging in the area.

I. **MINFILE NUMBER: 092ISE027**
   NAME(S): LUCKY MIKE

Status:	Past producer, open pit	Northing:	5574375
Latitude:	50 18 02	Easting:	664475
Longitude:	120 41 26	Elevation:	1591 m
Comments:	Skarn deposit.		
Commodities:	Tungsten, silver, copper, zinc, lead, gold		

MINERALS

Significant:	Scheelite, pyrite, pyrrhotite, chalcopyrite, galena, sphalerite
Associated:	Garnet, epidote, calcite

On the LUCKY MIKE property, a polymetallic skarn 110 m long with a NE strike occurs at the contact between andesitic breccias and felsic tuffs, within a lens of limy volcanic rocks, lithic tuffs and limestone. The skarn consists of interlacing garnet skarn (andradite garnet, magnetite, epidote, hornblende, chlorite and calcite) and carbonate skarn (coarse calcite, epidote, hornblende, chlorite, minor magnetite or hematite). The geometry is complex, with the skarn's edge having a tooth-like cross section. Tungsten mineralization is confined to the skarn with fine to coarse disseminated scheelite. Copper with silver and local zinc values is located along shallow E-dipping fault zones within the skarn and in the footwall volcanics. Tungsten occurs with the copper and silver where the structures cut through the skarn.

2. MINFILE NUMBER: 092ISE094
NAME(S): OLD ALAMEADA

Status:	Prospect	Northing:	5573580
Latitude:	50 17 36	Easting:	664700
Longitude:	120 41 16	Elevation:	1625 m

Commodities: Silver, lead, zinc, copper, gold

MINERALS

Significant: Pyrite, sphalerite, galena, chalcopyrite
Associated: Quartz

On the OLD ALAMEADA claim, a N-trending structure with shallow W dips (30 degrees to 40 degrees) hosts narrow quartz veins with significant sulfides. Minor historic underground workings have exploited a main vein 0.6 m wide, striking N. The vein is mineralized with pyrite, sphalerite, galena and chalcopyrite. Vein material in the dump showed quartz with a well-developed comb structure.

3. MINFILE NUMBER: 092ISE101
NAME(S): THELMA

Status:	Past producer, underground	Northing:	5570780
Latitude:	50 16 06	Easting:	664011
Longitude:	120 41 55	Elevation:	1554 m

Comments: Shaft located 3 km to S of Old Alameada.
Commodities: Silver, lead, zinc, gold, copper, limestone

MINERALS

Significant: Pyrite, galena, sphalerite, carbonate
Associated: Quartz

The property covers the contact zone between the volcanic and sedimentary sequences. Limestone and conglomerate beds strike N and dip steeply to the E. At the 1615 m contour, a 30 m wide band of dark gray limestone is exposed for 100 m. It contains scattered thin stringers of white calcite, some chert nodules, and vague shapes that may be fossils. Silver-lead-zinc mineralization is exposed in tabular and lenticular garnet-epidote skarn zones up to 5 m wide within the limestone. Pyrite, galena and sphalerite, with gold and silver values, occur as replacements along bedding planes and as disseminations throughout the limestone. Minor copper values are also associated with the skarn. The site consists of one shaft, underground workings and a number of surface trenches, all of which have collapsed and filled in since work ceased in 1940.

4. MINFILE NUMBER: 092ISE059
   NAME(S): SOPHIA

Status:	Showing	Northing:	5574822
Latitude:	50 18 19	Easting:	662062
Longitude:	120 43 27	Elevation:	1493 m
Commodities:	Lead, zinc, copper		

MINERALS

Significant: Pyrite, sphalerite, galena, chalcopyrite
Associated: Calcite, quartz

A 175 m wide limestone bed occurs for 600 m along a N-trending ridge. The gray, coarse-grained limestone contains numerous calcite stringers (generally less than 2 mm in width). In the central portion of the property, a feldspar porphyry intrusive with crystalline pyrite (up to 10 mm in size) contains quartz eyes throughout the matrix.

At the SOPHIA showing, mineralization occurs in a shear zone exposed in a trench. The zone is 8 m wide. Calcite and quartz occur as narrow stringers in andesitic porphyry and as a cement in brecciated volcanics. Pyrite, sphalerite, galena and chalcopyrite are associated with the quartz and calcite.

9.12.2 LOGAN LAKE

The Highland Valley porphyry copper deposits lie within a batholith dating back to the late Triassic. This large intrusive plug displaces sedimentary and volcanics. The major past producing mines were Highland Valley, OK, Bethlehem and Highmont, grading about 0.4% copper and 0.02% molybdenum. There are numerous other copper occurrences in the area.

I. MINFILE NUMBER: 092ISE001
   NAME(S): BETHLEHEM COPPER

Status:	Past producer, open pit	Northing:	5595731
Latitude:	50 29 53	Easting:	642814
Longitude:	120 59 11	Elevation:	1475 m
Comments:	Open pit.		
Commodities:	Copper, silver, gold, molybdenum		

MINERALS

Significant: Bornite, chalcopyrite, chalcocite, copper, cuprite, molybdenite
Associated: Quartz, calcite, zeolite, pyrite, specularite, magnetite, malachite, azurite

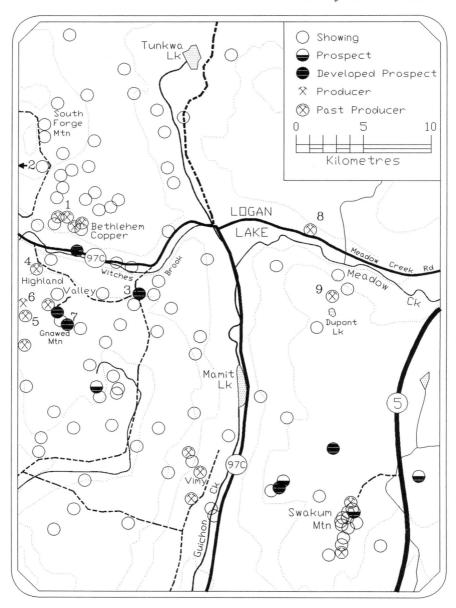

The Bethlehem ore deposits (EAST JERSEY 092ISE002, HUESTIS 092ISE004, IONA 092ISE006 and SNOWSTORM 092ISE005) are controlled by N-trending faults. Mineralization is concentrated in breccia bodies, faults and highly fractured areas. One such fault cuts right through the centre of the Jersey pit. Hydrothermal alteration is limited to the immediate area of the ore zones. Calcite, zeolite and quartz veining and vug-filling are common. The metal zones follow the alteration patterns. Bornite and chalcopyrite occur in the hydrothermal biotite zone, specularite in the epidote zone, and minor pyrite in the outer halo. Molybdenite, chalcocite and magnetite occur in minor amounts. Malachite, azurite, chrysocolla, cuprite, native copper, hematite, goethite and manganese oxides occur to shallow depths. Production from the Jersey pit began in 1964 and from the Jersey pit extension in 1977. The Bethlehem mine, which had been supplying ore to the Highland Valley Copper mill, was closed in June of 1989.

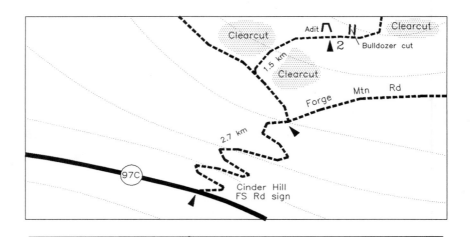

2.   MINFILE NUMBER: 092INW029
NAME(S): JOY

Status:	Prospect	Northing:	5604096
Latitude:	50 34 30	Easting:	635598
Longitude:	121 05 06	Elevation:	1733 m

MINERALS
Significant: Chalcopyrite, bornite, chalcocite, chrysocolla

The JOY prospect on Cinder Hill still shows the collapsed adit entrance. Pink calcite crystals and chalcocite are found in the dumps. Just 50 m up the track a recent bulldozer cut exposes extensive malachite, chrysocolla and azurite veinlets. Access is via Cinder Hill Forest Road.

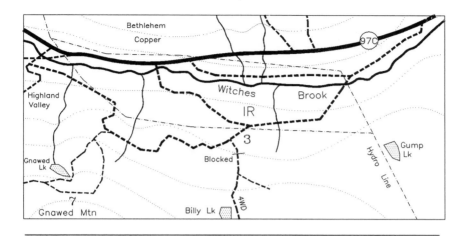

3. **MINFILE NUMBER: 092ISE011**
   NAME(S): JERICHO

Status:	Developed prospect	Northing:	5589909
Latitude:	50 26 40	Easting:	648243
Longitude:	120 54 44	Elevation:	1432 m
Comments:	On the S side of Witches Creek and Highway #97C, some 7 km W of the Logan Lake junction.		
Commodities:	Copper, molybdenum, silver		

MINERALS

Significant:	Bornite, chalcocite, chalcopyrite, molybdenite
Associated:	Quartz

The JERICHO adits are situated on the E flank of the Guichon Creek batholith. The property is underlain by medium to coarse-grained, cream gray-pink coloured granodiorite and quartz diorite, rich in biotite and plagioclase. A mineralized zone was discovered in 1956, and subsequently explored by two adits. The upper one, located on a low ridge, was driven over 250 m. Starting about 50 m from the portal, it intersects mineralized quartz veins. The principal sulfides are bornite associated with chalcocite, chalcopyrite, and seams and disseminations of molybdenite. The vein walls are sheared and strongly altered. From 200 m to its end, the upper adit intersects the mineralized zone. The lower adit was driven in a southerly direction. The mineral zone is about 700 m from the portal and was drifted on for short distances. Approximate reserves are 270,000 t grading 1% copper.

4. MINFILE NUMBER: 092ISW012
NAME(S): HIGHLAND VALLEY COPPER

Status:	Producer, open pit	Northing:	5594207
Latitude:	50 29 08	Easting:	638547
Longitude:	121 02 49	Elevation:	1275 m

Commodities: Copper, molybdenum, silver, gold, lead, zinc

MINERALS

Significant: Bornite, chalcopyrite, molybdenite, digenite, covellite, pyrite, pyrrhotite, sphalerite

Associated: Quartz, calcite

The HIGHLAND VALLEY deposit lies within the Guichon Creek batholith and is hosted by quartz monzonite and granodiorite. Feldspar porphyry and quartz feldspar porphyry dykes 0.5 m to 35 m wide occur in the deposit. They are cut by mineralized fractures and quartz veinlets. The granodiorite is also intruded by aplite dykes up to 30 cm wide, tan-coloured felsite dykes up to 4.5 m wide, and others (spessartite, hornblende, vogesite).

Production from the LORNEX mine (092ISW045) was combined with the Highland Valley operations in 1987. On the S side of the valley was the Lornex mine, which started in 1972. In 1981, its concentrator was expanded to become one of the largest in the industry. On the N side was BETHLEHEM COPPER (092ISE001), which began mining in 1963. In 1981, this operation was absorbed by Cominco, who already owned the Highland Valley orebody located W of the Lornex pit. Mining of the original Bethlehem Copper pits ceased in 1982.

Between the Highland Valley mine and the Lornex mine, measured ore reserves are over 500 million t grading 0.4% copper, 4.8 gm/t silver, 0.03 gm/t gold and 0.007% molybdenum. It is unclear if site tours of this active mine are currently permissible. Phone (250)523-3393 for details.

5. MINFILE NUMBER: 092ISW036
NAME(S): HIGHMONT (WEST)

Status:	Past producer, open pit	Northing:	5588881
Latitude:	50 26 13	Easting:	641603
Longitude:	121 00 22	Elevation:	1615 m

Commodities: Copper, molybdenum

The HIGHMONT deposits are located in the central core of the Guichon Creek batholith and are hosted primarily by quartz diorite and granodiorite. They are intruded by a dyke trending WNW, and consist of a biotite-quartz-feldspar porphyry. Small plagioclase/quartz porphyry and aplite dykes are scattered throughout the property. The principal economic minerals are chalcopyrite, bornite and molybdenite occurring in veins and fractures. Chalcocite is present in minor amounts. Pyrite and specular hematite are gangue minerals. Veins of gray, brecciated quartz up to 1 m wide are cut by seams of molybdenite and clay minerals.

---

6. MINFILE NUMBER: 092ISW045
NAME(S): LORNEX

Status:	Producer, open pit	Northing:	5590297
Latitude:	50 27 01	Easting:	639033
Longitude:	121 02 30	Elevation:	1550 m
Commodities:	Copper, molybdenum, silver, gold, zinc		

The LORNEX deposit is 1900 m long, 500 m wide and plunges NW to a depth of at least 750 m. Chalcopyrite, bornite and pyrite constitute 1.5% of the ore zone. Sulfides occur mainly with quartz as fracture-fillings and coatings. Veins average 5 mm to 15 mm in width. Molybdenite occurs as thin laminates in banded quartz veins, and less often as rosettes in vuggy quartz veins. The oxide zone averages 3 m to 30 m in thickness, and thins toward the E. Associated minerals are malachite, limonite, pyrolusite, azurite, cuprite, chalcocite, covellite and native copper. The Lornex mine produced 135 million t at 0.36% copper and 0.01% molybdenum.

---

7. MINFILE NUMBER: 092ISE152
NAME(S): ANN

Status:	Developed prospect	Northing:	5587377
Latitude:	50 25 23	Easting:	643085
Longitude:	120 59 09	Elevation:	1780 m

The ANN zone consists of a strong quartz stockwork hosted by breccia, and forms distinctive bluffs for several hundred metres along the W flank of Gnawed Mountain. Chalcopyrite, bornite, molybdenite and trace pyrite occur in quartz-filled fractures and hairline seams. Veins range in width from 2 cm to 10 cm, and occasionally up to 1 m. Numerous other workings show copper minerals on the NW and E flanks of Gnawed Mountain.

8. MINFILE NUMBER: 092ISE009
NAME(S): FORD

Status:	Past producer, underground		
Latitude:	50 29 11	Northing:	5594953
Longitude:	120 44 03	Easting:	660737
Elevation:	1172 m		

Comments: Located on N side of the Logan Lake to Lac Le Jeune road, 3 km E of the E end of Logan Lake.

Commodities: Copper, silver

MINERALS

Significant: Bornite, chalcocite

Associated: Chlorite, sericite, clinozoisite, zeolite, calcite

The FORD occurrence occupies the area N of Meadow Creek, which is underlain by dark gray to purplish red, porphyritic volcanic flows. The lavas are typically amygdaloidal and vary in composition from olivine basalt to augite/andesitic basalt. Thermal alteration has changed pyroxene to epidote, zoisite and calcite. The rock is locally shot through with sericite and epidote. Flows average 2 m in thickness.

The original open cuts (pre-1915) expose copper carbonate ore with occasional flecks of bornite and chalcocite along fracture planes in amygdaloidal flows. An adit follows a mineralized shear zone and intersects a set of faults. Chalcocite, bornite and some malachite occur in amygdules and associated veins. Some mineralization also occurs in a variety of veins.

9. MINFILE NUMBER: 092ISE012
NAME(S): BERTHA-MOLLY

Status:	Past producer, underground		
Latitude:	50 26 36	Northing:	5590211
Longitude:	120 42 36	Easting:	662600
Elevation:	1493 m		

Commodities: Copper, silver

MINERALS

Significant: Cuprite, malachite, azurite, chalcopyrite, pyrite

The Dupont Lake area is underlain mainly by volcanics, and lies approximately 8 km to the E of the contact with the Guichon Creek batholith. Quartz diorite outcrops SW of Dupont Lake. In 1942, a prospector did some surface-stripping on a copper showing, about 450 m W of an old shaft. Production from this occurrence, known as the Lost Group, was 31 t, yielding 218 gm of silver and 626 kg of copper.

The Bertha-Molly showing is hosted by purplish amygdaloidal andesites and reddish tuffs that are strongly fractured. The original shaft was sunk at a point where patches of cuprite occur in fractures. Small shipments were made. Recent development has exposed malachite, azurite, chalcopyrite, cuprite and pyrite hosted by shears and fracture-fillings in vesicular volcanics and red tuffs.

9.13 HOPE – PRINCETON

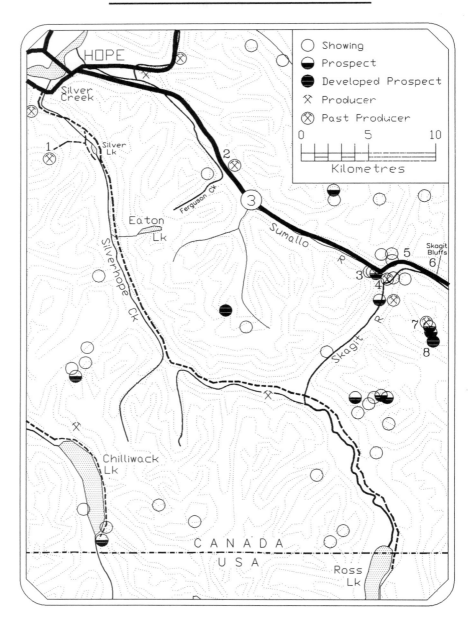

9.13.1 HOPE – MANNING PROVINCIAL PARK

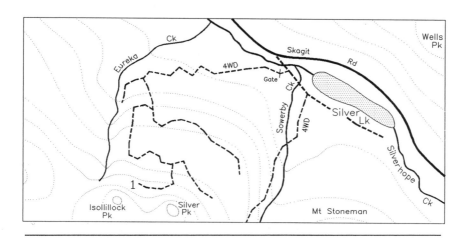

1. **MINFILE NUMBER: 092HSW011**
   NAME(S): EUREKA

Status:	Past Producer	Northing:	5462500
Latitude:	49 18 25	Easting:	611650
Longitude:	121 27 51	Elevation:	1585 m

Comments: Turn off just W of Hope and take Flood Rd W through town of Silver Creek. Head S on Silverhope Creek road 5.5 km to Silver Lake Prov Pk. Turn W up old Eureka Mine Rd (4WD).

Commodities: Silver, copper, lead

MINERALS

Significant: Tetrahedrite, pyrite

Associated: Siderite, limonite, quartz

Located high on the mountain, between 1,525 m and 1,750 m on N and W sides of Silver Peak. Considerable ore shipped 1868–1914. Some further work was done in 1924, including extending existing adits. The upper 600 m of the peak consist of conglomerate, which contacts a quartz diorite pluton on the W side. Cutting the conglomerate are a number of quartz porphyry dykes. The largest averages over 6 m wide and follows the line of Glory Hole Gulch. The chief gangue materials are siderite, limonite and quartz. One ore body has been traced across the summit for over 400 m. A second is found on the SW flank of the peak. Drifts, adits and a glory hole exist.

2. NAME(S): HOPE SLIDE

Status:	Showing	Northing:	5462600
Latitude:	49 18 05	Easting:	626700
Longitude:	121 15 00	Elevation:	750 m

Comments: Located on the N side of the Skagit River, opposite Ferguson Creek, about 11 km E of the highway junction at Hope where Highway #5 (Coquihalla) takes off. If you are heading W from Princeton and Manning Park, it is just 2 km W of Sunshine Valley ski area. Well sign-posted, with large parking and viewing areas.

MINERALS
Significant: Aplite
Associated: Picturestone

The Hope Slide occurred early on the morning of January 9, 1965, when some 46 million m³ of mountainside slipped into the Nicola Valley, burying the highway and an existing lake to a depth of 75 m, and killing four people in three cars who had, ironically, stopped on the highway because of snow drifts. Two of the bodies were never found. It's unclear what triggered the slide, although small seismic shocks some distance NE minutes earlier may have compounded an already unstable situation.

From the car park, a band of yellow aplite is visible about midway up the avalanche slope. This is the source for the enormous amount of picturestone material which lies everywhere among the debris. Although not a chert or jasper, it is quartz-rich, and takes a good polish. The area is currently under claim, so large specimens cannot be removed without permission.

On the S side of Highway #3, note the new forest growth above the road, where the avalanche debris swept up the slope, like a rogue wave, before settling back into the valley.

---

3. MINFILE NUMBER: 092HSW122
NAME(S): SUMALLO RIVER

A 200 m thick bed of massive, bluish gray and white limestone follows the Sumallo River for 3 km NW from its confluence with the Skagit River to Highway #3. The unit is underlain by impure limestone, argillite and breccia and overlain by interbedded quartzite and argillite.

4. MINFILE NUMBER: 092HSW042
NAME(S): BB, MAMMOTH, FOUNDATION MINES

Status:	Past producer, underground		
Latitude:	49 12 47	Northing:	5452704
Longitude:	121 04 32	Easting:	640158
Elevation:	914 m		

Comments: Located on the NE side of the Sumallo River opposite the confluence of the Sumallo and Skagit rivers. The area is known as Sumallo Grove, and is within Manning Park—collecting is prohibited.

Commodities: Silver, gold, zinc, copper, lead

MINERALS
Significant: Arsenopyrite, pyrrhotite, galena, sphalerite, chalcopyrite, pyrite, boulangerite, jamesonite

The regionally metamorphosed rocks generally contain fine-grained actinolite, epidote, chlorite and locally prehnite. Limestone is interbedded with greenstone. Three mineralized zones occur, paralleling the quartz diorite contact to the W. The middle zone occurs in a 3 m seam of altered limestone which hosts epidote, hornblende, pyroxene, wollastonite and garnet. Quartz occurs either as white, massive and sugary in form, or as clusters of individual, clear crystals. The scheelite fluoresces well under ultraviolet light. Development work consisted of a number of open cuts and short adits driven along narrow ore veins.

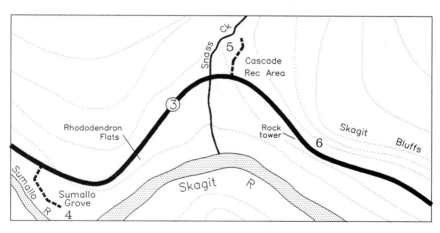

5. NAME(S): CASCADE RECREATION AREA

Latitude:	49 13 50	Northing:	5454690
Longitude:	121 03 20	Easting:	641560
Elevation:	1000 m		

Used partly to store road-building materials. There is a line of beautiful aplite (picturestone) boulders at the trail-head, including the red-brown of the Hope Slide, plus a black-brown variation.

---

6. NAME(S): SKAGIT BLUFFS

Latitude:	49 13 30	Northing:	5454680
Longitude:	121 03 00	Easting:	641964
Elevation:	1050 m		

Wedge-shaped crystals (6 mm in size) of axinite in violet, brown and black are reported associated with white, radiating aggregates of stilbite crystals, and greenish white prehnite crystals in tuffs and calcareous rocks along the highway at Skagit Bluffs, in the road-cut near km 38. At the W end of the bluffs, a 5 m high rock tower stands on the outside edge of the road. A lens of sulfide material shows 1 cm clear quartz in situ.

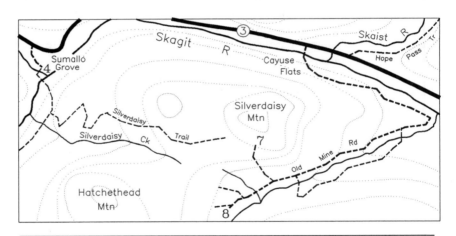

---

7. MINFILE NUMBER: 092HSW002
NAME(S): INVERMAY

Status:	Past Producer	Northing:	5448917
Latitude:	49 10 42	Easting:	643090
Longitude:	121 02 12	Elevation:	1733 m
Comments:	Park at Cayuse Flats. Cross the river and follow the true RH bank on the old mine road for 2 km before turning SW up creek for 5 km to INVERMAY on S side of Silverdaisy Mtn. GIANT COPPER is opposite, on S side of valley. In the fall, when river levels are lowest, it is sometimes possible to park 2 km further E and hop the Skagit River, cutting 4 km off the walk.		
Commodities:	Silver, gold, lead, zinc, copper		

MINERALS

Significant: Sphalerite, galena, arsenopyrite, chalcopyrite, jamesonite

The showing occurs in a quartz-rich diorite stock intruding pellite. A brecciated zone appears to host the mineralization. Shear zones from 6 cm to 100 cm contain lenses and bands of quartz, sphalerite and galena. Scattered pockets in tourmaline-rich layers at A and B adits include jamesonite, pyrite, arsenopyrite and chalcopyrite.

---

8.   MINFILE NUMBER: 092HSW001
NAME(S): GIANT COPPER

Status:	Developed prospect	Northing:	5447336
Latitude:	49 09 50	Easting:	644083
Longitude:	121 01 25	Elevation:	1800 m

MINERALS

Significant: Pyrrhotite, chalcopyrite, pyrite, arsenopyrite, molybdenite, galena, sphalerite, uraninite, monazite, scheelite

Associated: Quartz, calcite, tourmaline, feldspar, mica, magnetite

Mineralization occurs in a pipe-like zone of brecciated siliceous sediments of the Dewdney Creek formation. The zone measures 550 m by 360 m and comprises siliceous fragments in a gray matrix. Black tourmaline occurs in fractures and fragments.

9.13.2 EAST OF MANNING PROVINCIAL PARK

---

1.   NAME(S): BLACKWALL MOUNTAIN, LOOKOUT MOUNTAIN

Status:	Showing	Northing:	5437400
Latitude:	49 04 15	Easting:	661500
Longitude:	120 47 10	Elevation:	1400 m
Comments:	Over 160 Jurassic and Cretaceous era fossils sites are described within the park boundaries. One of the most scenic is the ValleyView Lookout Rd. Turn N on paved road opposite Manning Park Ski Lodge. Summer road only (July–September). Specimen collecting is prohibited in the park, so take only photos. The Visitor Centre, located on Hwy #3 just 500 m E of the start of Blackwall Road, has a small natural history exhibit that includes fossils. Call (250)840-8836.		
Commodities:	Fossils, fossil wood		

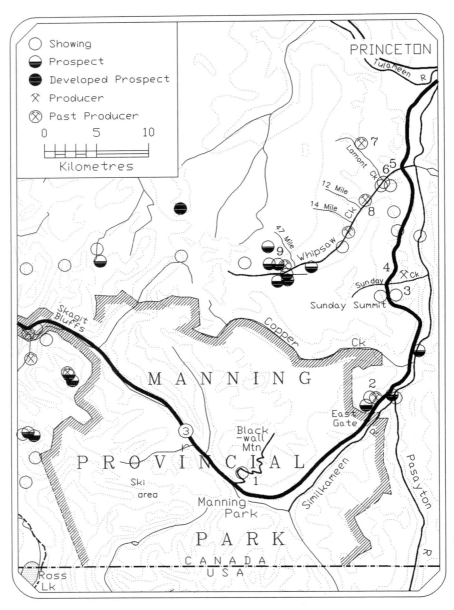

The first outcrops encountered going up the mountain (at 1.8 km, the bend on uphill side) are early Cretaceous coarse conglomerates. A few bivalves (*pelecypods*) suggest their marine origin. At 3.7 km, sparsely scattered fossils are found in talus slopes. About 5 km from start, a second outcrop hosts mid-Jurassic strata that dip near-vertically and are multi-layered, containing a wide variety of marine fossils. Bivalves are common, including the scallop *Syncycloneme* and the bivalve *Trigonia*. Ammonites and belemnites are rarer.

Under the cliff, beside the road and beyond Cascade Lookout, light coloured petrified wood is found.

Mineral exploration work has been conducted E of the Park, in the Bell Creek area, since 1900. Most of this work has focused on showings near the E boundary, just NE of the east gate. The RED STAR has received the most attention, although the KNOB HILL (092HSE069), GOLDEN CROWN (092HSE191) and PAW (092HSE093) have also been explored. Several adits were excavated on the better showings by early workers, extending over 300 m in length. There are at least five adits with raises and shafts on the former Red Star claims, with a total known length of 565 m. In 1964–65, 36 t of sorted ore were mined from the Main zone. Recent work included drilling, geo-surveys and sampling.

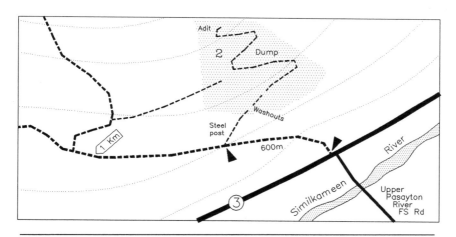

2. **MINFILE NUMBER: 092HSE067**
   NAME(S): RED STAR

Status:	Past producer, underground		
Latitude:	49 08 59	Northing:	5446640
Longitude:	120 36 32	Easting:	674360
Elevation:	1158 m		

Comments: Adit is at the top of a visible talus slope above Hwy #3 some 2 km E of East Gate. Upper Pasayton River Forest Road has its junction opposite, on Hwy #3.

Commodities: Zinc, copper, silver, gold, lead, molybdenum

MINERALS

Significant: Chalcopyrite, sphalerite, pyrite, galena, bornite, molybdenite, pyrrhotite, chalcocite

Associated: Quartz, barite, kaolinite, sericite

The RED STAR deposit is situated on the NW bank of the Similkameen River, above Highway #3, and is underlain by volcanics. Mineralization is hosted by a wide zone of strongly sheared schists containing large and small fractured quartz veins. The rocks have enriched silica, magnesium and barium contents. Barite is a significant component. Alteration of the mineralization has resulted in several types of ore: 1) general pyritization of the schists; 2) silicification of the fracture zones resulting in white, sugary quartz carrying pyrite, sphalerite, chalcopyrite and galena; 3) small but distinct veins of white quartz, usually less than 50 cm in width; and 4) glassy quartz with blebs of pyrite and chalcopyrite.

The upper adit, which extended N–S for 500 m, generally consisted of sphalerite and chalcopyrite in quartz veins. Sphalerite, chalcopyrite with galena, silver and gold mineralization were reported from the underground workings, which have since collapsed.

---

3. NAME(S): SUNDAY SUMMIT

Status:	Showing	Northing:	5458300
Latitude:	49 15 20	Easting:	675600
Longitude:	120 35 10	Elevation:	1300 m

Comments: Located E of Sunday Summit on Hope–Princeton Hwy #3.
Commodities: Agate, jasper

Fossil (agatized) wood is found on the S flank of a hill, 300 m SE of Sunday Summit, on the Hope–Princeton Highway #3. Leave the road where the N-bound traffic becomes a double lane. An old track leads up a slope around the S of the hill.

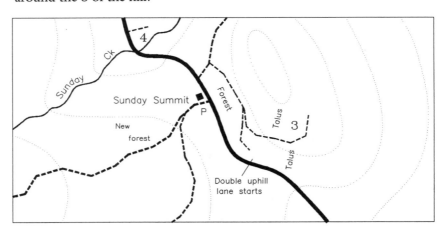

4.   MINFILE NUMBER: 092HSE168
NAME(S): SUNDAY CREEK

Status:	Prospect	Northing:	5457675
Latitude:	49 14 55	Easting:	675900
Longitude:	120 34 59	Elevation:	1231 m

Zeolite outcrops along Sunday Creek and Highway #3 just N of Sunday Summit, over a distance of 500 m along the W side of the highway, and in a 5 m high roadcut S of Sunday Creek. Several exposures also occur in Sunday Creek itself, just E of the highway. One of these, 100 m E off the highway, comprises a section of zeolitized tuff at least 30 m thick, overlain by sandstone, and underlain by volcanic pebble-cobble conglomerate. The mineralization consists of clinoptilolite, together with cristobalite, sanidine, plagioclase, quartz and biotite. Locally, the overburden has been stripped for mining, since the zeolite is a high quality clinoptilolite variety. Proven reserves are 3.5 million t, and probable reserves are 38 million t.

Carbonized wood, stained bright green by copper leaching, is reported in Sunday Creek.

9.13.3 WHIPSAW CREEK

Whipsaw Creek is a long, NE-flowing stream that drains the N perimeter of Manning Provincial Park, joining the Similkameen River about 9 km S of Princeton where Highway #3 makes a series of sweeping U-turns. Access is from the N hairpin bend. Currently an active logging road — drive with caution.

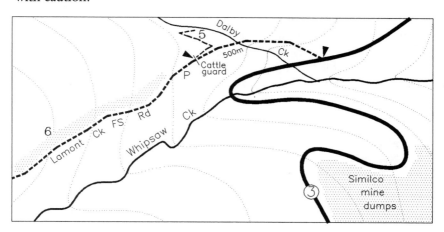

5.   NAME(S): DALBY CREEK AMBER

Status:	Showing	Northing:	5471750
Latitude:	49 22 30	Easting:	675730
Longitude:	120 34 45	Elevation:	1100 m

Park at the cattle guard 0.5 km from the turnoff, and walk back along N side of road to pick up old track that descends W into Dalby Creek. Coal seam is right at creek level. Be aware the water is used for cattle downstream, so don't pollute. Fossils in beige nodules are found in the stream.

6.   NAME(S): WHIPSAW FOSSILS

Status:	Showing

From the cattle grid at marker 0.5 km to marker 4 km, fossils are found, primarily in soft shales. Some also in beige sandstone nodules.

7.   MINFILE NUMBER: 092HSE231
NAME(S): LAMONT (9-MILE) CREEK PLACER

Status:	Past producer, open pit	Northing:	5473000
Latitude:	49 23 15	Easting:	671790
Longitude:	120 37 58	Elevation:	1128 m

Lamont (9-mile) Creek is a SW-flowing tributary of Whipsaw Creek, about 9 km long. The creek occupies a fairly broad and open valley extending SE from a divide separating it from Granite Creek to the W. Placer deposits were mined in this valley in the early 1900s, and are now reported to be exhausted. A syndicate held a lease on the creek in 1925.

8.   MINFILE NUMBER: 092HSE236
NAME(S): WHIPSAW CREEK PLACER

Status:	Past producer, open pit	Northing:	5464000
Latitude:	49 18 24	Easting:	670930
Longitude:	120 38 55	Elevation:	1155 m

The lower 2 km of Whipsaw Creek cut through a narrow, steep-sided valley, but the remainder flows over a more open valley floor. In 1887 it was noted that the gravels from this creek yielded "fine scales" of gold and platinum. The gravels were worked intermittently between 1887 and 1935. Total gold production is estimated at 3.5 kg. These deposits are now reported to be largely exhausted. An old log cabin remains, visible from the forestry road, 14.5 km from the turnoff on Highway #3.

---

9.   MINFILE NUMBER: 092HSE073
NAME(S): S AND M

Status:	Past producer, underground		
Latitude:	49 16 33	Northing:	5460370
Longitude:	120 44 06	Easting:	664750
Elevation:	1524 m		

At 15 km marker, take upper fork to Hope Pass. Site is at 20 km. The deposit is located on the NW side of Whipsaw Creek and is visible by the roof of the core shed, which still stands. The region in the headwaters of Whipsaw Creek is underlain to the W by intrusive and metamorphic rocks, and to the E by metamorphosed volcanics and sediments. The contact between the two strikes NNW, and continues S across Whipsaw Creek for at least 1.5 km and hosts several other deposits. Within the zone, pyrite, sphalerite, galena and chalcopyrite occur as disseminations and blebs in quartz-carbonate veinlets, and in narrow quartz veins generally. The deposit was explored as early as 1911, and trenched and tunnelled 1927–31.

9.14. PRINCETON

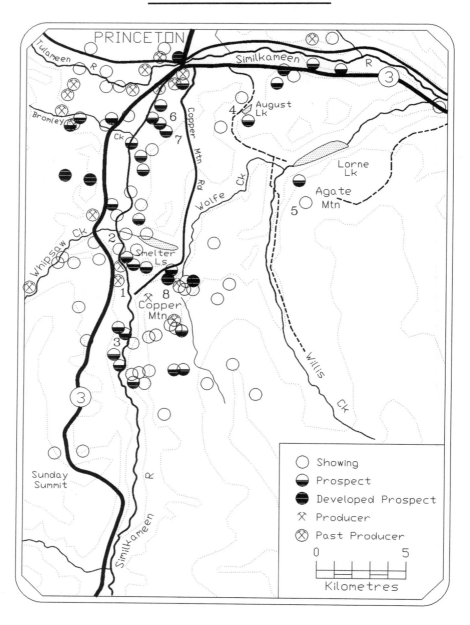

The area is dominated by volcanic rocks of the Intermontane Belt and sediments of the Triassic era, both of which have been intruded by various plutons. The area is known for its history of metal, coal and placer mining, which began in the 1880s. Porphyry copper deposits are abundant just N and S of Princeton. The area to the S, around Copper Mountain, has been worked since the early 1900s. The COPPER MOUNTAIN MINE (092HSE001) and VIRGINIA (092HSE242) were rich, grading about 5% copper.

To the W of Princeton, magnetite deposits are found at LODESTONE MOUNTAIN (092HSE034) and TANGLEWOOD HILL (092HSE035) nearby. Thermal coal was mined at BETHLEHEM COAL (092HSE227) SW of Princeton, and the COALMONT COLLIERY (092HSE157) W of the town. Fossil resin (amber) has been found. The valley also produced bentonite and zeolite.

Deposits of agate are known in the Tertiary basalts, and petrified wood, fossils and agatized limb casts have been found in the sedimentary rocks just W of the town at Vermilion Bluffs, Mount Jackman, Opal Mountain and S at Sunday Summit.

Eocene fossils in the form of leaf impressions, pine needle and cone imprints, insect imprints and root casts are common. Apart from the usual forms of preservation (shales, sandstones, coal seams), early paleo-botanists noted the remarkable selection of material preserved in chert: "The flora from the Princeton chert appears to be one of the most botanically significant assemblages thus far discovered from the Tertiary of North America". Fossils found to date include rosaceous flowers (an ancient form of rose), conifers, needles and dwarf shoots.

Cherty fossils are found in the Allenby formation. A famous site, named for the now-abandoned town of Allenby 8 km S of Princeton (now part of the Similco Mine dumps) gave its name—the Allenby formation—to the structure. Other examples are found right within Princeton city limits. The sandy, tilted structures are visible as you drive in on Highway #3 from Hope, and behind the stores on Vermilion Avenue. There are other bluffs S across the Similkameen River, beyond the Irly Bird store.

9.14.1 PLACER GOLD

The Similkameen River flows N for 60 km from the Cascade Mountains to Princeton, where it abruptly changes course and continues SE for 80 km before crossing into the United States. In the upper reaches, the valley gives way to a steep canyon that continues to the Pasayten River and Manning Park. Between Princeton and Whipsaw Creek, the middle section of the river runs through a wide valley containing deep gravels in many places. The lower part of the river, between Princeton and Hedley, flows in a broad valley flanked on either side by gravel terraces comprising reworked glacial material.

Gold was first discovered on the Similkameen River below Princeton in 1853, making it one of the very earliest gold discoveries in the province. The river was extensively worked, largely by individual placer miners, over a 40 km stretch, from 1860–1900. One operation in particular, 6 km upstream of the town, mined 600 m^3 of gravel in 1895, containing 1.2 gm/m^3 of gold and a considerable amount of platinum.

Since 1900, only minor production has been recorded, largely from dredging operations in the vicinity of Princeton. One dredge, operating 3 km upstream of Princeton, produced 1,400 gm of gold over a two-month period in 1941. Shortly afterwards, another consortium produced 4,320 gm of gold and 824 gm of platinum from about 6,000 m^3 of gravel at the same location.

A dragline dredge operated on the Similkameen River from 1947–50. It first mined a 2 km reach about 1.5 km upstream of Princeton. Subsequent work was conducted on a section beginning 300 m downstream of the confluence with the Tulameen River, and continuing E for 5 km. This operation recovered 50 kg of gold, 6.2 kg of silver and 10.6 kg of platinum from 434,000 m^3 of gravel. No production has been recorded since the termination of dredging operations in 1950. Total production from 1885–1950 is estimated at 229 kg of gold, 14.9 kg of platinum and 6.2 kg of silver.

Most recorded production and exploration has occurred along a stretch extending upstream from Princeton for 14 km, and continuing downstream past Princeton for 8 km. The alluvial gravels worked along the river yielded black sands containing fine platinum in addition to gold. The ratio of gold to platinum recovered was about 4:1.

In 1878, gold was reported to occur as "coarse scales", mixed with considerable platinum in similar-sized particles, at one point 5.5 km above Princeton. One of the larger gold nuggets found on the river weighed 160 gm. Precious metals in the gravels below Princeton occur in localized patchy concentrations, making them largely uneconomic for the early placer miners. One of the richer deposits occurred in an elevated bench at Princeton, and consisted of 1.5 m to 1.8 m of cemented gravel on a sand bed. Gravels tested on a bench 5 m above the river, just downstream of Princeton, averaged 1.8 gm of gold and 0.1 gm of platinum per m^3. Several shafts, 2 m to 3 m deep, sunk on a gravel bench near Bromley Creek, gave "colours" of gold and platinum. Higher values were found at bedrock in this bench.

Bromley Creek is an E-flowing tributary of the Similkameen River, about 10 km long. The lower half of the creek, in the vicinity of Highway #3, flows through an area of gravel terraces that may represent a S-trending abandoned channel of the Tulameen River, lying between the Similkameen River and the present Tulameen River. Various shafts sunk over an area extending N from the lower part of Bromley Creek to the Tulameen River are reported to have encountered "colours" of gold and platinum. The creek itself was noted in 1926 to contain "light, porous colours of gold in a surface residue". The creek and the surrounding area were first explored 1926–28.

Only minor prospecting has occurred since the 1950s. Some exploration work was conducted just S of Princeton and near the mouth of Whipsaw Creek between 1958 and 1969. More recently, gold and platinum were discovered in the early 1980s on the Rosch Ranch, on the E side of the Similkameen River, 7 km SW of Princeton. Work has outlined a channel, 2 m below surface, with coarse gold and platinum.

Further information is available from the Tourist Info Centre run by the Chamber of Commerce at (250)295-3103. Similkameen Gold Panning Tours run day excursions during the summer—call (250)295-7055.

9.14.2 PRINCETON SOUTH

Important copper deposits occur in a NW-trending belt of Nicola Group rocks, bounded on the S by the Copper Mountain stock, and on the W by a major fault known as the Boundary fault, that closely parallels Highway #3 from Sunday Summit to Princeton. While Copper Mountain itself is on the E side of the N-flowing Similkameen River, a number of past producing mines can be found on the W banks, notably the large INGERBELLE dumps adjacent to Highway #3 at the hairpin bends 10 km S of Princeton. The area has seen active mining since the 1890s.

I. **MINFILE NUMBER: 092HSE004**
    NAME(S): INGERBELLE

Status:	Past producer, open pit, underground		
Latitude:	49 20 22	Northing:	5467835
Longitude:	120 33 18	Easting:	677620
Elevation:	1097 m		

An open pit, 750 m W of the Similkameen River, across from Copper Mountain. The orebody, a skarn-porphyry deposit, has been developed by both underground and open pit methods, and is roughly L-shaped. The host rocks are mainly tuffs and andesite. An important feature is the very irregular distribution of copper mineralization. Chalcopyrite and pyrite were the main sulfide minerals, but the mix changed abruptly from place to place. Total sulfide content varied 2% to 5%, but some of the more pyritic material on the S side of the ore zones carried up to 10% sulfides. Production started in 1972.

2. MINFILE NUMBER: 092HSE006
NAME(S): RED BUCK

Status:	Past producer, underground		
Latitude:	49 20 51	Northing:	5468750
Longitude:	120 32 55	Easting:	678040
Elevation:	792 m		

The RED BUCK mine is on the steep W bank of the Similkameen River, about 1 km NE of INGERBELLE (092HSE004). Irregular and ill-defined bodies of mineralization occur in micromonzonite and diorite andesite. It is exposed in three adits over a vertical elevation of 50 m on the Red Buck claim. The host rocks are cut by pegmatite veins, comprised of orthoclase, albite and quartz. Mineralization consists of chalcopyrite and pyrite, associated with pegmatite. Stronger mineralization is localized along shears and joints.

The deposit was first explored before 1895. Extensive underground development was carried out in 1936–38. Production commenced in late 1938 with the completion of a 90 t/day flotation mill. However, operations were shut down in early 1939, after producing only 31 t of concentrate.

3. MINFILE NUMBER: 092HSE152
NAME(S): COPPER MOUNTAIN PEGMATITE

Status:	Prospect	Northing:	5464710
Latitude:	49 18 40	Easting:	678000
Longitude:	120 33 04	Elevation:	945 m

Coarse-grained pegmatite occurs in an oval-shaped intrusive body measuring 1200 m by 2000 m on both sides of the Similkameen River, and comprises the core of the Copper Mountain stock. Ten grab samples selected from fresh-looking, coarse-grained, orange to white pegmatite, collected from outcrops W of the Similkameen River, were found to be potentially suitable as a source of feldspar.

4. MINFILE NUMBER: 092HSE002
NAME(S): AUGUST LAKE

Status:	Showing	Northing:	5478900
Latitude:	49 26 13	Easting:	684040
Longitude:	120 27 41	Elevation:	914 m

Take Highway #3 E to Hedley and turn S at "Golf Course" sign, heading to Lorne Lake. August Lake is 5 km along this road. Scattered outcrops of white or cream-coloured moss agate are reported to occur in the valley and on the hillsides E and W of the lake. The area is underlain by volcanics and granodiorite.

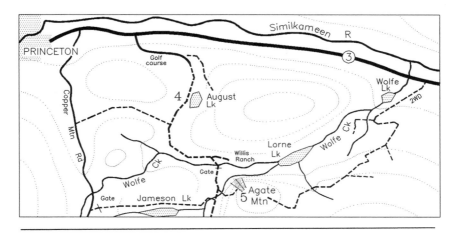

5. **MINFILE NUMBER: 092HSE147**
    NAME(S): AGATE MOUNTAIN, WILLIS RANCH

Status:	Showing	Northing:	5473350
Latitude:	49 23 09	Easting:	687550
Longitude:	120 24 57	Elevation:	1189 m

Same directions off Highway #3 as for AUGUST LAKE. The Willis Ranch is 11 km from Highway #3 turnoff. Ask permission here to drive through their yard, to park a km further. This site is only for the physically fit. The talus slope is on the NW corner of Agate Mountain (Wilbert Hills), just below a forestry lookout station, and involves up to a 600 m climb. The slope is highly visible throughout the Princeton area, particularly since the November 1996 rock slide which brought down tonnes of new rock. From the barn at the meadows, cross the rickety wooden bridge. A conical hill with a basalt tower atop splits the valley. Aim for the LH slope (500 m) and climb into the narrow valley, which is formed by two converging talus slopes. Stay in the bottom of the "V". After 200 m, a faint cattle trail appears that leads 500 m to where the valley is blocked by fresh avalanche debris.

The Agate Bluffs comprise a resistant capping of volcanics, resting on volcanics and granodiorite of the Bromley batholith. The volcanics consist mostly of basalt and andesite, with minor breccia and tuff. Agate is found in pieces, 5 cm to 50 cm in diameter, scattered throughout the talus, from just below the forestry look out station to near the meadows. Recent visits suggest the bottom third of the slope to be the best area. The middle third is steep and loose.

The agate is yellow to brown or green, and translucent to opaque.

Most of it is not well-banded, but some resembles opalized wood. The yellow-green material is frequently badly fractured and thus not suitable for cutting and polishing, although some of the larger chunks might yield suitable lapidary material. Trace calcite fluoresces green under short-wave ultraviolet light.

The upper third may be reached after a hard pull up-slope. Take water. Spectacular basalt columns serve as a central landmark. About 150 m L (N) of these columns, red jasper and a source of agate is found in situ.

The future of this site is uncertain, as recently the owners were considering selling the ranch to developers.

An alternate route of access is to take the Wolfe Creek turnoff 15 km E of Princeton and drive up to the fire lookout. From there, descend N and W (steep and loose) to the upper cliffs above the slide. Although this may appear less strenuous than the Willis Ranch access, it is not.

Still a third access route is available by taking the Copper Mountain road S. Near the top of Wolfe Creek Hill, a track takes off L, heading E for 4 km, to cross upper Willis Creek. About 500 m further, a track leads R up Agate Mountain. The top is 6 km further.

Copper deposits are found in a NW-trending belt across from INGERBELLE, extending over an area approximately 1 km wide and over 4 km long. They are bounded on the S by the Copper Mountain stock, on the W by a major fault known as the Boundary fault, and on the N by a complex of porphyries and breccias. They diminish to the E. Within a 5 km radius of the summit of Copper Mountain, no less than 25 sites, 15 pits, 50 adits and countless trenches provide access to the chalcopyrite, pyrite and bornite mineralization.

Access is from Highway #3, a km E of Princeton, via the Copper Mountain road that branches off at the RCMP station.

6. **MINFILE NUMBER: 092HSE139**
   NAME(S):ALLENBY TAILINGS

Status:	Prospect	Northing:	5477170
Latitude:	49 25 22	Easting:	679480
Longitude:	120 31 30	Elevation:	741 m

The ALLENBY TAILINGS consists of an old tailings dump from the nearby Allenby mill, which processed copper ores from the Similco mine (092HSE001) until 1957. The dump covers an area 450 m long and up to 200 m wide and is made up of about 2000 m³ of tailings from a pilot mill operating in 1977–78, in an attempt to recover gold and copper.

Well-formed leaf fossils are reported, taken from a cut in the railway tracks a few hundred metres SW of Allenby.

7. MINFILE NUMBER: 092HSE167
NAME(S): TAILINGS TEPHRA

Status:	Developed prospect	Northing:	5476725
Latitude:	49 25 07	Easting:	679850
Longitude:	120 31 13	Elevation:	823 m

This zeolite prospect outcrops on the abandoned Copper Mountain railway, and is contained in a waterlain, rhyolite tuff. A roadcut along the SE side of the railway exposes a section of vitric-crystal tuff, 3 m to 4 m thick, overlain by at least 6 m of mainly vitric rhyolite tuff. The upper and lower contacts of this zeolitized horizon are not exposed. The deposit is estimated to contain inferred reserves of 54,000 t over a SE strike extension of 70 m. The horizon continues W for 1,600 m across the Similkameen River, along the S flank of the W-trending TAILINGS syncline. Zeolite alteration is in the form of clinoptilolite, accompanied by plagioclase, potassium feldspar, quartz, clay, biotite, cristobalite and sanidine.

8. MINFILE NUMBER: 092HSE001
NAME(S): SIMILCO, COPPER MOUNTAIN

Status:	Past producer, open pit, underground		
Latitude:	49 19 52	Northing:	5466970
Longitude:	120 31 59	Easting:	679235
Elevation:	1188 m		

Situated on the E of the Similkameen River, on the slopes of Copper Mountain, some 20 km up the Copper Mountain road. The rocks in the vicinity are andesites and basalts, and are composed mostly of coarse agglomerate, breccia and tuff, with lesser amounts of volcanics and some layers of siltstone. The stock is elliptical and in plain view, being 10 km long in the NW–SE direction, with diorite at its outer edge grading through monzonite to syenite and pegmatite at the core. Development took place during the 1950s until 1969.

In 1977–78, the INGERBELLE mine (092HSE004) and COPPER MOUNTAIN consolidated operations. With the installation of an ore conveyor across the Similkameen River canyon, the delivery of Copper Mountain ore to the Ingerbelle mill began in 1980. The mining operation is currently called Similco mine, and is shut down.

9.14.3 PRINCETON NORTHWEST

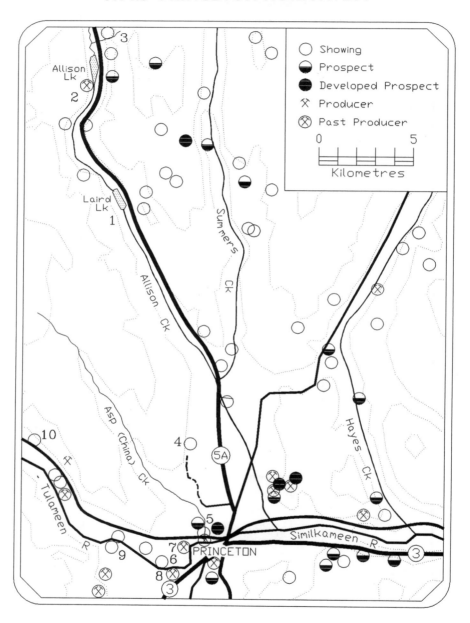

1. MINFILE NUMBER: 092HNE179
NAME(S): JOY MINING PLACER

Status:	Showing	Northing:	5488200
Latitude:	49 31 18	Easting:	680060
Longitude:	120 30 44	Elevation:	710 m

The placer occurrence is off Highway #5A, 20 km N of Princeton, at Laird Lake, and consists of a deposit of poorly sorted gravel containing rounded boulders from pebble size to 0.3 m or more in diameter, in a matrix of rusty-coloured sand. The sand contains a high percentage of heavy minerals, including visible gold and platinum.

On the way to this site, and 8 km N of Princeton, a prominent road cut exposes the Allenby formation, with fine fossils.

2. MINFILE NUMBER: 092HNE190
NAME(S): ALLISON LAKE

Status:	Past producer, open pit	Northing:	5505850
Latitude:	49 40 56	Easting:	672870
Longitude:	120 36 13	Elevation:	853 m

A marl deposit occurs at Allison Lake (Burns Lake), 25 km N of Princeton on Highway #5A. The deposit underlies a 180 m by 70 m area, at the S end of the lake, with thicknesses of up to 3 m. Indicated ore reserves are 16,000 t of marl, with an average thickness of 1.5 m. A sample of the marl analyzed 51% CaO. It was excavated along the S shores of the lake for agricultural markets between 1945–48. No production figures are available.

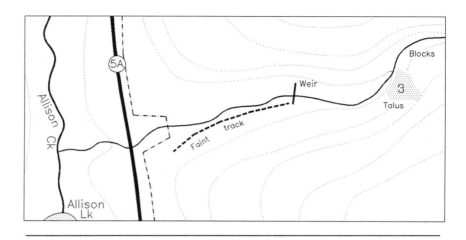

3.   NAME(S): BOUVETTE CREEK

Status:	Showing	Northing:	5505000
Latitude:	49 40 30	Easting:	672750
Longitude:	120 36 20	Elevation:	1035 m

Highway #5A crosses a creek 1 km N of the N end of Allison Lake. A faint track on the S bank leads 400 m to a broken weir. Upstream 100 m the S bank opens onto a small talus slope. At E end of talus, a rib of calcite and conglomerate shows travertine and pudding stone. Large blocks in the creek resemble concrete, but exhibit botryoidal and drusy forms.

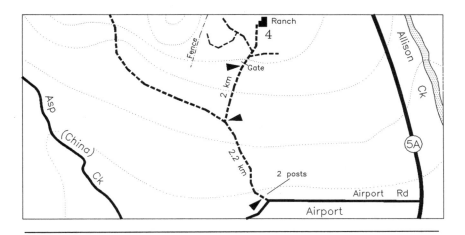

4. NAME(S): CURRIE RANCH

Status:	Showing	Northing:	5486700
Latitude:	49 30 30	Easting:	678000
Longitude:	120 32 30	Elevation:	955 m

Take Highway #5A and turn L after 1.5 km onto Airport Road. Unpaved road leaves far end of Airport Road. 4 km to ranch gate on Currie Road. Ask permission at the ranch about 0.5 km further. A hyalite (opal) deposit is located on the bare E slope of a ridge. Get directions from the ranch. The approach from the car involves a 300 m walk and a 70 m climb. The ridge is topped by thin basalt columns and has wonderful views. Fine-grained quartz (hyalite) is found on the slopes. A 10 cm wide band of the material occurs 15 m from the edge of the summit ridge. Thundereggs are also reported found in the area, and plant fossils in shale are common.

5. MINFILE NUMBER: 092HSE164
NAME(S): ASP CREEK, TULAMEEN BRIDGE

Status:	Showing	Northing:	5481600
Latitude:	49 27 45	Easting:	679530
Longitude:	120 31 21	Elevation:	671 m

The ASP CREEK zeolite showing outcrops along the river banks of Asp (China) Creek to the Tulameen River bridge, and 500 m NW of the creek's confluence with the Tulameen River. Zeolites are contained in a waterlain rhyolite tuff that consists of bedded white ash, with intercalations of vitric-crystal tuff. The cliff exposure exhibits a section of zeolitized tuff, 7 m thick, overlain by fine-grained sandstone, and underlain by carbonaceous shale. It is exposed over a length of 1000 m. The mineralization consists of clinoptilolite, which is accompanied by sanidine, plagioclase, quartz and biotite.

An adit on Asp (China) Creek, 650 m NW of the creek's confluence with the Tulameen River, just N of the Tulameen Road, exposes a 5 m thick coal-bearing section, with interbedded shale, clay and bentonite along the creek's S bank. It contains about 2 m of mostly dirty coal, concentrated near its base. One coal seam, 1.3 m thick, contains three thin bentonite partings and one 20 cm thick band of dirty coal. The seam comprises 90 cm of clean coal. The deposit was explored by a short adit some time before 1947.

Across the Tulameen River, leaf fossil imprints are found in a shale bank. Best access is from behind the hotel in Princeton, following the Tulameen River upstream on its S side.

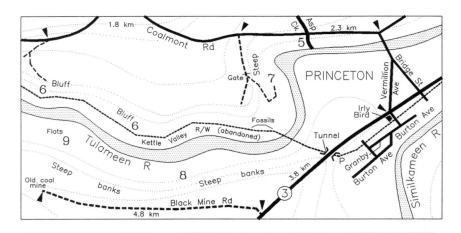

6. **MINFILE NUMBER: 092HSE146**
    NAME(S): VERMILION BLUFFS

Status:	Showing	Northing:	5479540
Latitude:	49 26 41	Easting:	677100
Longitude:	120 33 25	Elevation:	732 m

Possibly Princeton's most famous rockhound feature, this agate showing on a SW-facing bank of the Tulameen River is visible from the heights of the gravel pit 2 km SW of Princeton, on Highway #3. Visit in late afternoon, when the sun gives the bluff its best colours. The "bog" found here is a red-brown to black chert having small fossils. It takes a good polish.

The traditional access was to take the Tulameen Road W out of Princeton for 4.1 km from the bridge at the top of Bridge Street, before turning L (S) onto a logging road to park close to the old railway tracks.

A better route is to turn S off Highway #3 towards the Similkameen River, in the centre of town, at the Irly Bird Hardware. Follow Burton and Granby avenues and hence onto the Kettle Valley Railway right-of-way (unpaved). To the W, a tunnel under Highway #3 is visible. Park at the tunnel's gate, walk through (3 minutes), and over the Tulameen River bridge. The first cutting on the R after the bridge has fossils. Another 10 minute (level) walk along the right-of-way brings you to Vermilion Bluffs. Agate is hosted in andesite and basalt on both banks of the river, and is sometimes bluish in colour. One nodule weighed almost 25 kg. Farther W (500 m) on the N side of the river, banded agate, quartz crystals and calcite occur in seams with white plume on the side of a bluff. Petrified wood (root casts) are reported. The material replacing the wood is gray agate, and is found near the bottom of the bluff in a narrow dark seam of tuff. A further 500 m upstream, seam agate is reported in high bluffs.

Similar material, including amethyst crystals and crystal geodes, is reported on the S side of the river, opposite Vermilion Bluffs. Access is via the private property above (take the Black Mine road off Highway #3 S of Princeton).

---

7. NAME(S): SEQUOIA

Status:	Showing	Northing:	5480600
Latitude:	49 27 15	Easting:	678170
Longitude:	120 32 30	Elevation:	725 m

A 1966 report describes root casts of the giant fern *Metasequoia occidentalis* found at the base of gray tuff (weathered ash) on the W side of the Tulameen River just before it curves due E to flow into Princeton—2 km upstream of the bridge on Bridge Street. This is now private property. It is likely the structure extends across the river to the SE. An early photograph shows visitors digging at the foot of a banded rock bluff, very similar in structure to Vermilion Bluff. The material is reported to be at ground level.

Leaf imprints resembling modern ferns have also been reported. A close relative of the water pine and the sequoia, metasequoias were thought to have died out 25 million years ago, while the sequoias have become restricted to California. Recently, metasequoias were rediscovered in China, while another close relative, the ginkgo tree, flourishes in Japan.

---

8. MINFILE NUMBER: 092HSE211
NAME(S): PLEASANT VALLEY COAL

Status:	Past producer, underground	Northing:	5479220
Latitude:	49 26 30	Easting:	677840
Longitude:	120 32 48	Elevation:	671 m
Comments:	Off the Black Mine road, or access across the Tulameen River from the old Kettle Valley Railway tracks (see VERMILION BLUFFS access).		
Commodities:	Coal, selenite, fossils		

The old workings of the three Pleasant Valley Coal mines (Nos. 1, 2 and 4 mines) occur over a 2 km stretch along the S bank of the Tulameen River, 2.5 kn to 4.5 km SW of Princeton. The colliery was hosted in a sequence of sandstone, shale, waterlain rhyolite tephra (tuff) and coal, up to 2000 m thick.

The colliery's No. 1 mine was opened in 1928 and the No. 2 mine in 1929. The No. 1 mine closed in 1933. The company continued to produce coal from the No. 2 mine until 1937. The two mines produced 82,000 t of coal between 1928 and 1937. Tulameen Collieries opened up the No. 4 mine in 1947, after abandoning its operations across the Tulameen River in 1946. The company mined 100,000 t of coal from 1947–50. Selenite crystals are found in the dumps, and numerous fossils have been collected, including two fossil mammal teeth.

---

9. MINFILE NUMBER: 092HSE010
NAME(S): MCCORMACKS FLATS

Status:	Showing	Northing:	5480720
Latitude:	49 27 21	Easting:	674750
Longitude:	120 35 19	Elevation:	853 m

Agate showing, at the N end of McCormacks Flats, on the SW side of the Tulameen River, off the Black Mine Road. Now on private property. The N part of McCormacks Flats is underlain by andesite and basalt. These lavas are reported to contain agate, crystal geodes and amethyst. Agate and quartz crystal diggings are reported at the top of the bluffs.

---

10. NAME(S): BACON CUTTING

Status:	Showing	Northing:	5481500
Latitude:	49 27 45	Easting:	675360
Longitude:	120 34 48	Elevation:	780 m

Located in a yellow cutting on the N side of the Tulameen Road, 6 km W of the Bridge Sreet bridge in Princeton. Fossil wood and plant fossils in shale are common. Fragile septarian nodules (calcite) are also found in the highway slope.

9.15. COALMONT – TULAMEEN

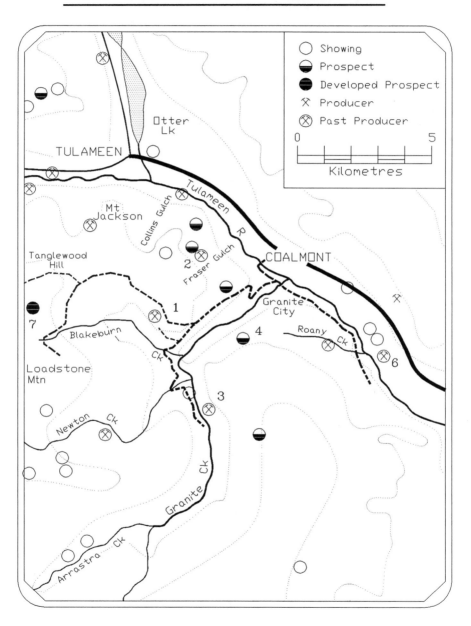

9.15.1 COALMONT AREA

The town of Coalmont is small, but boasts a hotel in the style of every western movie ever made. Half a km W of the hotel, generations of rockhounds have sifted through the coal piles in search of amber. Today, the piles have gone. But the source remains — COALMONT COLLIERY on Blakeburn Creek — and there is plenty of material there.

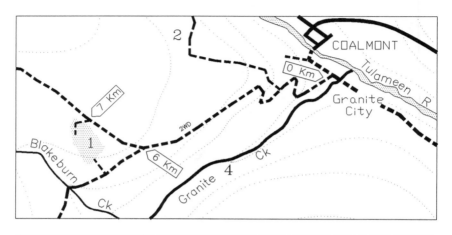

1. **MINFILE NUMBER: 092HSE157**
    NAME(S): COALMONT COLLIERY

Status:	Past Producer Open Pit/Underground		
Latitude:	49 29 21	Northing:	5484040
Longitude:	120 45 11	Easting:	662740
Elevation:	1250 m		
Commodities:	Coal, bentonite, amber, quartz		

When you reach the four-way stop in Coalmont, don't turn R to Tulameen, but drive straight on Parish Avenue. The road swings L and then R onto Bettes Avenue to cross the river on a bridge. On the far side, head downstream 700 m on the Granite City Road before turning SW onto the Blakeburn Road (marker 0 km). At marker 6 km choose either Arrastra Road or Blakeburn Road, depending on whether you want to walk up to, or down to, the site.

Various underground workings occur along the NE bank of Blakeburn Creek. The colliery comprised five mines, and was situated along the SW margin of the Tulameen Basin. The mines were in a coal-bearing shale approximately 130 m to 200 m thick, underlain by up to 120 m of sandstone, siltstone and volcanics, and overlain by 580 m to 700 m of sandstone and pebble conglomerate. The coal was generally poor coking quality. Freshly exposed, it is black with a bright luster, and is commonly banded.

Nodules of bright clear amber (resinite) are widely scattered throughout the coal. Mineral matter consists primarily of quartz and kaolinite, with occasional siderite, orthoclase and sepiolite.

The deposit was initially explored between 1908 and 1910. Production commenced in 1912, but at the deeper levels was limited by the squeezing of underground workings, associated in part with the swelling action of bentonite seams. Total underground production amounted to 2 million t.

About 200 m beyond the turn down to the mine site on Blakeburn Road, a road cut exposes further coal strata.

---

2. MINFILE NUMBER: 092HNE094
NAME(S): COLLINS GULCH

Status:	Past producer, underground	Northing:	5486820
Latitude:	49 30 50	Easting:	664050
Longitude:	120 44 01	Elevation:	1160 m

In the headwaters of Fraser Gulch (incorrectly labeled Bear's Den), and accessible from the Blakeburn Road some 6 km beyond COALMONT COLLIERY, a deposit is exposed in outcrop and various surface and underground workings for 2 km between Collins and Fraser gulches. Collins Gulch occurs along the NE margin of the Tulameen (sedimentary) Basin, and is hosted in a coal-bearing shale 130 m to 200 m thick with 600 m to 700 m of sandstone and pebble conglomerate overlaying it. The coal occurs in the lower 80 m, in a zone of mostly brown/gray/black shale and mudstone, with lesser coal and white/buff bentonite. It ranges from 10 m to 24 m in thickness, and contains 4 m to 17 m of clean coal. Resinite (amber) is reported.

Two seams of cleaner coal occur in Collins Gulch, 4 km SW of its confluence with the Tulameen River. The seams are at least 2 m thick and are separated by strata 6 m thick. Much of this intervening strata may also be coal.

At a prospect 1 km SE of Collins Gulch, three seams of coal (9 m, 9 m and 4 m thick) occur in a section 120 m thick. The two upper seams were explored by adits.

At the Fraser Gulch prospect, 2 km SE of Collins Gulch, coal-bearing strata are exposed discontinuously over a strike of 2 km.

The deposit was explored in early 1901 and a number of adits at Collins Gulch, Bear's Den and Fraser Gulch were excavated from 1910–13. The prospect was abandoned because of excessive shearing of the coal strata. The exposure at Collins Gulch was re-examined in 1948, leading to the excavation of two adits in 1950–51. Some 250 t of coal were produced in 1951.

9.15.2 GRANITE CITY

The discovery of gold at Granite Creek in 1885 by the aptly named Johnny Chance created boom times for Granite City. Today, nothing remains except a few sagging log buildings, and a cairn and plaque, at the confluence of Granite Creek with the Tulameen River. Yet at its peak, Granite City had over 15 hotels, and was the third largest city in western Canada! Access is the same as for COALMONT COLLIERY.

---

3.   MINFILE NUMBER: 092HSE230
NAME(S): GRANITE CREEK PLACER

Status:	Past Producer		Northing:	5480500
Latitude:	49 27 24		Easting:	664900
Longitude:	120 43 29		Elevation:	975 m

Granite Creek flows NE from Granite and Kettle mountains over a distance of some 27 km. The lower section cuts through a narrow rock-walled canyon that extends from its mouth upstream for 6 km, to the confluence with Newton Creek. Farther upstream, the creek occupies a broad valley floor that continues SW to Granite and Kettle mountains. The canyon contains shallow gravels varying from 0.5 m to 2.5 m thick, while the upper valley has gravels of much greater thickness. Gold- and platinum-bearing sections are generally found to occur on bedrock. These pay gravels are cemented by a stiff clay. Gold to platinum ratios average 3:1. The proportion of platinum increases upstream towards Newton Creek.

Early gold nuggets were coarse and rough, and frequently weighed 160 gm to 250 gm. One nugget obtained near the junction with Blakeburn Creek appeared to be made up of a number of smaller nuggets grown together. Some coarse nuggets found in the lower part of the creek contained a large amount of white quartz. Platinum occurred in smaller, silver-coloured nodules, generally not exceeding 16 gm, and usually round and pitted with holes.

Total gold production from 1885–1945 is estimated at 824 kg. Most of this production occurred between 1885 and 1890 from gravels in the canyon. The deeper gravels above Newton Creek were largely ignored until 1907 when two prospectors began to mine a section of the creek hydraulically, just above the mouth of Newton Creek. Mining on this part of the creek continued periodically until 1932.

4. MINFILE NUMBER: 092HSE103
NAME(S): GRANITE CREEK GYPSUM

Status:	Prospect	Northing:	5483320
Latitude:	49 28 54	Easting:	666080
Longitude:	120 42 26	Elevation:	1219 m

The GRANITE CREEK GYPSUM occurrence is reported along the E side of the Granite Creek valley for 800 m, with an average width of 6 m. Well-rounded lumps of pure white gypsum have been found in the bed of Granite Creek.

5. MINFILE NUMBER: 092HSE232
NAME(S): NEWTON CREEK PLACER

Status:	Past Producer	Northing:	5479400
Latitude:	49 26 52	Easting:	661000
Longitude:	120 46 44	Elevation:	1433 m

Newton Creek flows for a distance of 11 km into Granite Creek. The lower half of the creek cuts through a narrow, steeply sided valley, while the upper half flows over a broader, more open valley floor. Gold and platinum were produced from gravels in this creek from 1890–93. The gold to platinum ratios are reported to be 1:1. The gold is similar to that found at Granite Creek, being coarse and rough. Some of the larger nuggets contained quartz. Total gold production is estimated at 6.5 kg.

6. MINFILE NUMBER: 092HSE235
NAME(S): TULAMEEN RIVER

Status:	Past Producer	Northing:	5482950
Latitude:	49 28 37	Easting:	671800
Longitude:	120 37 42	Elevation:	707 m
Commodities:	Gold, platinum, iridium, palladium, rhodium, osmium, ruthenium		

MINERALS:
Associated: Quartz, chromite, magnetite, olivine

The placer lease is on the Tulameen River, about 6.5 km below Coalmont. Black sands produced by a dragline 4 km above Princeton assayed 250 gm/t gold and 40 gm/t platinum. Farther upstream, about 3 km below Coalmont, a sample of panned black sand assayed 27 gm/t gold and 21 gm/t platinum. A series of shafts and pits at this location below Coalmont encountered gravels averaging 1 gm/m³ of gold. Similar workings at Petersen Flat, 5 km

W of Princeton, averaged 1.2 gm/m³ of gold.

Minor production occurred during the 1940s and '50s, largely within 5 km of Princeton. This activity was centred 3 km W of Princeton, where for example, one operation recovered 1,534 gm of gold and 420 gm of platinum from 760 m³ of gravel in 1941.

Gold production for the entire river between 1885–1945 is estimated at close to 300 kg.

---

7. MINFILE NUMBER: 092HSE034
NAME(S): LODESTONE MOUNTAIN

Status:	Developed prospect	Northing:	5481000
Latitude:	49 27 48	Easting:	656810
Longitude:	120 50 09	Elevation:	1890 m
Comments:	Centre of ore reserves, at the summit of Lodestone Mtn. Take the Blakeburn Rd to marker 12 km, where a 4WD road turns R and leads another 10 km to Lodestone Lake. A steep track SE brings you 1.8 km to the summit (1895 m).		
Commodities:	Iron, vanadium, platinum, titanium		

MINERALS
Significant: Magnetite

The magnetite deposit occurs at the summit, intergrown with coarse-grained pyroxene and hornblende. Magnetite also forms semi-massive to massive lenses or vein-like bodies, with minor mica and pyroxene, up to 0.6 m in diameter. The lens masses occur in an ill-defined zone, about 100 m wide, that trends NW along the crest of Lodestone Mountain for at least 670 m. Drilling has outlined reserves of almost 90 million t, grading 15% soluble iron and 0.08% vanadium pentoxide.

---

8. MINFILE NUMBER: 092HSE035
NAME(S): TANGLEWOOD HILL

Status:	Developed prospect	Northing:	5484240
Latitude:	49 29 32	Easting:	657900
Longitude:	120 49 11	Elevation:	1588 m

Tanglewood Hill, 3 km NNE of LODESTONE MTN, is underlain by a mass of hornblende pyroxenite covering an area 2.5 km long and up to 1 km wide. Magnetite occurs in some two dozen lenses on the W and S slopes of Tanglewood Hill. Eight massive magnetite lenses exposed on the hill's W slope range from a few cm to 5.5 m wide. The largest is estimated to contain 54,000 t of magnetite, grading 50% to 60% iron and 2% titanium.

9.15.3 TULAMEEN AREA

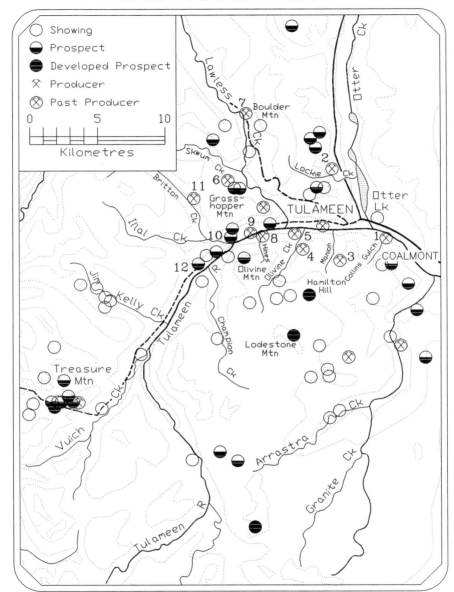

Legend:
○ Showing
◑ Prospect
● Developed Prospect
✗ Producer
⊗ Past Producer

0   5   10
Kilometres

The Tulameen River placers

The Tulameen River flows N from the Cascade Mountains for 30 km to Grasshopper Mountain, where it turns E for 10 km to the town of Tulameen. It then flows SE for 25 km before entering the Similkameen River at Princeton.

The upper part of the river runs through a wide valley extending from its headwaters in Paradise Valley N to Champion Creek. It continues through a narrow rock-walled canyon between Grasshopper and Olivine mountains, to the mouth of Olivine (Slate) Creek. The gravels in this canyon are generally not more than a metre thick, and occur in the creek bed and in benches on the sides of the valley, either in or above the level of the canyon. Below Olivine Creek, a broad valley floor with deep gravel deposits opens up and continues past the towns of Tulameen and Coalmont to a point 2 km below Granite Creek. The river then cuts through a canyon to a point 5 km W of Princeton. Here, the river enters a broad valley that eventually merges with that of the Similkameen River at Princeton.

Gold and platinum deposits have been found over the lower 40 km of the river. Most recorded production and exploration has occurred along two stretches. The upper stretch begins about 2 km W of Tulameen and continues up the river for 12 km to the mouth of Champion Creek. The lower stretch begins at Coalmont, just above the mouth of Granite Creek, and continues SE for 19 km to Princeton. Metals found along the Tulameen River tend to occur in old sinuous channels buried deep below glacial gravels, which yield only spotty values. Gold occurs in rough, angular or slightly flattened nuggets. Some contain abundant white quartz. One nugget found in 1931 near the mouth of Lawless (Bear) Creek weighed 250 gm. Platinum forms small rounded grains of uniform size, smaller than the gold nuggets, and commonly pitted. Such nuggets, produced at a hydraulic mine just below Britton (Eagle) Creek, weighed up to 16 gm. Larger platinum nuggets often have a coating or included crystals of cumulate chromite, sometimes with intergrown magnetite and inclusions of olivine. Platinum is also found to occur in pebbles of olivine and chromite. The gravels worked along the upper river also yielded black sands comprised of magnetite and chromite, with significant gold and platinum values. The ratio of gold to platinum recovered in this part of the river is generally about 1:1, but is observed to decrease upstream to the mouth of Britton Creek, where it is 1:2. Small quantities of native copper and gold-bearing pellets of tetrahedrite also occur in these placer deposits.

Some of the richest placers mined in the Tulameen district occur along the upper Tulameen River, in the canyon between Champion and Olivine creeks, both in the river bed and in adjacent gravel benches. Here, one deposit located 1 km below Eagle Creek and 13 km upstream from Tulameen (Sootheran lease), contained measured geological reserves of 200,000 m^3 grading over 3 gm/t of gold equivalent per m^3, for combined gold and platinum. A shaft sunk on a bench 11 km above Tulameen, also in the canyon, intersected coarse gold and platinum grading even higher values.

Precious metal grades continue to decline downstream. Just below the canyon, 4 km upstream of Tulameen, a hole drilled to a depth of 5 m yielded 1 gm of gold equivalent per m^3 for combined gold and platinum. Farther below the canyon, across from the mouth of Otter Creek at Tulameen, river gravels are estimated to yield only 0.5 gm of gold per m^3, with traces of platinum. Production of placer gold was first reported in 1877,

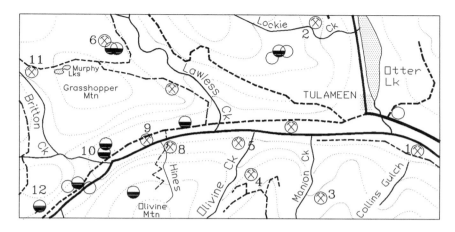

and may have commenced as early as 1860. By 1887, most of the shallower gravel deposits mined along the Tulameen River were reported to be exhausted. A few operators along the upper section persisted through the early 1900s. One operation 10 km above Tulameen, recovered 620 gm of gold and also some platinum from 1500 m³ of gravel. High platinum prices during the 1920s prompted a revival of placer mining along both the upper and lower sections of the river. Several deposits saw significant production during this time on the upper part of the river. Sporadic exploration and production occurred during the 1950s, '60s and '70s, mostly below the canyon, between Olivine Creek and the town of Tulameen. Crude gold production for the entire river between 1885 and 1945 is estimated at 297 kg.

I.   MINFILE NUMBER: 092HNE195
NAME(S): COLLINS GULCH PLACER

Status:	Past Producer	Northing:	5488900
Latitude:	49 31 57	Easting:	663570
Longitude:	120 44 22	Elevation:	853 m

Collins Gulch descends rapidly N on the S side of the Tulameen Valley, for 3.5 km, and then enters the Tulameen River 2 km SE of Tulameen. Some coarse gold was recovered from gravels over a section extending up to 800 m above the creek's mouth. This part of the creek lies in the floor of the Tulameen valley, below the canyon cut by the creek into the valley side. It has therefore been suggested that the gold-bearing gravels may have originated from the Tulameen River. The gravels were mined between 1886 and 1890. Estimated production for this period is 6.6 kg of gold. These placer deposits were reported to be largely exhausted by 1889.

2. MINFILE NUMBER: 092HNE193
NAME(S): LOCKIE (BOULDER) CREEK PLACER

Status:	Past Producer	Northing:	5494130
Latitude:	49 34 50	Easting:	660450
Longitude:	120 46 50	Elevation:	884 m

Lockie (Boulder) Creek initially flows S along the W flank of Boulder Mountain for 3 km, and then swings E for 4 km, entering Otter Lake 4.5 km N of Tulameen. The upper 4 km are a narrow valley, after which the creek enters a canyon, over 2 km long, before flowing out over a 500 m wide alluvial fan at Otter Lake.

At the placer occurrence, gold was recovered from gravels in the lower 2.5 km of the creek, as well as in a few places above the canyon. One nugget, found in 1887, likely the largest gold nugget from the Tulameen district, weighed 1.4 kg. Unlike most other streams in the district, no platinum was recovered from the creek's gravels. The creek was worked intermittently from 1886–1909.

3. MINFILE NUMBER: 092HNE194
NAME(S): MANION (CEDAR) CREEK PLACER

Status:	Past Producer	Northing:	5487590
Latitude:	49 31 18	Easting:	660200
Longitude:	120 47 12	Elevation:	1076 m

Manion (Cedar) Creek plunges steeply N from its headwaters on Hamilton Hill for 4 km, entering the Tulameen River some 2 km W of Tulameen. At the placer occurrence, gold- and platinum-bearing gravels were mined along the creek intermittently from 1886–1933. Some coarse gold and platinum, in nuggets weighing 3 gm to 6 gm, were recovered, in addition to finer dust, by ground sluicing.

4. MINFILE NUMBER: 092HNE198
NAME(S): OLIVINE (SLATE) CREEK PLACER

Status:	Past Producer	Northing:	5488930
Latitude:	49 32 04	Easting:	657640
Longitude:	120 49 17	Elevation:	942 m

Olivine (Slate) Creek flows NE from the W flank of Lodestone Mountain for 11 km, before entering the Tulameen River 5 km W of Tulameen. The stream initially passes through a deep but flat-floored valley, 6 km long, before encountering a short canyon, and then a series of waterfalls, just above its mouth. The more extensive gravel deposits are found in the broader parts of the valley above the falls. In one section, the gravels are over 2 m deep and thicken downstream. A large amount of coarse gold and platinum was recovered from the creek's gravels, mostly from the valley above the canyon. One gold nugget found in 1886 weighed 393 gm. The gravels were mined from 1886–1900. Estimated production for this period is 38 kg of gold. The creek was extensively explored underground (looking for old river channels) above and below the falls, and at its mouth, from 1925–31. One tunnel excavated above the falls was 670 m long. A shaft sunk from this tunnel is reported to have intersected gold- and platinum-bearing gravels containing boulders of pyroxenite, peridotite and dunite.

---

5. MINFILE NUMBER: 092HNE022
NAME(S): EL ALAMEIN

Status:	Past Producer	Northing:	5489450
Latitude:	49 32 22	Easting:	656380
Longitude:	120 50 19	Elevation:	838 m

MINERALS

Significant:	Gold, pyrite, chalcopyrite
Associated:	Calcite, quartz

The EL ALAMEIN mine is on the S bank of the Tulameen River, 200 m SE of the mouth of Lawless Creek. The Tulameen River valley, in this vicinity, is underlain by greenstone (chlorite schist) with lesser volcanics and minor sediments. These rocks strike NW, and are regionally metamorphosed. The mine is in a shear zone up to 9 m wide, and roughly follows the contact between argillite to the NE and rhyolite porphyry to the SW. It has been traced SE from the river bank up the N slope of Olivine Mountain for 850 m. The zone contains narrow stringers of calcite and quartz, erratically mineralized with native gold. The stringers are narrow (2 cm to 15 cm wide) and from 0.3 m to 1 m long. The gold occurs as wavy layers and wisps within calcite-quartz stringers. Pyrite and chalcopyrite occur in the veinlets and in the sheared and brecciated diorite.

The deposit was discovered in 1937, when a slide exposed showings of native gold in the river bank. It was eventually mined from three adits developed in the steep S bank of the river. Gold production between 1949 and 1951 amounted to 6.2 kg, recovered from an unknown amount of ore.

6. MINFILE NUMBER: 092HNE064
NAME(S): ST GEORGE

Status:	Past producer, underground		
Latitude:	49 34 23	Northing:	5493060
Longitude:	120 54 17	Easting:	651480
Elevation:	1378 m		

MINERALS

Significant: Pyrite, pyrrhotite, chalcopyrite, sphalerite, galena
Associated: Calcite, quartz

Area of shafts are about 1 km SW of the confluence of Skwum and Lawless (Bear) creeks, 11 km NW of Tulameen. The ST. LAWRENCE prospect (092HNE065) is some 400 m SE. The LIVERPOOL prospect (092HNE066) lies a further 400 m SE of ST. LAWRENCE. Access is via Britton Creek FS Road (active logging in 1998) and then 3 km past the Murphy Lakes Rec Site.

The area is underlain by dark gray/black schist, limestone (marble) and chlorite schist (greenstone). The upper part is intruded by porphyritic dykes and sills. Massive sulfides are developed where non-calcareous schists grade into the overlying calcareous schists and marbles.

The deposit consists of a lens of dispersed/consolidated sulfides, and has been traced along strike for 27 m, and downdip for 55 m in two shafts. The sulfides occur in limestone over widths of up to 4 m. The deposit lies 100 m E of a porphyritic dyke; mineralization consists of pyrite and pyrrhotite, with lesser chalcopyrite and minor sphalerite and galena, in a gangue of calcite and minor quartz. A grab sample of pyrite and pyrrhotite in limestone from the dump of the W shaft analyzed 1% copper. The prospect was explored by two shafts with several drifts and crosscuts, from 1903–13. A total of 27 t were mined in 1916.

The ST. LAWRENCE deposit 400 m to the SE consists of a massive sulfide lens, up to 1.8 m thick, exposed in three partially caved-in shafts. It is hosted in limestone and schist. Mineralization consists of pyrrhotite, pyrite and sphalerite, with minor galena, chalcopyrite and magnetite.

The LIVERPOOL prospect 400 m S of St Lawrence was explored as early as 1901. The showing was periodically tunnelled from 1921–29. It shows similar geology.

Similar mineralization is exposed in trenches on the CHICAGO (092HNE016) claim 200 m to the S. Here, pyrite, chalcopyrite and sphalerite occur in limestone. The limestone (hosting the sulfides) outcrops to the W as two NW-trending, parallel bands. Most of the limestone is coarse-grained and white, and contains relatively abundant veins and pods of quartz. The S exposures reveal bluish gray/white banded, coarse-grained limestone with a few inclusions of schist.

7. MINFILE NUMBER: 092HNE192
NAME(S): LAWLESS (BEAR) CREEK PLACER

Status:	Past Producer	Northing:	5498250
Latitude:	49 37 10	Easting:	652360
Longitude:	120 53 26	Elevation:	1180 m

Lawless (Bear) Creek is a S-flowing tributary of the Tulameen River, some 22 km long, situated 13 km NW of Tulameen. The lower 9 km of the creek flow through a narrow deep valley, while upstream the landscape widens to a broader, more open valley. The narrow lower section contains shallow gravels confined to the creek bed.

At the placer occurrence, some gold and minor platinum were recovered from gravels near the mouth of a creek. One gold nugget, found in 1886, weighed 585 gm. The gravels were mined intermittently from 1886–99. Estimated production for 1886 was 1.8 kg. Some development work on the placer leases was done in 1982.

8. MINFILE NUMBER: 092HNE197
NAME(S): HINES CREEK PLACER

Status:	Past Producer	Northing:	5489130
Latitude:	49 32 13	Easting:	654580E
Longitude:	120 51 49		

Hines Creek plunges rapidly N from its headwaters on Olivine Mountain for 2.3 km, entering the Tulameen River 7.5 km W of the town of Tulameen. Platinum and gold were recovered from gravels a short distance above the Tulameen River. The quantity of gravel in this creek is now quite limited. The deposits were worked as early as 1885.

9. MINFILE NUMBER: 092HNE199
NAME(S): TULAMEEN RIVER PLACER, SOOTHERAN

Status:	Past Producer	Northing:	5488740
Latitude:	49 32 02	Easting:	652810
Longitude:	120 53 17	Elevation:	870 m

The Sootheran lease, 1 km below the Britton (Eagle) Creek mouth, was operated intermittently from 1925–47, and produced 3.9 kg of platinum and 530 gm of gold from 1926–28.

10. MINFILE NUMBER: 092HNE128
NAME(S): D, R, CREEK ZONE

Status:	Prospect	Northing:	5487990
Latitude:	49 31 39	Easting:	651850
Longitude:	120 54 06	Elevation:	908 m
Comments:	Zone sampled is 50 m NW of the confluence of Britton (Eagle) Creek with the Tulameen River, 11 km W of Tulameen.		

MINERALS
Significant: Chromite, chalcopyrite, sperrylite, millerite, asbestos

The D showing occurs is in the dunite-rich core of an intrusive complex. Mineralization occurs in a serpentine breccia zone containing fragments of dunite/peridotite cemented by a matrix of serpentine. The zone is 200 m long, up to 150 m wide, and lies mostly north of the river, on either side of the creek. Chromite occurs in the breccia and the surrounding dunite, in areas of strong magnesium alteration, mostly along Britton Creek. The mineral forms irregular lenses up to 20 cm long and 10 cm wide, fracture fillings up to 2 cm wide, and primary layers up to 15 cm thick.

Platinum occurs in elevated values in the breccia and in the surrounding dunite/peridotite. Two samples from the breccia assayed between 2 gm/t and 4 gm/t platinum.

11. MINFILE NUMBER: 092HNE196
NAME(S): BRITTON (EAGLE) CREEK PLACER

Status:	Past Producer	Northing:	5491600
Latitude:	49 33 39	Easting:	648490
Longitude:	120 56 48	Elevation:	1200 m

Britton (Eagle) Creek flows SE for 12 km before entering the Tulameen River, 10 km SW of Tulameen. The lower part of the creek descends rapidly into the Tulameen River through a narrow V-shaped canyon, 4 km long. In contrast, the upper part of the creek and its various tributaries flow through broader, flaring valleys. The stream contains gravel deposits of limited extent, especially in the lower sections. Above the canyon, the gravels are deeper and more widespread. Coarse gold and platinum were recovered near the mouth of the creek. These deposits were prospected and mined as early as 1885.

12. MINFILE NUMBER: 092HNE097
NAME(S): CHAMPION CREEK

Status:	Prospect	Northing:	5486000
Latitude:	49 30 36	Easting:	649880
Longitude:	120 55 47	Elevation:	1006 m

A molybdenum-copper showing outcrops on both sides of the Tulameen River. Hosted in metamorphic rocks, a zone of disseminated molybdenite, chalcopyrite, bornite, pyrite and trace covellite occurs in the roadside quarry on the N side of the river, 250 m W of the mouth of Champion Creek. Most of the mineralization is in the marble, and lies close to the contact zone (0 m to 10 m distance). Similar mineralization occurs sporadically along a stretch of Champion Creek, beginning near the creek's mouth, and continuing upstream for about 1.5 km. Disseminated molybdenite, pyrite, chalcopyrite, sphalerite and tetrahedrite are found in skarn-altered limestones in a gangue of quartz, reddish garnet, epidote, hornblende and pyroxene. High gold and silver assays are reported from this mineralization. There is an old adit, 200 m S of the creek mouth.

CHAPTER 10: ADDRESSES

While every effort has been made to obtain current addresses and phone numbers, be aware that institutions close, stores move, and clubs change executives.

Reference Libraries:

Vancouver   **Geological Survey of Canada**
Suite 1500, 605 Robson Street
Vancouver, BC V6B 5J3
phone: (604)666-3812, fax: (604)666-7186

Victoria   **Energy, Mines & Petroleum Resources Library**
Ground Floor, 1810 Blanshard Street
PO Box 9321
Station Provincial Government
Victoria, BC V8W 9N3
phone: (250)952-0583, fax: (250)952-0581

Ottawa   **Geological Survey of Canada**
601 Booth Street
Ottawa, ON K1A 0E8
phone: (613)995-0947

Maps and reports:

Vancouver   **Geological Survey of Canada**
Map & Publication Sales
Suite 1500, 605 Robson Street
Vancouver, BC V6B 5J3
phone: (604)666-3812, fax: (604)666-7186

Victoria   **Energy, Mines & Petroleum Resources**
Geological Survey Branch
5th Floor, 1810 Blanshard Street
Victoria, BC V8V 1X4
phone: (250)952-0583, fax: (250)952-0381

Crown Publications Inc.
521 Fort Street
Victoria, BC V8W 1E7
phone: (250)386-4636, fax: (250)386-0221

Ottawa   **Geological Survey of Canada**
601 Booth Street
Ottawa, ON K1A 0E8
phone: (613)995-0947

Claim Maps and Free Miner Certificates

To find the location of the office serving your community, contact BC Enquiry toll free at 1-800-663-7867.

Gold Commissioners' Offices:

(Some of these offices have a mines inspector, but not a resident geologist.)

Alberni Mining Div., 4515 Elizabeth St., Port Alberni, BC V9Y 6L5 (250)724-9204
Atlin Mining Div., Third St., Box 100, Atlin, BC V0W 1A0 (250)651-7595
Cariboo Mining Div., 102 – 350 Barlow St., Quesnel, BC V2J 2C1 (250)992-4301
Clinton Mining Div., 1423 Cariboo Hwy, Clinton, BC V0K 1K0 (250)459-2268
Fort Steele Mining Div., 102 – 11th St., Cranbrook, BC V1C 2P2 (250)426-1211
Golden Mining Div., 606 – 6th St. North, Box 39, Golden, BC V0A 1H0
(250)344-7550
Greenwood Mining Div., 524 Central Ave., Box 850, Grand Forks, BC V0H 1H0
(250)442-5444
Kamloops Mining Div., 250 – 455 Columbia St., Kamloops, BC V2C 6K4
(250)828-4540
Liard Mining Div., 302 – 865 Hornby St., Vancouver, BC V6Z 2C5 (604)660-2672
Lillooet Mining Div., 615 Main St., Court House, Bag 700, Lillooet, BC V0K 1V0
(250)256-7548
Nanaimo Mining Div., 13 Victoria Cres., Nanaimo, BC V9R 5B9 (250)755-2200
Nelson Mining Div., 310 Ward St., Nelson, BC V1L 5S4 (250)354-6104
New Westminster Mining Div., 100 – 635 Columbia St., New Westminster, BC
V3M 1A7 (604)660-8666
Nicola Mining Div., 1840 Nicola Ave., Box 4400, Merritt, BC V0K 2B0
(250)378-9343
Omineca Mining Div., 3793 Alfred St., Box 5000, Smithers, BC V0J 2N0
(250)847-7207
Osoyoos Mining Div., 112 – 100 Main St., Penticton, BC V2A 5A5 (250)492-1211
Revelstoke Mining Div., 1100 West 2nd St., Box 380, Revelstoke, BC V0E 2S0
(250)837-7636
Similkameen Mining Div., 151 Vermilion Ave., Box 9, Princeton, BC V0W 1W0
(250)295-6957
Skeena Mining Div., 100 Market Pl., Prince Rupert, BC V8J 1B7 (250)627-0415
Slocan Mining Div., Box 580, Kaslo, BC V0G 1M0 (250)353-2219
Trail Creek Mining Div., 2888 Columbia Ave., Rossland, BC V0G 1Y0
(250)326-7324
Vancouver Mining Div., 302 – 865 Hornby St., Vancouver, BC V6Z 2C5
(604)660-2672
Vernon Mining Div., #102, 3001 – 27th St., Vernon, BC V1T 4W5 (250)549-5511
Victoria Mining Div., 3rd Fl., 1810 Blanshard St., Victoria, BC V8W 9N3
(250)952-0542

Mining & Exploration Information

District Geologist's Offices, Ministry of Employment & Investment:
Cranbrook: 100 Cranbrook St. N., V1C 3PQ (250)426-1658
Fernie: Bag 1000, V0B 1M0 (250)423-6884
Kamloops: #200, 2985 Airport Dr., V2B 7W8 (250)828-4566
Nanaimo: 2080B Labieux Rd., V9T 6J9 (250)751-7374
Prince George: 3990 – 22nd Ave., V2N 3A1 (250)565-6125
Smithers: 3793 Alfred Ave., V0J 2N0 (250)847-7391
Vancouver: Rm 301, 865 Hornby St., V6Z 2G3 (604)660-0223
Victoria: PO Box 9320, Stn. Prov.Gov. V8W 9N3 (250)952-0403

Mining Museums

Barkerville, Barkerville Historic Town, at the end of Hwy 26. (250)994-3332
Britannia Beach, British Columbia Museum of Mining, on Hwy #99, 52 km from
  Vancouver. (604)688-8735
Cumberland, Cumberland Museum, off Island Hwy near Comox. (250)336-2445
Rossland, Rossland Mining Museum, junction Hwys 3B/22. (250)362-7722
Silverton, Silverton Outdoor Mining Exhibit, on Hwy 6, nr Silverton Village.
  (250)358-7788
Woodberry Creek, Woodberry Mining Museum, Hwy 31, 2 km north of Ainsworth
  Hot Springs. (250)353-2592

Mineral Displays in BC

Abbotsford Museum, 2313 Ware St., Abbotsford *(Mining exhibit)*
Ashcroft Museum, 404 Brink St., Ashcroft *(Mining & mineralogical displays)*
Atlin Museum, 3rd & Trainor Sts., PO Box 111, Atlin *(Gold rush material)*
BC & Yukon Chamber of Mines, 860-1066 West Hastings St., Vancouver *(Small
  museum)*
BC Provincial Archives, Parliament Buildings, Victoria *(Manuscripts, historical
  documents)*
Boundary Museum, PO Box 17, Grand Forks *(Mining equipment)*
Bulkley Valley Historical & Museum Society, PO Box 2615, Smithers *(Some fossil
  material)*
Courtenay & District Museum, 360 Cliffe Ave., PO Box 3128, Courtenay *(Fossils)*
Dawson Creek Museum, 13 St. & Alaska Ave., Dawson Creek *(Fossils, mammoth
  tusk)*
Energy, Mines & Petroleum Resources, 1st Fl., 1810 Blanshard St., Victoria *(Rock &
  mineral displays)*
Fernie Museum, 502 – 5th Ave., PO Box 1527, Fernie *(Coal mining gear & history)*
Fort George Regional Museum, PO Box 1779, Prince George *(Mineral displays)*
Fort Steele Heritage Town, 16 km N Cranbrooke, Hwys 93/95 *(Mining exhibit)*
Grand Forks Boundary Museum, Hwy 3, 7370 – 5th St., Grand Forks *(Mining
  exhibit)*
Greenwood Museum, 214 South Copper St., Greenwood *(Mining exhibit)*
Hope Museum, 919 Water St., Hope *(Mining exhibit)*
Hudson's Hope Museum, PO Box 98, Hudson's Hope *(Fossils, dinosaur & gold
  panning history)*
Kaatza Museum, Lake Cowichan, Vancouver Island *(Mining exhibit)*

Kamloops Museum, 207 Seymour St., Kamloops *(Local geology)*
Kelowna Centennial Museum, 470 Queensway, Kelowna *(Mining exhibit)*
Kettle River Museum, Hwy 3 (CPR Station), Midway *(Mining exhibit)*
Kimberley Heritage Museum, 105 Spokane St., Kimberley *(Mining exhibit)*
Kitimat Smelter, Kitimat *(Public tours daily)*
Lillooet Museum, PO Box 441, Lillooet *(Mining & gold rush history)*
Mineral World, 9891 Seaport Pl., Sidney, ph:(250)655-4367, fax:(250)656-2350
   (Mineral displays)
Mission Museum, 33201 Second Ave., Mission *(Mineral collection)*
Museum of Northern BC, PO Box 669, Prince Rupert *(Rock collection, mining history)*
Nanaimo Centennial Museum, 100 Cameron Rd., Nanaimo *(Coal mining history,
   simulated mine tunnel)*
Nelson Centennial Museum, 402 Anderson St., Nelson *(Geology & mining history)*
Nicola Valley Museum, 2202 Jackson Ave., Merritt *(Mining exhibit)*
Osoyoos Museum, PO Box 791, Osoyoos *(Mining samples, fossils)*
Peace Island Park Museum, Taylor, nr Fort St John *(Fossils, rocks)*
Powell River Historical Museum, PO Box 42, Powell River *(International sand
   collection)*
Quesnel Historical Museum, le Bourdais Park, 405 Barlow Ave., Quesnel *(Rock &
   mining displays)*
R.N. Atkinson Museum, 785 Main St., Penticton *(Mineralogy & natural history
   displays)*
Rossland Historical Museum, PO Box 26, Hwys 22/38, Rossland *(Underground
   tours of LeRoy Mine)*
Royal BC Provincial Museum, 601 Belleville St., Victoria *(Some displays)*
Sandon Museum, PO Box 303, Sandon *(Mining history)*
Science World, 1455 Quebec St., Vancouver, ph:(604)268-6363, fax:(604)682-2923
   (Mineral displays)
The Rockhound Shop, 777 Cloverdale Rd, Victoria, ph:(250)475-2080 *(Mineral
   displays)*
Wells Historical Society, PO Box 244, Wells *(Mining history)*
Williams Lake Museum, Williams Lake *(Mining history)*
Yale Museum, 31179 Douglas St., Yale *(Mining exhibit)*

Rock Collecting Magazines

BC Rockhounder, 60, 15875 - 20th Ave., Surrey, BC V4A 2V1
Cab & Crystal, 7 Elizabeth St N., Unit 406, Mississauga, ON L5G 2Y8
Lapidary Journal, Suite 201, 60 Chestnut Avenue, Devon, PA 19333-1312
Rock & Gem, 4880 Market St., Ventura, CA 93003-7783
Rock & Minerals, 1319 Eighteenth St. NW, Washington DC 20036-1802

BC Clubs & Associations

Most clubs change their president, address and phone number every few years. For
the latest information, contact your nearest Visitor Information service, Chamber of
Commerce or Municipality, or write to: The Lapidary Rock & Mineral Society of BC,
13515 - 112 Ave., Surrey, BC V3R 2E9 ph: (604)584-5592, fax:(604)584-5570

Publications of the Gem & Mineral Foundation of Canada are available from affiliated clubs and societies, or from the Foundation's Secretary at 3492 Dundas Street, Vancouver, BC V5K 1R8.

On-line information on the clubs is available via the Canadian Rockhound website. It, too, changes its address periodically. Search for it using key words "Canadian Rockhound".

Lower Mainland:
Lapidary Rock & Mineral Society of British Columbia
4705 – 4th Avenue
Delta, BC V4K 1P5

Fraser Valley Rock & Gem Club
c/o M. Lindberg
5543 – 238th Street
Langley, BC V2Z 2P1
Meeting: OAP Hall, 273rd St., Aldergrove, 2nd Fri/mth, 7:30pm

Maple Ridge Lapidary Club
PO Box 142
Maple Ridge, BC V2X 7E9
Meeting: Craft Studio, 11963 Haney Pl., Maple Ridge, 1st Thur/mth, 7:30pm

Surrey Rockhound Gem & Mineral Club
PO Box 9060, Unit 160
Surrey, BC V3T 5P8
Meeting: Bear Creek Park Pavilion, 13750 – 38th Ave., 4th Wed/mth, 7:30pm

Burnaby Laphounds Club
PO Box 72046
4429 Kingsway
Burnaby, BC V5H 4P9
Meeting: Bonsor Recreation Centre, 2nd Tues/mth, 8:00pm

Delta Rockhound Gem & Mineral Club
c/o 5247 Crescent Drive
Ladner, BC V4L 1T5
Meeting: South Delta Rec Centre, 1720 – 56th St., 3rd Mon/mth, 7:30pm

Port Moody Rock & Gem Club
c/o Kyle Centre
125 Kyle Street
Port Moody, BC V3H 2V7
Meeting: Parks & Rec Bldg., 300 Loco Rd., Pt Moody, last Tues/mth, 7:30pm

Creative Jewellers Guild of BC
c/o Richmond Cultural Centre
7700 Minoru Gate
Richmond, BC V6Y 1R9
Meeting: Richmond Art Centre, 3rd Sun/mth, 1– 4pm

Richmond Gem & Mineral Club
c/o Richmond Art Centre
7700 Minoru Gate
Richmond, BC V6Y 1R9
Meeting: Richmond Cultural Centre, 1st Fri/mth, 7:30pm

BC Faceters Guild
c/o Hastings Community Centre
3096 East Hastings Street
Vancouver, BC V5K 2A3
Meeting: Hastings Comm. Centre, 2nd Sat/mth, 9am – 12:30pm

Canada Rock Association
2620 West Broadway
Vancouver, BC V6K 2G3
Meeting: 2620 West Broadway, 1st & 3rd Sat/mth, 2pm

Dunbar Lapidary Club
c/o Dunbar Community Centre
4747 Dunbar Street
Vancouver, BC V6S 2H2
Meeting: Dunbar Comm. Centre, 2nd Tues/mth, 7:30pm

Hastings Centre Rockhounds
c/o Hastings Community Centre
3096 East Hastings Street
Vancouver, BC V5K 2A3
Meeting: Hastings Comm. Centre, 4th
Wed/mth, 7:30pm

Lapidary Club of Vancouver
c/o 6317 Crescent Place
Delta, BC V4K 4V2
Meeting: Marpole–Oakridge Comm.
Centre, 59th & Oak, 1st Tues/mth,
7:30pm

Tiffany Gem Cutters of BC
c/o 4116 Inverness Street
Vancouver, BC V5V 4W7

Lapidary Club of West Vancouver
PO Box 91233
West Vancouver, BC V7V 2N6
Meeting: Marpole–Oakridge Comm.
Centre, 59th & Oak, 1st Tues/mth,
7:30pm

Interior:
Shuswap Rock Club
c/o S23, RR#2
Chase, BC V0E 1M0
Meeting: Chase Library meeting room,
1st Tues/mth, 7:30pm

Thompson Valley Rock Club
957 Holt Street
Kamloops, BC V2B 5H1
Meeting: Parkview Activity Centre, 500
McDonald Ave., 1st Mon/mth, 7:30pm

Lillooet Rock & Gem Club
PO Box 633
Lillooet, BC V0K 1V0

High Country Rockhound Club
PO Box 1182
Logan Lake, BC V0K 1W0
Meeting: Community Gallery, 1st Fri/mth,
7:00pm

Creston Valley Rock & Mineral Club
RR#2, Site 23, PO Box 14
Creston, BC V0B 1G0
Meeting: 1913 Elm St., 1st Thur/mth,
1:00pm

Kokanee Rock Club
1416 Vancouver Street
Nelson, BC V1L 1E4
Meeting: Selkirk College/Nelson
Campus, last Tues/mth, 7:30pm

1120 Rock Club
PO Box 182, Station A
Kelowna, BC V1Y 7N5
Meeting: 100F Hall, 2597 Richter St.,
last Tues/mth, 7:30pm

Penticton Geology & Lapidary Club
c/o Leir House Cultural Centre
220 Manor Park Avenue
Penticton, BC V2A 2R2
Meeting: Leir House Cultural Centre,
1st Wed/mth, 7:30pm

Spruce City Rock & Gem Club
c/o Studio 2880
2880 – 15th Avenue
Prince George, BC V2M 1T1
Meeting: Studio 2880, 1st Tues/mth,
7:30pm

Golden Rock & Fossil Club
PO Box 2542
Golden, BC V0A 1H0
Meeting: Members' homes, 2nd Wed/
mth, 8:00pm. Call (250)344-2010

Vancouver Island:
Ripple Rock Gem & Mineral Club
PO Box 6
Campbell River, BC V9W 4Z9
Meeting: North Island College, 2nd
Fri/mth, 7:30pm

Courtenay Gem & Mineral Club
PO Box 3025
Courtenay, BC V9N 5N3
Meeting: Tsolum Building, Lewis Park,
3rd Tues/mth, 7:30pm

Cowichan Valley Rockhound Club
PO Box 232
Duncan, BC V9L 3X3
Meeting: 375 Brea Road, Duncan, 3rd
Mon/mth, 7:30pm

Parksville and Dist. Rock & Gem Club
PO Box 812
Parksville, BC V9P 2G8
Meeting: 215 Evergreen Street, 2nd
Tues/mth, 1:30pm

Alberni Valley Rock & Gem Club
PO Box 1291, Postal Station A
Port Alberni, BC V9Y 7M2
Meeting: Cherry Creek Hall, Moore
Road, 1st Sun/mth, 7:00pm

Victoria Lapidary & Mineral Society
PO Box 5114, Postal Station B
Victoria, BC V8R 6N3
Meeting: Burnside Bowling Clubhouse,
273 Hampton, 1st Mon/mth, 7:30pm

Powell River Lapidary Club
c/o 4871 Saskatchewan Avenue
Powell River, BC V8A 3G5
Meeting: members' homes, 2nd Wed/
mth. Call (604)483-4168

Retail Rock & Mineral Outlets

Ages Rockwood Art, 224-757 West Hastings, Vancouver, BC (604)681-2868

Amethyst Creations, 2746 W 4th Street, Vancouver, BC (604)736-7015

Barnabas Kiss Minerals, 20297 Stanton Avenue, Maple Ridge, BC

Bridal Falls Restaurant & Rock Shop, 53560 Bridal Falls Rd, Rosedale, BC
  (604)794-3003

C&D Gemcraft, P.O.Box 136, Slocan, BC (250)355-2471

Canadian Institute of Geology, P.O.Box 57010, Vancouver, BC

Capilano Rock & Gem, 1406 Pemberton Street, N.Vancouver, BC (604)987-5311

Cariboo Jade & Gems, 24km E of Princeton on Hwy #3, Princeton, BC
  (250)295-7133

Creative Fluorescents & Jewellery, 4260 Dallyn Road, Richmond, BC
  (604)278-5141

Eagle Gem & Gifts, 102-2270 Cliffe Avenue, Courtenay, BC (250)897-0502

Earth Magic Enterprises, 4888 Ridgelawn Drive, Burnaby, BC

Happy Prospector, 3005 Hot Springs Road, Agassiz, BC (604)796-3118

J.S.Gemstones, Powell River, BC

Jade West, 796-176th St, Surrey, BC (604)538-4525

Jade World, 1696 West First Avenue, Vancouver, BC (604)733-7212,
  (800)563-8881

Joan's Gems & Minerals, 810 Quayside N, W. Vancouver, BC (604)524-8540

Kamloops Rock Shop, 234 Victoria Street, Kamloops (250)314-6609

Latin American Imports, P.O.Box 430, Nelson, BC (250)359-7007, (800)287-1477

Mineral World, 9891 Seaport Place, Sidney, BC (250)655-4367, (800)879-0733

Mountain Gems, 4611 Hastings Street, Burnaby, BC (604)298-5883

O'Fergusen Rocks & Grits, 23537 40th Avenue, RR#12, Langley, BC
  (604)530-4254

Okanagan Opal Inc., P.O.Box 298, Vernon, BC (250)542-5173

Osirus Enterprises, 5-2330 Tyner Street, Port Coquitlam, BC

Pebble Peddlar, 12297 Roach Street, Mission, BC (604)820-1077

Rock Crystal House, 243 W.Broadway, Vancouver, BC (604)879-3238

Rockhound Shop, 777 Cloverdale Avenue, Victoria, BC (250)475-2080

Terra Crystal Galleries, 54-650 Terminal Avenue, Nanaimo, BC

Tierney's Crystals & Crafts, P.O.Box 27123, Collingwood PO, Vancouver, BC
  (604)435-6777

Tony's Rocks & Minerals, 2330 Benvoulin St, Kelowna, BC (250)860-3831

Western Gem & Minerals, 5631A-176A St, Surrey, BC (604)574-1980,
  (800)946-8170

White Stetson Motel & Rock Shop, 2248 King George Hwy, Surrey, BC
  (604)536-6216

CHAPTER 11: GLOSSARY OF TERMS

Acicular ("a-sick-u-lar") – needle-shaped.

Adit – horizontal or inclined passage entering a mine.

Alluvial – sand, silt or gravel deposited by water.

Amorphous ("a-more-fuss") – having no crystal structure.

Amygdaloidal ("a-mig-de-loy-dal") – small, round gas cavities in rock.

Anticline – strata folded like the letter "A".

Asteriated – showing a star-like pattern.

Bar – sand or gravel bed in river.

Basal – cleavage parallel to base of the crystal.

Batholith – igneous rock formed deep underground and of huge size.

Bladed – elongated, flat and thin.

Bloom – decomposed ore by surface oxidation.

Botryoidal ("bot-ree-oi-dahl") – rounded masses, resembling a bunch of grapes.

Brecciated ("bree-she-ated") – material made of sharp-edged rock fragments cemented together with other minerals.

Cabachon ("cab-o-shon") – (or "cab"), an oval stone with convex face, popular for broaches, buckles, etc.

Carat – unit of weight = one fifth of a gram, or 200 milligrams.

Carbonization – chemical alteration to a carbonate (CO_3).

Chatoyant ("shat-oy-ant") – reflecting light in a streak, like a cat's eye.

Cleavage – tendency of a crystal to split along a face or plane.

Columnar – like a column.

Conchoidal (con-koy-dahl") – clam shell-shaped, cupped surface.

Concretion ("con-cree-shun") – lump of dissimilar rock in sedimentary matrix.

Coulee ("coo-lee") – steep-sided, small valley.

Craze – tendency for gemstone to develop tiny cracks.

Crust – outer layer of earth's surface.

Cryptocrystalline ("kripto-kristal-een") – having crystals so small as to be invisible to the naked eye.

Crystal – regular, repeating arrangement of atoms, often showing symmetrical planar faces.

Dendritic – branching or fern-like shape of one mineral crystallizing inside another.

Dip – angle from the horizontal (0) to vertical (90) that orebody/strata makes with the ground.

Drusy – surface covered in small crystals.

Dyke – body of rock cutting through major rock matrix.

Element – single substance having all the same atoms; i.e. silver, carbon.

Escarpment (scarp) – sharp rise in land, often a cliff.

Extrusive – igneous rock that solidifies on the surface.

Facet – flat surface polished onto a gemstone.

Fault – displacement of rocks along a fracture zone.

Felsic – rocks containing mostly quartz and feldspar.

Fibrous – thread-like or needle-like crystals.

Fire – gemstone's brilliance.

Fissure – crack in rock; may be empty or filled.

Float – rock fragments found on surface some distance from outcrop.

Foliated – capable of being separated into thin sheets, like mica.

Fracture – the texture or shape of a broken surface.

Gemstone – any stone considered precious or semi-precious when cut or polished.

Geode ("gee-ode") – a hollow or crystal/chalcedony-filled nodule.

Glacial drift – material carried by advancing ice.

Gossanous – oxidized, near-surface iron deposit

Habit – characteristic manner or occurrence of a mineral.

Hackly – a jagged fracture.

Hydrous ("hi-druss") – containing chemically bonded water.

Inclusion – foreign material in a mineral.

Intrusive – rock that has pushed into pre-existing matrix or rock, solidifying below the surface.

Karat – measure of gold purity, where 24 is pure gold.

Lamellar – parallel arrangement of platy crystals.

Lode – economic concentration of mineral or ore.

Loess ("low-ess") – silt deposited by the wind.

Lustre – appearance of light on a fresh surface.

Magma – molten rock or lava from deep within the earth.

Marl – mixture of clay and calcite.

Massive – mineral formed in large, homogeneous mass.

Matrix – the rock or mineral mass.

Metamorphic – change in mineral or crystal due to heat, pressure or chemical change.

Mineral – naturally occurring substance with defined chemical composition.

Moraine – stones and boulders scraped into piles by a glacier's edges.

Mucking – removal of waste material, usually during mining operations.

Nodule – a ball-like mineral mass.

Opaque – material through which light cannot pass.

Orbicular – having circular patterns.

Outcrop – exposed rock on earth's surface.

Overburden – rock or soil to be removed before reaching economic ore.

Pan – wash gravels for gold and other heavy minerals.

Percolating – filtering action of underground water or mineral solutions through the matrix.

Petrify – reformed as a stone.

Pitch – angle of dip or inclination of a mineral bed or vein, at right angles to its strike.

Placer – stream separation of heavy minerals.

Pluton – igneous intrusive that doesn't reach the surface.

Primary stone – one that has not been changed by natural forces since its formation.

Prismatic – splitting light into its component colours and reflecting some or all of same.

Pseudomorph ("sue-doe-morf") – where one mineral replaces another, but keeps the previous one's shape.

Refraction – bending of light as it passes from one medium (air) into another (gemstone).

Reniform – kidney-shaped form.

Rough – uncut gem material.

Sagenitic ("saj-e-nit-ick") – having needle-like crystals of a foreign mineral.

Schiller – lustre or iridescence due to internal reflection of light.

Seam – mineral mass in a crack or between strata.

Secondary stone – natural alteration of existing rock or mineral.

Sectile – capable of being cut into shavings, like wax.

Sediment – Rock or mineral produced by weathering or erosion, and then deposited.

Shaft – vertical or sloping mine entrance.

Silicify – change into chalcedony or opal.

Sintering – melting an ore and removing the silica-rich liquids.

Smelt – melt a rock, ore or mineral to remove some fraction.

Steatitization – hydrothermal action, changing magnesium-rich minerals into talc.

Stratum (plural "strata") – single, distinct sedimentary layer.

Strike – direction orebody makes compared to north (000-360 degrees).

Suite – group of minerals or rocks occurring together.

Syncline – folded strata like the letter "U".

Tabular – shaped like a table.

Talus – rock debris at foot of cliff or slope.

Translucent – allows light, but not detail, to pass through.

Transparent – allows both light and detail to pass through.

Tumble – method of polishing rocks in a rotary drum.

Twin – symmetrical intergrowth of two or more crystals of the same species.

Ultramafic – high ferromagnesium content: olivine, pyroxene, amphibole.

Vein – thin sheet or stringer of mineral deposit.

Vesicles – spherical or oval cavities formed in lava by gas bubbles.

Vitreous – glass-like lustre.

Vug – small cavity in rock, often containing a mineral.

Approximate field conversions

Metric to Imperial:

Length:	1 cm = 0.4 inches = width of fingernail
	1 m = 39.2 inches = long yard (three paces)
	1 km = 0.63 miles
Weight:	1 gm = 5 carats = 1/28th of troy ounce
	1 kg = 2.2 lb = weight of rock hammer

Imperial to Metric:

Length:	1 inch = 2.54 cm = distance between 2 knuckle lines
	1 ft = 30 cm = 1 adult shoe length
	1 yard = 0.92 m = 3 paces
Weight:	1 oz = 28.4 gm
	1 lb = 0.46 kg = 460 gm

List of monthly birthstones

January	garnet	July	ruby
February	amethyst	August	sardonyx
March	bloodstone	September	sapphire
April	diamond	October	opal
May	emerald	November	topaz
June	pearl	December	turquoise

Wedding anniversary list

	Traditional	*Modern*
1	Paper	Clocks, plastics
2	Calico	China, cotton
3	Muslin	Crystal, glass, leather
4	Silk	Electrical, linen, silk
5	Wood	Silverware, wood
6	Iron	Wood, iron
7	Copper	Desk sets, wool, copper
8	Bronze	Linens & laces, bronze
9	Pottery	Leather, pottery, glass
10	Tin	Diamond, tin, aluminum
11	Steel	Fashion, steel
12	Fine linen	Pearl, gemstones
13	Lace	Textiles
14	Ivory	Gold
15	Crystal	Watches
20	China	
25	Silver	
30	Pearl	
35	Coral	
40	Ruby	
50	Gold	
60	Diamond	
70	Platinum	

Common chemical elements of mineralogy and their symbols

Aluminum	Al	Molybdenum	Mo
Antimony	Sb	Nickel	Ni
Arsenic	As	Nitrogen	N
Barium	Ba	Oxygen	O
Beryllium	Be	Phosphorus	P
Bismuth	Bi	Platinum	Pt
Boron	B	Potassium	K
Cadmium	Cd	Radium	Ra
Calcium	Ca	Selenium	Se
Carbon	C	Silicon	Si
Chlorine	Cl	Silver	Ag
Chromium	Cr	Sodium	Na
Cobalt	Co	Strontium	Sr
Copper	Cu	Sulfur	S
Fluorine	F	Tellerium	Te
Gold	Au	Thorium	Th
Hydrogen	H	Tin	Sn
Iron	Fe	Titanium	Ti
Lead	Pb	Tungsten	W
Lithium	Li	Uranium	U
Magnesium	Mg	Vanadium	V
Manganese	Mn	Zinc	Zn
Mercury	Hg	Zirconium	Zr

Partial list of minerals that have been identified in BC

Actinolite
Aegerite
Agate
Alabaster
Albite
Allemontite
Almandite
  (garnet)
Amber
Amethyst
Amphiboles
Analcite
Andalusite
Andesite
Andradite
  (garnet)
Anglesite
Ankerite
Antigorite
Apatite
Apophyllite
Aragonite
Argentite
Argillite
Arsenic (native)
Arsenopyrite
Asbestos
Augite
Aventurine
Axinite
Azurite
Barite
Basalt
Bentonite
Beryl
Biotite
Bornite
Bournonite
Breccia
Calcite
Carnelian
Cassiterite
Celestite
Cerrusite
Chabazite
Chalcedony
Chalcocite
Chalcopyrite
Chlorite

Chromite
Chrysocolla
Chrysotile
Cinnabar
Clevelandite
Clinozoisite
Coal (bituminous)
Colemanite
Collinsite
Concretions
Copper
Corundum
Cosalite
Covellite
Crocidolite
Cuprite
Cyanite
Dallasite
Danburite
Diopside
Dioptase
Dolomite
Epidote
Erythrite
Feldspar
Ferrierite
Fluorite
Gabbro
Galena
Garnet
Geode
Gneiss
Gold
Gossan
Granite
Graphite
Greenstone
Grossularite
Gypsum
Hematite
Heulandite
Hornblende
Idocrase
Ilmenite
Jade
Jamesonite
Jasper
Kaolinite
Kyanite

Lazulite
Lazurite
Leonhardite
Limestone
Limonite
Lizardite
Magnesite
Magnetite
Malachite
Marble
Marcasite
Marl
McGillite
Mesolite
Mica
Millerite
Molybdenite
Muscovite
Nephrite
Obsidian
Olivine
Opal
Pastelite
Pegmatite
Pentlandite
Peridot
Perthite
Petrified wood
Phosphate
Plagioclase
Platinum
Porphyry
Prehnite
Pyrargyrite
Pyrite
Pyrolusite
Pyromorphite
Pyrophyllite
Pyroxene
Pyrrhotite
Quartz
Quartzite
Realgar
Rhodochrosite
Rhodonite
Rhyolite
Rodingite
Rutile
Sagenite

Sandstone
Scapolite
Scheelite
Selenite
Serpentine
Shattuckite
Siderite
Sillimanite
Silver
Smithsonite
Soapstone
Sodalite
Specularite
Spessartite
Sphalerite
Spinel
Staurolite
Steatite
Stellerite
Stibnite
Stilbite
Talc
Tetradymite
Tetrahedrite
Thomsonite
Thundereggs
Tonalite
Topaz
Tourmaline
Travertine
Tremolite
Trilliumite
Tuff
Uraninite
Uvarovite
Vesuvianite
Williamsite
Wolfenite
Wolframite
Wollastonite
Zeolite
Zircon

CHAPTER 12: BIBLIOGRAPHY

Arem, J., 1991. *Gems and Jewelry.* Bantam Books, Toronto, ON.

Armstrong, J.E., 1990. *Vancouver Geology.* Geological Assoc. of Canada, Cordilleran Section.

Bacon, C., 1996. *Rockhounding British Columbia.* Self-published photocopy.

Baird, D.M., 1962. *Yoho National Park, British Columbia: The mountains, the rocks, the scenery.*

Baird, D.M., 1964. *Kootenay National Park, British Columbia: Wild mountains and great valleys.*

Baird, D.M., 1965. *Glacier and Mount Revelstoke National Park, British Columbia: Where rivers are born.* Misc. Report No.11. Geological Survey of Canada, Ottawa, ON.

Barlee, N.L., 1975. *Similkameen: The pictographic country.* Canada West Publications, Summerland, BC.

Barlee, N.L., 1976. *Gold creeks and ghost towns.* Canada West Publications. Summerland, BC.

Barlee, N.L., 1978. *Historic treasures and lost mines.* Canada West Publications, Summerland, BC.

Barlee, N.L., 1979. *The guide to gold panning in British Columbia.* 2nd ed. Canada West Publications, Summerland, BC.

Barlee, N.L., 1984. *Gold creeks and ghost towns.* Canada West Publications. Summerland, BC.

Basque, G., 1991. *Gold panner's manual.* Stagecoach Publishing, Langley, BC.

Battey, M.H., 1972. *Mineralogy for students.* Oliver & Boyd, Edinburgh, UK.

Bertalan, Stephen, 1997. *Gemstones of British Columbia.* Special publication. Canadian Institute of Gemmology, Vancouver, BC.

Cole, S.K., 1987. *Spud's dream: The story of how a Canadian mountain-man helped create a world-class city.* Rand & Sarah Publishing, Richmond, BC.

Collings, R.K. and Andrews, P.R., 1991. *Mica and vermiculite.* Summary Report No.5. CANMET, Ottawa, ON.

de Hullu, E., 1993. *Bridge River Gold.* Bralorne Pioneer Community Club, Bralorne, BC.

Downing, P.B., 1992. New discoveries. *Rock & Gem.* 10: 45–46.

Downs, A., 1969. *Wagon road north.* Foremost Publishing, Surrey, BC.

Eisbacher, G.H., 1973. *Vancouver Geology: A short guide.* Geological Association of Canada, Cordilleran Section.

Fay, G.S., 1972. *The rockhound's manual.* Harper & Row, New York, NY.

Gait, R.I., 1972. *Exploring Minerals & Crystals.* McGraw-Hill Ryerson Ltd., Toronto, ON.

Grice, J.D., 1989. *Famous mineral localities of Canada.* Fitzhenry & Whiteside Ltd., Markham, ON.

Griffiths, D., 1995. *Heather's Amazing Discovery.* Courtenay & District Museum, Courtenay, BC.

Guppy, W., 1988. *Wet Coast Adventures: Mine-finding on Vancouver Island.* Cappis Press, Victoria, BC.

Hudson, R., 1997. *A field guide to gold, gemstone & mineral sites of British Columbia, Volume I: Vancouver Island.* Orca Book Publishers, Victoria, BC.

Hutchinson, B. and Hutchinson, J., 1975. *Rockhounding & beachcombing on Vancouver Island.* The Rockhound Shop, Victoria, BC.

Ince, B., 1982. *Collecting minerals: A handbook for the amateur.* McClelland & Stewart, Toronto, ON.

1987. Jade, stone of heaven. *National Geographic* 172 (no. 3): 282.

Johnson, B. and Johnson, C., 1985. *Pacific northwest gold and gem atlas.* Private publishing, Susanville, CA.

Johnston, R.A.A., 1915. *A list of Canadian mineral occurrences.* Govt. Printing Bureau, Dept Mines, Ottawa, ON.

Kunz, G.F., 1892. *Gems and precious stones of North America.* Dover Publications Inc., New York, NY.

Leaming, S. and Leaming, C., 1980. *Guide to rocks and minerals of the northwest.* Hancock House, N.Vancouver, BC.

Leaming, S.F., 1973. *Rock and mineral collecting in British Columbia.* Geological Survey of Canada Paper 72–53. Geological Survey of Canada, Ottawa, ON.

Leaming, S.F., 1977. *Jade in Canada.* GSC Paper 78–19. GSC, Ottawa, ON.

Ludvigsen, R. and Beard, G., 1997. *West Coast Fossils.* Whitecap Books, Vancouver, BC.

Metz, R., 1974. *Gems and minerals in color.* Hippocrene Books, Inc., New York, NY.

1989. *George's guide to claimstaking in British Columbia.* Ministry of Energy, Mines & Petroleum Resources, Mineral Titles Branch, Victoria, BC.

Gem Materials of BC. Special Publication No.74. Montana Bureau of Mines & Geology.

Mulligan, R., 1968. *Geology of Canadian beryllium deposits.* Department of Energy, Mines & Resources, Ottawa, ON.

Mussio, R. and Mussio, W., 1994. *Backroad & outdoor recreation mapbook of Vancouver Island.* Mussio Ventures Ltd., Surrey, BC.

Paterson, T.W., 1980. *British Columbia. The pioneer years.* 3 vols. Stagecoach Publishing, Langley, BC.

Pearsons, H., 1973. *BC gem trails.* 4th ed. Private printing.

Pell, J., 1988. *The industrial potential of kyanite and garnet in British Columbia.* Province of British Columbia, Energy, Mines & Petroleum Resources, Victoria, BC.

Pough, F.H., 1953. *A field guide to rocks and minerals.* Houghton Mifflin Co., Boston, MA.

Purvis, R., 1962. *Canadian Gem Stones.* Lillooet, BC.

Purvis, R., 1971. *Treasure hunting in British Columbia.* McClelland & Stewart, Toronto, ON.

Richmond, A.M., 1932. *Asbestos in British Columbia.* BC Department of Mines, Victoria, BC.

Sabina, A., 1972. *Rock & mineral collecting in Canada: Yukon, British Columbia, Alberta, Saskatchewan, Manitoba.* Vol. 1, no.1. Geological Survey of Canada, Ottawa, ON.

Sabina, A., [1973] 1993. *Rocks and minerals for the collector: The Alaska Highway: Dawson Creek, BC to Yukon/Alaska border.* Geological Survey of Canada Paper 72–32, Geological Survey of Canada, Ottawa, ON.

Shewchuck, M., 1975. *Fur, gold & opals in the Thompson River Valley.* Hancock House, Surrey, BC.

Sinkankas, J., 1959. *Gemstones of North America*. D.Van Nostrand Co. Inc., Princeton, NJ.

Steele, P., 1995. *Atlin's Gold*. Caitlin Press, Prince George, BC.

Thornton, M., 1975. *Dredging for gold: The gold divers' handbook*. Keene Industries, Northridge, CA.

Van der Flier-Keller, E. and McMillan, W.J., 1987. *The identification of common rocks*. Information Circular 1987–5. Energy, Mines & Petroleum Resources, Mineral Resources Division, Victoria, BC.

Wayland, S.F., 1997. *Guide for weekend prospectors: Easy tests for rocks and minerals*. Hancock House, Surrey, BC.

West, J. and Stirling, D., 1986. *Naturalist's Guide to the Victoria Region*. Victoria Natural History Society, Victoria, BC.

White, D.E., 1988. *The Fraser Valley Story*. Hancock House, Surrey, BC.

Yorath, C.J., 1990. *Where terranes collide*. Orca Book Publishers, Victoria, BC.

Yorath, C.J. and Nasmith, H.W., 1995. *The geology of southern Vancouver Island: A field guide*. Orca Book Publishers, Victoria, BC.

Additional reading

Publications of the 24th International Geological Congress, Montreal, 1972 (available from the GSC, Ottawa):

Mineral Deposits along the Pacific Coast of Canada, AC–06
Copper & molybdenum deposits of the Western Cordillera, AC–09
Major lead-zinc deposits of Western Canada, AC–24
Coal, oil & gas and industrial mineral deposits of the Interior Plains, Foothills and Rocky Mountains of Alberta and British Columbia, AC–25

Gemmology Canada (Vancouver, Canadian Institute of Gemmology).

MacFall, Russell P., *Gem Hunter's Guide*, Department of Mines and Resources.

Resources, Source Files., BC Ministry of Energy, Mines and Petroleum Resources.

Gem & Mineral Federation , 1995. *Rockhounding in the four western provinces, the NWT, the Yukon and Nova Scotia*.

INDEX

A

Aberdeen, 204

acid, 16

aerolites, 58

Agassiz, 58, 105

agate, 26, 63, 121, 131, 132, 133, 135, 137, 138, 139, 143, 147, 153, 154, 209, 234, 243, 250, 252

Agate Mountain, 27, 43, 243

alabaster, 27

Alberta Plain, 6

Allenby, 239, 244

amber, 20, 27, 142, 144, 236, 239, 254, 255

amethyst, 28, 147

analcite, 28

Anderson Lake, 97

Anglesey Lookout, 139

anhydrite, 28

ankerite, 29

anniversary, 279

apatite, 29

aplite, 29, 228

apophyllite, 29

aragonite, 29

argentite, 29

argillite, 29

arsenopyrite, 30, 177, 229

asbestos, 30

Ashcroft, 43, 134, 135, 140

Aspen Grove, 207

axinite, 30

B

Back Valley, 137

barite, 30, 199

Barker, Billy, 13, 55

Barkerville, 13

basalt, 6, 30, 73, 243

BC Energy, Mines & Petroleum Resources, 268

BC Forest Service, 67

Bennett, W.A.C., 63, 119

beryl, 31

Bethlehem Copper, 218

Big Bend, 13

birthstones, 279

Black Tusk, 6

Blackdome Mountain, 43, 49

Blackwell Mountain, 231

bloodstone, 31

bornite, 31, 200, 205, 222

bournonite, 32

Bowen Island, 71, 90

Bralorne, 180, 182, 186

Bridge River, 63, 119, 155, 168, 169, 178

Britannia Mine, 72, 89, 90

Brokenback Hill, 113

Burrard Inlet, 71

C

Cache Creek, 44, 134, 136

Cadwallader Creek, 62, 182, 184

calcite, 32

Cariboo, 55, 145

carnelian, 32

Carpenter Lake, 178, 188

Cassiar, 13

cassiterite, 32

Central System, 31

chabazite, 32

chalcedony, 33

chalcocite, 204, 205, 207

chalcopyrite, 33, 75, 76, 81, 90, 110, 112,
    201, 202, 220, 222, 231, 233

chert, 33, 239, 250

Chilliwack River, 58, 104

chrysocolla, 33, 220

Cinder Hill, 220

cinnabar, 33, 165, 171, 173, 174, 175

cleavage, 24

Clinton, 146, 148

Coalmont, 254

Coastal Belt, 1

colour, 22

commodities, 70

concretions, 33

Congress Mine, 179

conversions, 279

Copper Mountain, 239, 241, 245

Coquihalla Highway, 193

Cordillera, 1, 8, 9

corundum, 34

Craigmont Mine, 203

Crown Publications, 68, 268

crystallography, 21

Cultural Properties Act, 19

D

dallasite, 34

Dana, James Dwight, 16

Dawson, G.M., 60, 131

density, 24

developed prospect, 69

diamond, 34

diopside, 34

diorite, 6

Douglas, Sir James, 12, 151

Duffy Lake Road, 153

E

Eastern System, 4

Ecological Reserve Act, 19

epidote, 35

ethics, 10

Eureka, 227

F

feldspar, 35

ferrierite, 35

flowerstone, 84

fluorite, 35

fossil wood, 35, 142, 135, 234, 252

fossils, 57, 80, 86, 104, 111, 113, 138,
    148, 176, 231, 236, 239, 247, 250,
    251, 252

fracture, 24

Fraser Canyon, 12

Fraser River, 12, 58, 65, 104, 116, 119

Fraser River Jade Reserve, 119

Fraser Valley, 103

Free Miner Certificates, 269

G

gabbro, 6

galena, 35, 95, 199, 211, 212

Gambier Island, 71

Garibaldi Lake, 93

Garibaldi Park, 6

garnet, 36, 104, 115

Geological Survey of Canada, 268

Global Positional System, 16, 69

gold, 37, 52, 53, 81, 83, 152, 156, 166,
179, 180, 181, 182, 236, 239, 256, 260

Gold Bridge, 32, 62, 180

Gold Commissioner, 10, 13, 14, 18, 68,
269

granite, 20

Granite City, 254, 256

Granite Creek, 256

Grant Hill, 71

grossularite, 37

gypsum, 37, 133, 257

H

habit, 20

hammer, 15

hardness, 22

Harrison Hot Springs, 109, 114

Harrison Mills, 111

Hat Creek, 140

Hat Valley, 44

hematite (haematite), 38

Hemlock Valley, 111

Heritage Conservation Act, 19, 57

heulandite, 38

hexagonal, 21

Highland Valley, 33, 218

Highland Valley Copper, 222

Hope, 108, 192, 226

Hope Slide, 29, 228

Horseshoe Bay, 30

Horseshoe Bend, 156

hot springs, 102

Howe Sound, 71, 88

hyalite, 38, 249

I

idocrase, 38, 128

igneous rocks, 6

ilmenite, 38

Indian artifacts, 65

Interior System, 4

iolite, 38

isometric, 21

J

jade, 38, 59, 98, 121, 128, 129, 153, 156,
167, 170, 171, 186, 193

jadeite, 60

jasper, 39, 139, 140, 143, 153

K

karat, 56

Kentucky–Alleyne Provincial Park, 207

kimberlite, 36

Kitsilano Beach, 71

Kootenays, 13

kyanite, 39

L

Land Act, 18

lazulite, 39

Leech River, 13

Lighthouse Park, 71

Lillooet, 49, 119, 150

Lillooet Lake, 100

limestone, 39, 77, 82, 133, 146, 148

Logan Lake, 33, 218

longitude, 69

loupe, 15

Lucky Strike, 177

lustre, 23

Lynn Creek, 89

Lytton, 129

M

magnesite, 40, 176

magnetism, 25

magnetite, 40, 80, 85, 203, 258

malachite, 40

Manning Provincial Park, 227

maps, 67

marble, 7, 40, 86, 144, 264

marcasite, 40

Marshall Creek, 170

Merritt, 199, 206, 215

metamorphic rocks, 7

meteorites, 58

Mineral Hill, 77, 209

Mineral Tenure Act, 18

MINFILE number, 67, 68

Mohs, Friederich, 22

molybdenite, 40

monoclinic, 21

Mount St. Helens, 4

Murrin Provincial Park, 91

muscovite, 40

N

Nahatlatch River, 122

National Meteorite Collection, 58

natrolite, 41

Nelson Island, 77

nephrite, 41, 60, 98

nickel, 43, 117, 120

Nicoamen Plateau, 27, 131

Northair, 95

O

obsidian, 6, 41

ocean ridge, 8

olivine, 42

Omineca, 13

opal, 42, 138, 146, 149, 249

orthorhombic, 21

P

Painted Chasm, 149

panning, 53, 54, 55

past producer, 69

pastelite, 43

Peace-Omineca, 13

pegmatite, 6, 43, 196

Pemberton, 6

pentlandite, 43, 117

peridot, 43

peridotite, 6

perlite, 43

petrified wood, 44

picturestone, 228

piezoelectric, 25

Pioneer, 181, 183

plaster of Paris, 37

plate tectonics, 8

platinum, 44, 129, 237, 260

porphyry, 44

Powell River, 44, 79

prehnite, 45, 146

Princeton, 27, 42, 44, 238

producer, 69

prospect, 69

pyrite, 45, 75, 76, 83, 95, 202, 208, 211, 213, 227, 237, 264

pyrolusite, 45

pyrophyllite, 45, 140

pyrrhotite, 45, 117, 231

Q

quartz, 45, 95, 190

Queen Charlotte Islands, 4, 12, 29, 30, 46

R

radioactivity, 25

realgar, 45

rhodochrosite, 46

rhodonite, 46, 121

rhyolite, 6, 46

Richardson, Sir John, 60

Rocky Mountain, 6, 7

Rocky Mountain Trench, 4

rodingite, 46

S

sard, 46

sardonyx, 46

scheelite, 47, 171, 173, 216

Scottie Creek, 28, 34, 146

Sechelt Peninsula, 75

sedimentary rocks, 7

selenite, 47, 147

serpentine, 47

shattuckite, 47

Shaw Springs, 27, 132

showing, 69

siderite, 47, 58

siderolites, 58

silica, 3

sillimanite, 47, 126

silver, 47

Silverdale Hill, 71

Similkameen River, 239

Simon Fraser University, 63

site name, 68

Skagit Bluffs, 230

skarn, 48

soapstone, 48

sodalite, 48

specific gravity, 24

Spences Bridge, 133

sphalerite, 48, 89, 112, 231, 237

spinel, 48

Stanley Park, 71, 72

steatite, 48

stibnite, 48, 171, 173, 179, 189

Stikine, 13

stilbite, 49

streak, 25

Stump Lake, 209

subduction zone, 8

Sunday Summit, 234

Swakum Mountain, 216

T

talc, 49, 99, 123, 124, 125, 126, 127, 153, 168, 185

tektites, 59

tetragonal, 21

tetrahedrite, 227

Texada Island, 36, 58, 79

Thompson River, 12, 130

thompsonite, 49

thundereggs, 49, 65, 154, 249

tonalite, 49

tourmaline, 49

transform plate, 8

travertine, 50, 148, 152, 165, 248

Trespass Act, 18

triclinic, 21

troy ounces, 56

tuff, 50

Tulameen, 34, 259

Tulameen River, 34, 240, 257, 259

turquoise, 50

Tyax Creek, 171

Tyax Lake, 176

U

Universal Transverse Mercator (UTM),
      69

uraninite, 50

V

Vancouver, 71, 77, 78

Vancouver Island, 4

Vermilion Bluffs, 239, 250

vesuvianite, 50

Vimy Mine, 205

W

weight, 56, 279

Western System, 4, 31

Whipsaw Creek, 235

Whistler, 88, 92

Whistler Valley, 35

wollastonite, 51

Y

Yalakom River, 51, 119, 151, 155

yalakomite, 51

Z

zeolite, 51

zircon, 51

Zofka Ridge, 118